Nostradamus

The Complete Prophecies, in French and English

Michel de Nostredame

ZEM BOOKS

Nostradamus

The Complete Prophecies,

in French and English

By

Michel de Nostredame

ISBN 978-1-387-86416-4

Online Bookstore: www.lulu.com/zem66

Visit us on Facebook at: www.facebook.com/zembooks

Contact us:

zemrocksme99@gmail.com

Contents

Century I

I 1
Estant assis de nuict secret estude,
Seul reposé fus la selle d'airain;
Flambe exigue sortant de solitude
Feit proferer qui n'est à croire en vain.

Sitting alone at night in secret study;
it is placed on the brass tripod.
A slight flame comes out of the emptiness and
makes successful that which should not be believed in vain.

I 2
La verge en main mise au milieu des branches,
De l'onde il moulle le limbe & le pied,
Vn peur & voix fremissent par les manches,
Splendeur diuine, le diuin pres s'assied.

The wand in the hand is placed in the middle of the tripod's legs.
With water he sprinkles both the hem of his garment and his foot.
A voice, fear: he trembles in his robes.
Divine splendor; the God sits nearby.

I 3
Quand la litiere du tourbillon ver*f*ee,
Et *f*eront faces de leurs manteaux couvers,
La republique par gens nouveaux vexée,
Lors blancs & rouges iugeront à l'enuers.

Quand la lictiere du tourbillon versee
Et seront faces de leurs manteaux couuerts,
La republique par gens nouueaux vexee,
Lors blancs & rouges iugeront à l'enuers.

Quand la litiere du tourbillon ver*f*ee,
Et *f*eront faces de leurs manteaux couuers,
La Republique par gens nouueaux vexée :
Lors Blancs & Rouges iugeront à l'enuers.

When the litters are overturned by the whirlwind

1

and faces are covered by cloaks,
the new republic will be troubled by its people.
At this time the reds and the whites will rule wrongly.

I 4
Par l'vniuers sera fait vn Monarque,
Qu'en paix & vie ne sera longuement,
Lors se perdra la piscature barque,
Sera regie en plus grand detriment.

In the world there will be made a king
who will have little peace and a short life.
At this time the ship of the Papacy will be lost,
governed to its greatest detriment.

I 5
Chassez seront sans faire long combat,
Par le pays seront plus fort greuez :
Bourg & Cité auront plus grand debat
Carcas, Narbonne, auront cœurs esprouvez,

They will be driven away for a long drawn out fight.
The countryside will be most grievously troubled.
Town and country will have greater struggle.
Carcassonne and Narbonne will have their hearts tried.

I 6
L'œil de Rauenne sera destitué,
Quand à ses pieds les aisles failliront,
Les deux de Bresse auront constitué,
Turin, Verseil, que Gaulois foulleront.

The eye of Ravenna will be forsaken,
when his wings will fail at his feet.
The two of Bresse will have made a constitution
  for Turin and Vercelli, which the French will trample
underfoot

I 7
Tard arriué l'execution faite,
Le vent contraire, lettres au chemin prinses
Les coniurez quatorze d'vne fecte,
Par le Rosseau senez les entreprinses.

2

Arrived too late, the act has been done.
The wind was against them, letters intercepted on their way.
The conspirators were fourteen of a party.
By Rousseau shall these enterprises be undertaken.

I 8
Combien de fois prinse Cité solaire,
Seras, changeant les loi barbares & vaines
Ton mal s'approche, plus seras tributaire,
Le grand Hadrie recouurira tes vaines.

How often will you be captured, O city of the sun ?
Changing laws that are barbaric and vain.
Bad times approach you. No longer will you be enslaved.
Great Hadrie will revive your veins.

I 9
De l'Orient viendra le cœur Punique,
Facher Hadrie & les hoirs Romulides,
Accompagné de la classe Libique
Trembler Mellites, & proches Isles vuides.

From the Orient will come the African heart
to trouble Hadrie and the heirs of Romulus.
Accompanied by the Libyan fleet
the temples of Malta and nearby islands shall be deserted.

I 10
Serpens transmis dans la cage de fer,
Oú les enfans septains du Roy sont pris
Les vieux & peres sortiront bas d'enfer,
Ains mourir voir de son fruict mort & cris.

A coffin is put into the vault of iron,
where seven children of the king are held.
The ancestors and forebears will come forth from the depths
of hell,
lamenting to see thus dead the fruit of their line.

I 11
Le mouuement de sens, cœur, pieds & mains
Seront d'accord, Naples, Leon, Secile.

3

Glaiues, feux, eaux, puis aux nobles Romains
Plongez, tuez, morts par cerueau debile.

The motion of senses, heart, feet and hands
will be in agreement between Naples, Lyon and Sicily.
Swords fire, floods, then the noble Romans drowned,
killed or dead because of a weak brain.

I 12
Dans peu dira fauce brute fragile,
De bas en haut, efleué promptement,
Puis en intant desloayale & labile,
Qui de Veronne aura gouuernement.

There will soon be talk of a treacherous man, who rules a
short time,
quickly raised from low to high estate.
He will suddenly turn disloyal and volatile.
This man will govern Verona.

I 13
Les Exilez par ire, haine inteſtine
Feront au Roy grand coniuration :
Secret mettront ennemis par la mine.
Et ſes vieux ſiens contre eux ſedition.

Les exilez par ire, haine intestine
Feront au Roy granp'coniuration,
Secret mettront ennemys par la mine,
Et ses vieux siens contre eux sedition.

Les exilez par ire, haine inteſtine
Feront au Roy grand coniuration :
Secret mettront ennemis par la mine,
Et ſes vieux ſiens contr'eux ſedition.

Through anger and internal hatreds, the exiles
will hatch a great plot against the king.
Secretly they will place enemies as a threat,
and his own old (adherents) will find sedition against them.

I 14
De gens eſclaue, chanſons, chants & requeſtes,

Captifs par Princes, & Seigneurs aux pri∫ons.
A l'advenir par idiots ∫ans te∫tes,
Seront receus par divins orai∫ons.

De gens esclaue, chansons, chants & requestes
Captifs par Princes & Seigneur aux prisons.
A l'aduenir par idiots sans testes,
Seront receus par diuins oraisons.

De gen∫ e∫claue chan∫ons, chants & reque∫tes,
Captifs par Princes & Seigneurs aux pri∫ons,
A l'aduenir par idiots ∫ans te∫tes
Seront receus pour diuins orai∫ons.

From the enslaved populace, songs, chants and demands,
while Princes and Lords are held captive in prisons.
These will in the future by headless idiots
be received as divine prayers

I 15
Mars nous menace par la force bellique,
Septante fois fera le ∫ang e∫pandre :
Auge & ruyne de l'Eccle∫fia∫tique,
Et plus ceux qui d'eux rien voudront entendre.

Mars nous menace par ∫a force bellique,
Septante fois faire le ∫ang e∫pandre :
Auge & ruine de l'Eccle∫fia∫tique,
Et plus ceux qui d'eux rien voudront entendre.

Mars nous menasse par sa force bellique,
Septante fois fera le sang espandre,
Auge & ruyne de l'Ecclesiastique,
Et plus ceux qui d'eux rien voudront entendre.

Mars threatens us with the force of war
and will cause blood to be spilt seventy times.
The clergy will be both exalted and reviled moreover,
by those who wish to learn nothing of them.

I 16
Faux à l'e∫tang, ioint vers le Sagittaire,
En ∫on haut AUGE de l'exaltation,

5

Pe*f*te, famine, mort de main militaire,
Le *f*iecle approche de renovation.

Faux à l'estang, ioint vers le Sagittaire.
En son haut auge de l'exaltation
Peste, famine, mort de main militaire,
Le Siecle approcher de renouation.

Faux à l'E*f*tang, ioint vers le Sagittaire,
En *f*on haut auge & l'exaltation,
Pe*f*te, famine, mort de main militaire.
Le *f*iecle approche de renouation.

A scythe joined with a pond in Sagittarius
at its highest ascendant.
Plague, famine, death from military hands;
the century approaches its renewal.

I 17
Par quarante ans l'iris n'apparoistra.
Par quarante ans tous les iours fera veu
La terre aride en siccite croistra
Et grands deluges quand sera apperceu.

For forty years the rainbow will not be seen.
For forty years it will be seen every day.
The dry earth will grow more parched,
and there will be great floods when it is seen.

I 18
Par la discorde negligence Gauloise,
Sera passage à Mahommet ouuert
De sang trempé la terre & mer Senoyse
Le port Phocen de voiles & nefs couuert.

Because of French discord and negligence
an opening shall be given to the Mohammedans.
The land and sea of Siena will be soaked in blood,
and the port of Marseilles covered with ships and sails.

I 19
Lors que Serpens viendront à circuir l'are
Le sang Troyen vexé par les Espagnes,

Par eux grans nombre en sera faicte rare,
Chef fuit, caché aux mares dans les saignes.

When the snakes surround the altar,
and the Trojan blood is troubled by the Spanish.
Because of them, a great number will be lessened.
The leader flees, hidden in the swampy marshes.

I 20
Tours, Orleans, Blois, Angers, Reims & Nantes
Citez vexées par ʃubit changement :
Par langues eʃtranges ʃeront tendués tentes,
Fleuues, dards, Renes, terre & mer tremblement.

Tours, Orleans, Bloys, Angers, Reims, Nantes,
Citez vexez par subit changement,
Par langues estranges seront tendues tentes
Fleuues, dards, renes, terre & mer tremblement

Tours, Orleans, Blois, Angiers, Rheims & Nantes
Citez vexées par ʃubit changement.
Par langue' eʃtranges ʃeront tendues tentes,
Fleuues, dars, Renes, terre & mer tremblement.

The cities of Tours, Orleans, Blois, Angers, Reims and
Nantes
are troubled by sudden change.
Tents will be pitched by (people) of foreign tongues;
rivers, darts at Rennes, shaking of land and sea.

I 21
Profonde argille blanche nourrir rocher
Qui d'vn abysme y stra lacticineuse :
En vain troubles ne l'oseront toucher,
Ignorans estre au fond terre arguilleuse.

The rock holds in its depths white clay
which will come out milk-white from a cleft
Needlessly troubled people will not dare touch it,
unaware that the foundation of the earth is of clay.

I 22
Ce que viura & n'ayant aucun sens,

Viendra leser à mort son artifice.
Authun, Chaalon, Langres & les deux Sens,
La gresle & glace fera grand malefice.

A thing existing without any senses
will cause its own end to happen through artifice.
At Autun, Chalan, Langres and the two Sens
there will be great damage from hail and ice.

I 23
Au maoys troisiesme se leuant du Soleil,
Sanglier, Liepard au champ Mars pour combattre
Liepard laissé, au ciel extend son œil,
Vn Aigle autour du solei voir s'esbatre.

In the third month, at sunrise,
the Boar and the Leopard meet on the battlefield.
The fatigued Leopard looks up to heaven
and sees an eagle playing around the sun.

I 24
A Cité neufue pensif pour condamner,
L'oysel de proye au ciel, se vient offrir
Apres victoire à captifs pardonner,
Cremone & Mantoue grand maux aura à souffrir.

At the New City he is thoughtful to condemn;
the bird of prey offers himself to the Gods.
After victory he pardons his captives.
At Cremona and Mantua great hardships will be suffered.

I 25
Perdu, trouué, caché de si long siecle,
Sera pasteur demy Dieu honoré,
Ains que la Lune acheue son grand cycle,
Par autres vieux sera deshonoré.

The lost thing is discovered, hidden for many centuries.
Pasteur will be celebrated almost as a God-like figure.
This is when the moon completes her great cycle,
but by other rumors he shall be dishonored.

I 26

Le grand du foudre tombe d'heure diurne,
Mal & predit par porteur postulaire,
Suyuant presage tombe d'heure nocturne
Conflit, Reims, Londres, Etrusque pestfere.

The great man will be struck down in the day by a
thunderbolt.
An evil deed, foretold by the bearer of a petition.
According to the prediction another falls at night time.
Conflict at Reims, London, and pestilence in Tuscany.

I 27
Dessous de chaine Guien du Ciel frappé,
Non loing de là, caché le thresor,
Qui par long siecles auoit esté grappé,
Trouué mourra, l'œil creué de ressort.

Beneath the oak tree of Gienne, struck by lightning,
the treasure is hidden not far from there.
That which for many centuries had been gathered,
when found, a man will die, his eye pierced by a spring.

I 28
La tour de Bouq craindra fuste Barbare
Vn temps, long temps apres barque hesperique,
Bestail, gens, meubles tuous deux ferot grand'tare
Taurus & Libra quelle mortelle picque.

Tobruk will fear the barbarian fleet for a time,
then much later the Western fleet.
Cattle, people, possessions, all will be quite lost.
What a deadly combat in Taurus and Libra.

I 29
Quand le poisson terrestre, & aquatique
Par forte vague au grauier sera mis,
Sa forme estrange, suaue & horrifique,
Par mer aux murs bien tost les ennemys.

When the fish that travels over both land and sea
is cast up on to the shore by a great wave,
its shape foreign, smooth and frightful.
From the sea the enemies soon reach the walls.

I 30

La nef estrange par le tourment marin
Abordera pres de port incogneu,
Nonobstant signes du rameau palmerin,
Apres mort, pille, bon auis tard venu.

Because of the storm at sea the foreign ship
will approach an unknown port.
Notwithstanding the signs of the palm branches,
    afterwards there is death and pillage. Good advice comes
too late.

I 31

Tant d'ans les guerres, en Gaule dureront
Outre la course du Castulon Monarque,
Victoire incerte trois grands courouneront
Aigle, Coq, Lune, Lyon, Soleil en marque.

The wars in France will last for so many years
beyond the reign of the Castulon kings.
An uncertain victory will crown three great ones,
    the Eagle, the Cock, the Moon, the Lion, the Sun in its
house.

I 32

Le grand empire sera tost translaté
En lieu petit, qui bien tost viendra croistre
Lieu bien infime, d'exigué comté.
Ou au milieu viemdra poser son Sceptre.

The great Empire will soon be exchanged
for a small place, which soon will begin to grow.
A small place of tiny area
in the middle of which he will come to lay down his scepter.

I 33

Pres d'vn grand pont de plaine spacieuse,
Le grand lyon par forces Cesarees
Fera abbatre hors cité rigoureuse
par effroy porte luy seront resserrees.

Near a great bridge near a spacious plain

the great lion with the Imperial forces
will cause a falling outside the austere city.
Through fear the gates will be unlocked for him.

I 34
L'oyseau de proye volant à la fenestre,
Auant conflit fait aux François parure.
L'vn bon prendra, l'autre ambigue sinistre,
La partie foible tiendra par bonne augure.

The bird of prey flying to the left,
   before battle is joined with the French, he makes
preparations.
   Some will regard him as good, others bad or uncertain.
   The weaker party will regard him as a good omen.

I 35
Le Lyon ieune, le vieux surmontera,
En champ bellique par singuliere duelle,
Dans cage d'or les yeux luy creuera,
Deux classes vne, pour mourir mort cruelle.

Le Lyon ieune le vieux ſurmontera
En champ bellique par ſingulier duelle,
Dans cage d'or les yeux luy creuera :
Deux claſſes vne, puis mourit, mort cruelle.

The young lion will overcome the older one,
in a field of combat in single fight:
He will pierce his eyes in their golden cage;
two wounds in one, then he dies a cruel death.

I 36
Tard le Monarque ſe viendra repentir
De n'auoir mis à mort ſon aduerſaire.
Mais viendra bien à plus haut conſentir,
Que tout ſon ſang par mort fera défaire.

Tard le Monarque ſe viendra repentir
De n'anoir mis à mort ſon adverſaire :
Mais viendra bien à plus haut conſentir
Que tout ſon ſang par mort fera defaire.

11

Tard le Monarque se viendra repentir,
De n'auoir mis à mort son aduersaire,
Mais viendra bien à plus haut consentir,
Que tout son sang par mort fera deffaire.

Too late the king will repent
that he did not put his adversary to death.
But he will soon come to agree to far greater things
which will cause all his line to die.

I 37
Vn peu deuant que le Soleil s'ab∫con∫e
Conflit donné, grand peuple dubieux.
Profligez port marin ne fait re∫pon∫e.
Pont & ∫epulchre en deux e∫tranges lieux.

Vn peu deuant que le Soleil s'esconse
Conflit donné, grand peuple dubieux,
Profigez, port marin ne faict response
Pont & sepulchre en deux estranges lieux.

Vn peu devant que le Soleil s'ab∫con∫e
Conflit donné, grand peuple dubieux :
Profigez, port marin ne fait re∫pon∫e,
Pont & ∫epulcre en deux e∫tranges lieux.

Shortly before sun set, battle is engaged.
A great nation is uncertain.
Overcome, the sea port makes no answer,
the bridge and the grave both in foreign places.

I 38
Le Sol & l'Aigle au vi¢teur paroi∫tront.
Re∫pon∫e vaine au vaincu lon a∫∫eure.
Par cor ne cris harnois n'arre∫teront.
Vindi¢te. paix par mort s'acheue à l'heure.

Le Sol & l'Aigle au victeur paroistront,
Response vaine au vaincu l'on asseure,
Par cor, ne cris harnois n'arresteront
Vindicte paix, par mort l'acheue à l'heure.

Le Sol & l'Aigle au vi¢teur paroi∫tront,

12

Re*fpon∫e* vaine au vaincu l'on a*∫∫*eure :
Par cor, ne crys harnois n'arre*∫*teront
Vindi¢te, paix, morts *∫*i acheue à l'heure.

The Sun and the Eagle will appear to the victor.
An empty answer assured to the defeated.
Neither bugle nor shouts will stop the soldiers.
Liberty and peace, if achieved in time through death.

I 39
De nuict dan le lict le supresme estrangle
Pour trop auoir subiourné blond esleu
Par trois l'Empire subroge exancle,
A mort mettra carte, pacquet ne leu.

At night the last one will be strangled in his bed
because he became too involved with the blond heir elect.
The Empire is enslaved and three men substituted.
He is put to death with neither letter nor packet read.

I 40
La trombc fausse dissimulant folie,
Fera Bisance vn changement de loix,
Hystra d'Egypte qui veut que l'on deslie
Edict changeant monnoyes & alloix.

The false trumpet concealing madness
will cause Byzantium to change its laws.
From Egypt there will go forth a man who wants
the edict withdrawn, changing money and standards.

I 41
Siege en Cité & de nuict assaillie
Peu eschappez non loing de mer conflit,
Femme de ioye, retours fils defaillie,
Poison & lettte cachée dans le olic.

The city is besieged and assaulted by night;
few have escaped; a battle not far from the sea.
A woman faints with joy at the return of her son,
poison in the folds of the hidden letters.

I 42

Les dix Kalendes d'Auril de fait Gotique
Ressuscité encor par gens malins,
Le feu estaint, assemleee diabolique,
Cerchant les os du d'Amant & Pselin,

The tenth day of the April Calends, calculated in Gothic
fashion
   is revived again by wicked people.
   The fire is put out and the diabolic gathering
   seek the bones of the demon of Psellus.

I 43
Auant qu'aduienne le changement d'Empire,
Il aduiendra vn cas bien merueilleux,
Le champ mué, le piller de Porphire
Mis translaté sur le rocher noisleux.

Auant qu'aduienne le changement d'empire,
Il aduiendra vn cas bien merueilleux,
Le champ mué, le pillier de porphire
Mis, tran*f*laté *f*ur le rocher nouailleux.

Auant qu'aduienne le changement d'Empire,
Il adviendra vn cas bien merveilleux :
Le champ mué, le piller de porphire,
Mis, tran*f*laté *f*ur le rocher noi*f*eux.

Before the Empire changes
a very wonderful event will take place.
The field moved, the pillar of porphyry
put in place, changed on the gnarled rock.

I 44
Cha*ff*er *f*eront moines, abbez, nouices :
Le miel *f*era beaucoup plus cher que cire.
En brief *f*eront de retour *f*acrifices,
Contreuenans *f*eront mis à martire.

En bref seront de retour sacrifices,
Contreuenans seront mis à martyre,
Plus ne seront Moines, Abbez, Nouices,
Le miel sera beaucoup plus cher que cire.

14

En breb, ƒeront de retour ƒacrifices,
Contrevenant ƒeront mis à martire :
Plus ne ƒeront Moines, Abbez, ne novices,
Le miel ƒera beaucoup plus cher que cire.

In a short time sacrifices will be resumed,
those opposed will be put (to death) like martyrs.
The will no longer be monks, abbots or novices.
Honey shall be far more expensive than wax.

I 45
Secteur de sectes grand peine au delateur,
Beste en Theatre, dressé le ieu scenique,
Du faict inique ennobly l'inuenteur,
Par sectes, monde confus & scismatique,

Se¢teur de ƒe¢tes grand preme au delateur.
Beƒte en theatre, dreƒƒé le ieu ƒcenique.
Du fait antique ennobli l'inuenteur.
Par ƒe¢tes monde confus & ƒchiƒmatique.

Se¢teur de ƒe¢tes grand peine au delateur,
Beƒte en theatre, dreƒƒé le ieu ƒcenique,
Du fait antique ennobli l'inuenteur,
Par ƒe¢te monde confus & ƒchiƒmatique.

A founder of sects, much trouble for the accuser:
A beast in the theater prepares the scene and plot.
The author ennobled by acts of older times;
the world is confused by schismatic sects.

I 46
Tout aupres d'Aux, de Lectore & Mirande,
Grand feu du Ciel en trois nuicts tombera,
Cuase aduiendra bien stupende & mirande,
Bien peu apres la terre tremblera.

Very near Auch, Lectoure and Mirande
a great fire will fall from the sky for three nights.
The cause will appear both stupefying and marvelous;
shortly afterwards there will be an earthquake.

I 47

Du Lac Leman, les sermons fascheront.
Des iours seront reduicts par les sepmaines,
Puis mois, puis an, puis tous deffailliront
Les Magistrats damneront les loix vaines.

The speeches of Lake Leman will become angered,
the days will drag out into weeks,
then months, then years, then all will fail.
The authorities will condemn their useless powers.

I 48
Vingt ans du regne de la Lune passez,
Sept mil ans autre tiendra sa Monarchie :
Quand le Soleil prendra ses iours lassez,
Lors accomplit & mine ma prophetie.

When twenty years of the Moon's reign have passed
another will take up his reign for seven thousand years.
When the exhausted Sun takes up his cycle
then my prophecy and threats will be accomplished.

I 49
Beaucoup, beaucoup auant telles menees,
Ceux d'Orient, par la vertu Lunaire,
L'an mil sept cens seront grands emmenees,
Subiugant presque le coing Aquilonaire.

Long before these happenings
the people of the East, influenced by the Moon,
in the year 1700 will cause many to be carried away,
and will almost subdue the Northern area.

I 50
De l'aquatique triplicité naistra,
D'vn qui fera le Ieudy pour sa feste.
Son bruit, los, regne, sa puissance croistra,
Par terre & mer,aux Oriens tempeste.

From the three water signs will be born a man
who will celebrate Thursday as his holiday.
His renown, praise, rule and power will grow
on land and sea, bringing trouble to the East.

I 51
Chef d'Aries, Iupiter & Saturne,
Dieu eternel quelles mutations !
Puis apres long siecle son malin temps
(tetourne,
Gaule & Italie, quelles emotions.

The head of Aries, Jupiter and Saturn.
Eternal God, what changes !
Then the bad times will return again after a long century;
what turmoil in France and Italy.

I 52
Les deux malins de Scorpion conioints,
Le grand Seigneur meurtry dedans sa salle,
Peste à l'Eglise par le nouueau Roy ioints,
L'Europe basse & Septentrioanle.

Les deux malins de Scorpion conioints,
Le grand Seigneur murtri dedans la *f*ale.
Pe#&131;te à l'Eglise le nouueau Roy ioint
L'Europe ba*ff*e & Septentrionale.

Les deux malins de Scorpion conioint,
Le grand Seigneur meurtry de dans *f*a *f*alle :
Pe*f*te à l'Egli*f*e par le nouueau Roy ioint.
L'Europe ba*ff*e, & Septentrionale.

Two evil influences in conjunction in Scorpio.
The great lord is murdered in his room.
A newly appointed king persecutes the Church,
the lower (parts of) Europe and in the North.

I 53
Las qu'on verra grand peuple tourmenté,
Et la Loy saincte en totale ruyne,
Par autres loix toute la Chrestienté,
Quand d'or, d'argent trouue nouulelle mine.

Alas, how we will see a great nation sorely troubled
and the holy law in utter ruin.
Christianity (governed) throughout by other laws,
when a new source of gold and silver is discovered.

17

I 54
Deux reuolts faits du malin falcigere
Du regne & siecles fait permutation,
Le mobil signe en son endroit s'ingere,
Aux deux esguax & d'inclination.

Two revolutions will be caused by the evil scythe bearer
making a change of reign and centuries.
The mobile sign thus moves into its house:
Equal in favor to both sides.

I 55
Soubz l'opposite climat Babylonique,
Grande sera de sang effusion,
Que terre & mer, air, Ciel sera inique,
Sectes, faim, regnes, pestes, confusion,

In the land with a climate opposite to Babylon
there will be great shedding of blood.
Heaven will seem unjust both on land and sea and in the air.
Sects, famine, kingdoms, plagues, confusion.

I 56
Vous verrez toſt & tard faire grand change,
Horreurs extremes & vindications,
Que ſi la Lune conduite par ſon Ange,
Le ciel s'approche des inclinations.

Vous verrez tost & tard faire grand change
Horreurs extresmes & vindications,
Que si la Lune conduite par son ange,
Le ciel s'approche des inclinations.

Vous verrez toſt & tard faire grand change,
Horreurs extremes & vindications.
Que ſi la Lune conduite par ſon ange,
Le ciel s'approche des inclinations.

Sooner and later you will see great changes made,
dreadful horrors and vengeances.
For as the moon is thus led by its angel
the heavens draw near to the Balance.

18

I 57
Par grand discord la trombe tremblera,
Accord rompu, dressant la teste au ciel,
Bouche sanglante dans le snag nagera,
Au sol sa face oingte de laict & miel.

The trumpet shakes with great discord.
An agreement broken: lifting the face to heaven:
the bloody mouth will swim with blood;
the face anointed with milk and honey lies on the ground.

I 58
Trenché le ventre, naistra auec deux teste
Et quatre bras, quelques sna entiers viura
Iour qui Alquilloye celebrera ses festes,
Fousssan, Thurin, chef Ferrare suyura.

Through a slit in the belly a creature will be born with two heads
and four arms: it will survive for some few years.
The day that Alquiloie celebrates his festivals
Fossana, Turin and the ruler of Ferrara will follow.

I 59
Les Exilez deportez dans les iſles :
Au changement d'vn plus cruel Monarque
Seront murtris, & mis dans les ſcintilles,
Qui de parler ne ſeront eſté parques.

Les exilez deportez dans les Isles,
Au changement d'vn plus cruel Monarque,
Seront meurtris, & mis deux des scintilles
Qui de parler ne seront esté parques,

Les exilez deportez dans les Iſles,
Au changement d'vn plus cruel Monarque
Seront meurtris, & mis deux des ſcintilles,
Qui de parler ne ſeront eſté Parques.

The exiles deported to the islands
at the advent of an even more cruel king
will be murdered. Two will be burnt

19

who were not sparing in their speech.

I 60

Vn Empereur naistra pres d'Italie,
Qui à l'Empire sera vendu bien cher,
Diront auec quels gens il se ralie
Qu'on trouuera moins Prince que boucher.

An Emperor will be born near Italy,
who will cost the Empire very dearly.
They will say, when they see his allies,
that he is less a prince than a butcher.

I 61

La republique miserable infelice,
Sera vastée du nouueau Magistrat,
Leur grand amas de l'exil malefice,
Fera Sueue rauir leur grand contract.

The wretched, unfortunate republic
will again be ruined by a new authority.
The great amount of ill will accumulated in exile
will make the Swiss break their important agreement.

I 62

La grande perte, laslque feront les lettres,
Auant le cicle de Latona parfait :
Feu, grand deluge, plus par ignares ∫ceptres,
Que de long ∫iecle ne ∫e verra refait.

La grande perte laslque feront les lettres
Auant le cicle de laton a parfaict,
Feu, grand deluge, plus par ignares sceptres
Que de long siecle ne se verra refaict.

La grande perte laslque feront les lettres
Auant le cycle de Latone parfait !
Feu, grand deluge, plus par ignares ∫ceptres :
Que de long temps ne ∫e verra refait.

Alas! what a great loss there will be to learning
before the cycle of the Moon is completed.
Fire, great floods, by more ignorant rulers;

how long the centuries until it is seen to be restored.

I 63
Les fleaux passees diminué le monde,
Long-temps la paix, terres inhabitees.
Seur marchera par le ciel, terre, mer & onde,
Puis de nouueau les guerres suscitees.

Pestilences extinguished, the world becomes smaller,
for a long time the lands will be inhabited peacefully.
People will travel safely through the sky (over) land and
seas:
then wars will start up again.

I 64
De nuict soleil penseront auoir veu,
Quand le pourceau demy homme on verra,
Bruit, chant, bataille au Ciel battre apper ceu
Et bestes brutes à parler on orra.

At night they will think they have seen the sun,
when the sec the half pig man:
Noise, screams, battles seen fought in the skies.
The brute beasts will be heard to speak.

I 65
Enfant sans mains, iamais veu si grand foudre
L'enfant Royal au ieu d'esteuf blessé :
Au puy brisez, fulgures allant moudre,
Trois sur les chaines par le milieu troussé.

A child without hands, never so great a thunderbolt seen,
the royal child wounded at a game of tennis.
At the well lightning strikes, joining together
three trussed up in the middle under the oaks.

I 66
Celuy qui lors portera les nouuelles,
Apres vn peu il viendra respirer,
Viuiers, Tournon, Montferrant & Pradelles,
Gresle & tempeste, les fera suospirer.

He who then carries the news,

21

after a short while will (stop) to breathe:
Viviers, Tournon, Montferrand and Praddelles;
hail and storms will make them grieve.

I 67
La grand famine que ie sens approcher,
Souuent tourner puis estre vniuerselle,
Si grande & longue qu'on viendra arracher,
Du bois racine, & l'enfant de mamelle.

La grand famine que ie ſens approcher,
Souuent tourner, puis eſtre univerſelle,
Si grande & longue qu'on viendra arracher
Du bois racine, & l'enfant de mammelle.

La grand famine que ie ſens approcher!
Souuent tourner, puis eſtre vniuerſelle :
Si grande & longue, qu'on viendra arracher
Du bois racine, & l'enfant de mamelle.

The great famine which I sense approaching
will often turn (in various areas) then become worldwide.
It will be so vast and long lasting that (they) will grab
roots from the trees and children from the breast.

I 68
O quel horrible & malheureux tourment !
Trois innocens qu'on viendra à liurer,
Poison suspecte, mal garde tradiment,
Mis en horreur par bourreaux enyurez

O to what a dreadful and wretched torment
are three innocent people going to be delivered.
Poison suggested, badly guarded, betrayal.
Delivered up to horror by drunken executioners.

I 69
La grand montagne ronde de sept estades,
Apre???s paix, guerre, faim, inondation,
Roulera loing, abysmant grand contrades,
Mesmes antigues, & grand fondation.

The great mountain, seven stadia round,

after peace, war, famine, flooding.
It will spread far, drowning great countries,
even antiquities and their mighty foundations.

I 70
Pluye, faim, guerre, en Perse non cessee,
La foy trop grande trahyra le Monarque
Par la finie en Gaule commencee,
Secret augure pour à vn estre parque.

Rain, famine and war will not cease in Persia;
too great a faith will betray the monarch.
Those (actions) started in France will end there,
a secret sign for on to be sparing.

I 71
La Tour Mariue trois fois prinse & reprinse
Par Espagnols, Barbares, Ligurins,
Marseille & Aix, Arles par ceux de Pise
Vast, feu, fer, pille, Auignon des Thurins.

The marine tower will be captured and retaken three times
by Spaniards, Barbarians and Ligurians.
Marseilles and Aix, Ales by men of Pisa,
devastation, fire, sword, pillage at Avignon by the Turinese.

I 72
Du tout Marseille des habitans changee
Course & pour fuitte iusques pres de Lyon.
Narbon, Tholoze par Bordeaux outragee,
Tuez, captifs, presque d'vn million,

The inhabitants of Marseilles completely changed,
fleeing and pursued as far as Lyons.
Narbonne, Toulouse angered by Bordeaux;
the killed and captive are almost one million.

I 73
France à cinq parts par neglect assaillie
Tunys, Argiels esmeuz par Persiens,
Leon, Seuille, Barcelone faillie
N'aura la classe par les Venitiens.

France shall be accused of neglect by her five partners.
Tunis, Algiers stirred up by the Persians.
Leon, Seville and Barcelona having failed,
they will not have the fleet because of the Venetians.

I 74
Apres seiourné vogueront en Epire
Le grand secours viendra vers Antioche,
Le noir poil crespe tendra fort à l'Empire
Barbe d'airain le rostira en broche.

After a rest they will travel to Epirus,
great help coming from around Antioch.
The curly haired king will strive greatly for the Empire,
the brazen beard will be roasted on a spit.

I 75
Le tyran Siene occupera Sauone,
Le fort gaigné tiendra classe marine,
Les deux armées par la marque d'Ancone
Par effrayeur le chef s'en examine.

The tyrant of Siena will occupy Savona,
having won the fort he will restrain the marine fleet.
Two armies under the standard of Ancona:
the leader will examine them in fear.

I 76
D'vn nom farouche tel proferé ƒera,
Que les trois Sœurs auront FATO le nom.
Puis peuple grand par langue & fait duira :
Plus que nul autre aura bruit & renom.

D'vn nom farouche tel proferé sera,
Que les trois sœurs auront fato le nom :
Puis grand peuple par langue & fait duira,
Plus que nul autre aura bruit & renom.

D'vn nom farouche tel proferé ƒera,
Que les trois ƒœurs auront fato le nom :
Puis grand peuple par langue & fai¢t dira,
Plus que nul autre aura bruit & renom.

24

The man will be called by a barbaric name
that three sisters will receive from destiny.
He will speak then to a great people in words and deeds,
more than any other man will have fame and renown.

I 77
Entre deux mers dressera promontoire
Que puis mourra par le mords du cheual,
Le sien Neptune pliera voile noire,
Par Calpte & classe aupres de Rocheual.

A promontory stands between two seas:
A man who will die later by the bit of a horse;
Neptune unfurls a black sail for his man;
the fleet near Gibraltar and Rocheval.

I 78
D'vn Chef vieillard naiſtra ſens hebeté,
Degenerant par ſçauoir & par armes.
Le Chef de France par ſa fœur redoubté.
Champs diuiſez, concedez aux gens gendarmes.

D'vn chef vieillard naiſtre ſens hebeté
Degenerant par ſçauoir & par armes,
Le chef de France par ſa fœur redouté,
Champz diuiſez, concedez aux gens gendarmes.

D'vn chef vieillard naistra sens hebeté,
Degenerant par sçauoir & par armes :
Le chef de France par sa sœur redouté,
Champs diuisez, concedez aux gens d'armes.

To an old leader will be born an idiot heir,
weak both in knowledge and in war.
The leader of France is feared by his sister,
battlefields divided, conceded to the soldiers.

I 79
Bazax, Lectore, Condon, Ausch, Agine,
Esmeus par loix, querelles & monopole,
Car Bourd, Thoulouse, Bay mettra enruyne
Renouueller voulant leur tauropole.

Bazas, Lectoure, Condom, Auch and Agen
are troubled by laws, disputes and monopolies.
Carcassone, Bordeaux, Toulouse and Bayonne will be ruined
when they wish to renew the massacre.

I 80

De la fixiesme claire splendeur celeste,
Viendra tonner si fort eu la Bourgongne :
Puis naistra monstre de tres-hydeuse beste,
MArs, Auril, May, Iuin, grand charpin & rongne

From the sixth bright celestial light
it will come to thunder very strongly in Burgundy.
Then a monster will be born of a very hideous beast:
In March, April, May and June great wounding and worrying.

I 81

D'humain troupeau neuf feront mis à part,
De iugement & conseil feparez.
Leur fort fera diuifé en depart,
... . , ... morts, bannis, efgarez.

D'humain troupeau neuf seront mis à part :
De iugement & conseil separees,
Leur sort sera diuisé en depart,
Cap, Thita, Lambda morts, bannis esgarez,

D'humain troupeau neuf feront mis à part,
De iugement & confeil feparez :
Leur fort fera diuifé en depart,
Kappa, Thita, Lambda mors bannis efgarez.

Nine will be set apart from the human flock,
separated from judgment and advise.
Their fate is to be divided as they depart.
K. Th. L. dead, banished and scattered.

I 82

Quand colomnes de bois grande tremblee
D'auster conduicte couuerte de rubriche,
Tant vuidera dehors vne assemblee,

26

Trembler Vienne & le pays d'Austriche.

When the great wooden columns tremble
in the south wind, covered with blood.
Such a great assembly then pours forth
that Vienna and the land of Austria will tremble.

I 83
La gent estrange diuisera butins
Saturne & Mars son regard furieux,
Horrible strage aux Toscans & Latins,
Grecs qui seront à frapper curieux.

The alien nation will divide the spoils.
Saturn in dreadful aspect in Mars.
Dreadful and foreign to the Tuscans and Latins,
Greeks who will wish to strike.

I 84
Lune obscurcie aux profondex tenebres,
Son frere passe de couleur ferrugine :
Le grand caché long temps soubs les tenebres,
Tiendra fer dans la playe sanguine.

The moon is obscured in deep gloom,
his brother becomes bright red in color.
The great one hidden for a long time in the shadows
will hold the blade in the bloody wound.

I 85
Par la response de Dame, Roy troublé,
Ambassadeurs mespriseront leur vie,
Le grand ses freres contrefera doublé,
Par deux mourront ire, haine, enuie.

Par la reſponſe de Dame Roy troublé.
Ambaſſadeurs meſpriſeront leur vie.
Le Grand, ſes freres contrefera, doublé.
Par deux mourront ire, haine, enuie.

Par la reſponſe de Dame, Roy troublé,
Ambaſſadeurs meſpriſeront leur vie :
Le grand ſes freres contrefera doublé,

27

Far deux mourront ire, haine, & envie.

The king is troubled by the queen's reply.
Ambassadors will fear for their lives.
The greater of his brothers will doubly disguise his action,
two of them will die through anger, hatred and envy.

I 86
La grande Royne qaund se verra vaincue
Fera excez de masculin courage :
Sur cheual fleuue passera toute nué,
Suitte par fer, à soy fera outrage.

When the great queen sees herself conquered,
she will show an excess of masculine courage.
Naked, on horseback, she will pass over the river
pursued by the sword: she will have outraged her faith

I 87
Ennosigée feu du centre de terre,
Fera trembler autour de Cité neufue :
Deux grands rochers long temps ferôt la guerre,
Puis Arethusa rougira nouueau Fleuue.

Earthshaking fire from the center of the earth
will cause tremors around the New City.
Two great rocks will war for a long time,
then Arethusa will redden a new river.

I 88
Le diuin mal surprendra le grand Prince,
Vn peu deuant aura femme espousee:
Son puy & credit à vn coup viendra mince,
Conseil mourra pour la teste rasee.

The divine wrath overtakes the great Prince,
a short while before he will marry.
Both supporters and credit will suddenly diminish.
Counsel, he will die because of the shaven heads.

I 89
Toust ceux de Ilerde seront dedans Moselle
Mettans à mort tous ceux de Loyre & Saine,

Secours marin viendra pres d'haute velle,
Quand l'Espagnol ouurira toute veine.

Those of Lerida will be in the Moselle,
kill all those from the Loire and Seine.
The seaside track will come near the high valley,
when the Spanish open every route.

I 90
Bourdeaux, Poitiers, au son de la campane,
A grande classe ira iusques à l'Angon,
Contre Gaulois sera leur tramontane,
Quand monstres hydeux naistra pres d'Orgon,

Bordeaux and Poitiers at the sound of the bell
will go with a great fleet as fast as Langon.
A great rage will surge up against the French,
when a hideous monster is born near Orgon.

I 91
Les Dieux feront aux humains apparence,
Ce qu'ils scront autheurs de grand conflit.
Auant ciel veu serain, espee & lance
Que vers main gauche sera plus grand afflict,

Les dieuz feront aux humains apparence
Ce qu'ils *f*eront auteurs de grand conflit.
Auant ciel veu *f*erein e*f*pée & lance :
Que vers main gauche *f*era plus grand afflit.

Les Dieux feront aux humains apparence,
Ce qu'ils *f*eront autheurs de grand confli¢t :
Auant ciel *f*eu *f*erain, e*f*pée & lance,
Que vers main gauche *f*era plus grand affli¢t.

The Gods will make it appear to mankind
that they are the authors of a great war.
Before the sky was seen to bee free of weapons and rockets:
the greatest damage will be inflicted on the left.

I 92
Sous vn la paix par tout sera clamee
Mais non long temps, pille & rebellion

29

Par refus, ville, terre & mer entammee,
Morts & captifs, le tiers d'vn milion.

Soubs vn la paix par tout *f*era clamée :
Mais non long temps pille & rebellion.
Par refus ville terre & mer entamée :
Mors & captifs le tiers d'vn milion.

Sous vn la paix par tout *f*era clamée,
Mais non long temps, pille & rebellion,
Par refus ville, terre & mer entamée,
Morts & captifs le tiers d'vn milion.

Under one man peace will be proclaimed everywhere,
but not long after will be looting and rebellion.
Because of a refusal, town, land and see will be broached.
About a third of a million dead or captured.

I 93
Terre Italique pres des monts tremblera,
Lyon & Coq; non trop confederez,
En lieu de peur, l'vn l'autre s'aidera,
Seul Castulon & Celtes moderez.

The Italian lands near the mountains will tremble.
The Cock and the Lion not strongly united.
In place of fear they will help each other.
Freedom alone moderates the French.

I 94
Au port Selin le tyran mis à mort,
La liberté non pourtant recouuree
Le nouueau Mars par vindicte & remort,
Dame par la foere de frayeur honoree.

The tyrant Selim will be put to death at the harbor
but Liberty will not be regained, however.
A new war arises from vengeance and remorse.
A lady is honored through force of terror.

I 95
Deuant monstier trouué enfant besson
D'heroicq sang de moyne vestutisque,

Son bruit par secte, langue & puissance son,
Qu'on dira soit efleué le Vopisque, Celuy

In front of a monastery will be found a twin infant
from the illustrious and ancient line of a monk.
His fame, renown and power through sects and speech
is such that they will say the living twin is deservedly
chosen.

I 96
Celuy qu'aura la charge de destruire
Temples & fectes changees par fantasie,
Plus aux rochers qu'aux viuans viendra nuyre,
Par langue ornee d'oreilles ressaisies.

Celuy qui aura la charge de deſtruire
Temples, & fe¢tes changez par fantaſie :
Plus aux rochers qu'aux viuans viendra nuire,
Par langue ornée d'oreilles raſſaſie.

Celuy qu'aura la charge de deſtruire
Temples & fc¢tes changez par fantaſie,
Plus aux rochers qu'aux viuans viendra nuire.
Par langue ornée oreilles reſſaſie.

A man will be charged with the destruction
of temples and sects, altered by fantasy.
He will harm the rocks rather than the living,
ears filled with ornate speeches.

I 97
Ce que fer, flamme, n'a sceu paracheuer,
La douce langue au conseil viendra faire
Par repos, songe, le Roy fera resuer,
Plus l'ennemy en feu, sang militaire.

Ceque fer, flamme n'a ſceu paracheuer,
La douce langue au conſeil viendra faire.
Par repos ſonge le Roy fera reſuer.
Plus l'ennemi en feu, ſang militaire.

Ce que fer flàme, n'a ſceu paracheuer,
La douce langue au conſeil viendra faire :

31

Par repos *f*onge, le Roy fera re*f*uer,
Plus l'ennemy en feu, *f*ang militaire.

That which neither weapon nor flame could accomplish
will be achieved by a sweet speaking tongue in council.
Sleeping, in a dream, the king will see
the enemy not in war or of military blood.

I 98
Le chef qu'aura conduit peuple infiny
Loing de son ciel, de mœurs & langue estrange
Cinq mil en Grete, & Thessale finy,
Le chef fuyant sauué en la marine grange,

The leader who will conduct great numbers of people
far from their skies, to foreign customs and language.
Five thousand will die in Crete and Thessaly,
the leader fleeing in a sea going supply ship.

I 99
Le grand Monarque qui fera compagnie,
Auec deux Roys vnis par amitié,
O quel souspir fera la grande mesnie,
Enfans Narbon à l'entour quel pitié.

The great king will join
with two kings, united in friendship.
How the great household will sigh:
around Narbon what pity for the children.

I 100
Long temps au ciel sera veu gris oyseau,
Aupres de Dole & de Tosquane terre,
Tenant au bec vn verdoyant rameau
Mourra tost grand, & finira la guerre.

For a long time a gray bird will be seen in the sky
near Dôle and the lands of Tuscany.
He holds a flowering branch in his beak,
but he dies too soon and the war ends.

Century II

II 1
Vers Aquitaine par insuls Britaniques
Et par eux mesmes grandes incursions
Pluyes, gelees feront terroirs iniques
Port Selyn fortes fera inuasions.

Towards Aquitaine by the British Isles
By these themselves great incursions.
Rains, frosts will make the soil uneven,
Port Selyn will make mighty invasions

II 2
La teste bleuë fera la teste blanche
Autant de mal que France à fait leur bien,
Mort à l'anthenne, grand pendu sur la branche,
Quand des prins siens le Roy dira combien.

La te*f*te bleue fera la te*f*te blanche,
Autant de mal, que France a fait leur bien :
Mort à l'anthenne, grand pendu *f*ur la branche,
Quand prins des *f*iens, le Roy dira combien.

La Tc*f*te bleuë fera la Te*f*te blanche,
Autant de mal que France a fait leur bien.
Mort à l'auton. Grand pendu *f*ur la branche,
Quand pris des *f*iens le Roy dira combien.

The blue head will inflict upon the white head
As much evil as France has done them good:
Dead at the sail-yard the great one hung on the branch.
When seized by his own the King will say how much.

II 3
Pour la chaleur solaire sus la mer
De Negrepont les poissons demy cuits,
Les habitans les viendront entamer
Quand Rod & Gennes leur faudra le biscuit.

Because of the solar heat on the sea
From Negrepont the fishes half cooked:
The inhabitants will come to cut them,
When food will fail in Rhodes and Genoa.

II 4
Depuis Monech iusqu'au pres de Sicile
Toute la plage demourra desolee,
Il n'y aura faux-bourgs, Cité ne Ville
Que par Barbare pillee & vollee.

From Monaco to near Sicily
The entire coast will remain desolated:
There will remain there no suburb, city or town
Not pillaged and robbed by the Barbarians.

II 5
Quand dans poisson fer & lettre enfermee
Hors sortira qui pis fera la guerre,
Aura par mer sa classe bien ramee
Apparoissant pres de Latine terre.

That which is enclosed in iron and letter in a fish,
Out will go one who will then make war,
He will have his fleet well rowed by sea,
Appearing near Latin land.

II 6
Aupres des portes & dedans deux citez
Seront deux fleaux onc n'apperceu vn tel,
Faim dedans peste, de fer hors gens boutez,
Crier secours au grand Dieu immortel.

Near the gates and within two cities
There will be two scourges the like of which was never seen,
Famine within plague, people put out by steel,
Crying to the great immortal God for relief.

II 7
Entre plusieurs aux isles deportees,
L'vn estre nay à deux dents en la gorge
Mourront de faim, les arbres esbroutees
Pour eux neuf Roy nouuel edit leur forge.

Entre plu*f*ieurs aux i*f*les deportez,
L'vn e*f*tre nay à deux dents en la gorge
Mourront de faim les arbres ébroutez.

Pour eux neuf Roy nouuel edi¢t leur forge.

Entre plu*f*ieurs aux i*f*les deportez,
L'vn e*f*tre né à deux dents à la gorge :
Mourront de faim, les arbres esbroutez :
Pour eux neuf Roy nouuel edit leur forge.

Amongst several transported to the isles,
One to be born with two teeth in his mouth
They will die of famine the trees stripped,
For them a new King issues a new edict.

II 8
Temples sacrez prime façon Romaine,
Reietteront les goffes fondemens,
Prenant leurs loix premieres & humaines
Chassant, non tout, des saints les cultemens.

Temples consecrated in the original Roman manner,
They will reject the excess foundations,
Taking their first and humane laws,
Chasing, though not entirely, the cult of saints.

II 9
Neuf ans le regne le maigre en paix tiendra
Puis il cherra en soif si sanguinaire
Pour luy grand peuple sans foy & loy mourra,
Tué par vn beaucoup plus debonnaire.

Nine years the lean one will hold the realm in peace,
Then he will fall into a very bloody thirst:
Because of him a great people will die without faith and law
Killed by one far more good-natured.

II 10
Auant long temps le tout sera rangé
Nous esperons vn siecle bien senestre,
L'estat des masques & des seule bien changé
Peu trouueront qu'à son rang vueillent estre

Before long all will be set in order,
We will expect a very sinister century,
The state of the masked and solitary ones much changed,

Few will be found who want to be in their place.

II 11
Le prochain fils de l'ANICR paruiendra
Tant esleué iuſqu'au regne des Forts.
Son aſpre gloire vn chacun la craindra :
Mais ſes enfans du regne iettez hours.

Le prochain fils de l'asnier paruiendra
Tant esleué iusques au regne des forts,
Son aspre gloire vn chacun la craindra,
Mais ses enfans du regne iettez hours.

Le prochain fils de l'aſnier paruiendra,
Tant eſleué iuſqu au regne des fors,
Son aſpre gloire vn chacun la craindra,
Mais ſes enfans du regne iettez hours.

The nearest son of the elder will attain
Very great height as far as the realm of the privileged:
Everyone will fear his fierce glory,
But his children will be thrown out of the realm.

II 12
Yeus clos ouuerts d'antique fantasie
L'habit des seules seront mis à néant :
Le grand monarque chastira leur frenaisie
Rauir des temples le thresor par deuant.

Yeus clos ouuerts d'antique fantaſie,
L'habit des ſeuls ſeront mis à neant :
Le grand Monarque chaſtiera leur freneſie,
Rauir des temples le threſor par deuant.

Yeus clos ouuerts d'antique fantaſie.
L'habit des Seuls ſera mis à neant.
Le grand Monarque chaſtira freneſie :
Threſor raui des temples par deuant.

Eyes closed, opened by antique fantasy,
The garb of the monks they will be put to naught:
The great monarch will chastise their frenzy,
Ravishing the treasure in front of the temples.

36

II 13
Le corps sans ame plus n'estre en sacrifice,
Iour de mort mis en natiuité
L'esprit diuin fera l'ame felice
Voyant le verbe en son eternité.

The body without soul no longer to be sacrificed:
Day of death put for birthday:
The divine spirit will make the soul happy,
Seeing the word in its eternity.

II 14
A Tours, Gien, gardé seront yeux penetrans,
Descouuriront de loing la grand'seraine,
Elle & sa suitte au port seront entrans,
Combats, poussez, puissance souueraine.

At Tours, Gien, guarded, eyes will be searching,
Discovering from afar her serene Highness:
She and her suite will enter the port,
Combat, thrust, sovereign power.

II 15
Vn peu deuant monarque trucidé,
Castor Pollux en nef, astre crinite,
L'erain public par terre & mer vuidé,
Pise, ast, Ferrare, Turin, terre interdicte.

Shortly before the monarch is assassinated,
Castor and Pollux in the ship, bearded star:
The public treasure emptied by land and sea,
Pisa, Asti, Ferrara, Turin land under interdict.

II 16
Naples, Palerme, Sicile, Syracuses,
Nouueaux tyrans, fulgures, feux celestes
Forces de Londres, Gands, Bruxelles & Suses,
Grand hecatombe, trumphe, faire festes.

Naples, Palermo, Sicily, Syracuse,
New tyrants, celestial lightning fires:
Force from London, Ghent, Brussels and Susa,

Great slaughter, triumph leads to festivities.

II 17
Le camp du temple de la vierge vestale,
Non esloigné d'Ethene & monts Pyrenées :
Le grand conduit est caché dans la male,
North, getez, fleuues, & vignes mastinees.

The field of the temple of the vestal virgin,
Not far from Elne and the Pyrenees mountains:
The great tube is hidden in the trunk.
To the north rivers overflown and vines battered.

II 18
Nouuelle & pluye subite, impetueuse
Empeshera subit deux exercices,
Pierre, ciel, feux faire la mer pierreuse
La mort de sept, terre & marin subites.

New, impetuous and sudden rain
Will suddenly halt two armies.
Celestial stone, fires make the sea stony,
The death of seven by land and sea sudden.

II 19
Nouueau venus lieu baſti ſans defenſe,
Occuper place alors inhabitable.
Prez, maiſons, champs, villes prendre à plaiſance.
Faim, peſte, guerre. arpen long labourable.

Nouueaux venus, lieu basty sans deffence
Occuper place par lors inhabitable,
Prez, maisons, champs, villes prendre à plaisance,
Faim, peste, guerre, arpen long labourable.

Nouueaux venus, lieu baſty sans defence,
Occuper place, pour lors inhabitable :
Prez, maiſons, champs, villes prendre à plaiſance,
Faim, peſte, guerre arpen, long labourage.

Newcomers, place built without defense,
Place occupied then uninhabitable:
Meadows, houses, fields, towns to take at pleasure,

Famine, plague, war, extensive land arable.

II 20
Freres & *f*œurs en diuers lieux captifs,
Se trouueront pa*ff*er pres du Monarque,
Les contempler *f*es rameaux ententifs,
De*f*plai*f*ant voir menton, frond, nez les marques.

Freres & Sœurs en plusieurs lieux captifs,
Se trouueront passer pres du Monarque
Les contempler ses rameaux ententifs,
Desplaisant voir menton, frond, nez les marques.

Freres & *f*œurs en diuers lieux captifs :
Se trouueront pa*ff*er pres du Monarque :
Les contempler *f*es rameaux ententifs,
Deplai*f*ans voir menton, frond, nez les marques.

Brothers and sisters captive in diverse places
Will find themselves passing near the monarch:
Contemplating them his branches attentive,
Displeasing to see the marks on chin, forehead and nose.

II 21
L'ambassadeur enuoyé par Byremes,
A my-chemin d'incogneus repoussez,
De tel renfort viendront quatre triremes,
Cordes & chaines en Negrepont troussez.

The ambassador sent by biremes,
Halfway repelled by unknown ones:
Reinforced with salt four triremes will come,
In Euboea bound with ropes and chains.

II 22
Le camp Aso, d'Eurotte partira,
S'adioignant proche de l'isle submergee,
D'Arton classe phalange pliera.
Nombril du monde plus grand voix subroges.

The imprudent army of Europe will depart,
Collecting itself near the submerged isle:
The weak fleet will bend the phalanx,

39

At the navel of the world a greater voice substituted.

II 23
Palais oyseaux, par oyseau dechassé,
Bien tost apres le prince paruenu,
Combien qu'hors fleuue ennemy repoussé,
Dehors saisi trait d'oyseau soustenu.

Palace birds, chased out by a bird,
Very soon after the prince has arrived:
Although the enemy is repelled beyond the river,
Outside seized the trick upheld by the bird.

II 24
Bestes farouches de faim fleuues tranner,
Plus part du camp encontre Hister sera,
En cage de fer le grand fera trainner,
Qunad Rin enfant Germain obseruera.

Beasts ferocious from hunger will swim across rivers:
The greater part of the region will be against the Hister,
The great one will cause it to be dragged in an iron cage,
When the German child will observe nothing.

II 25
La garde estrange trahyra forteresse,
Espoir & ombre du plus haut mariage,
Garde deceue, fort prinse dans la presse,
Loyre, Son, Rosne, Gar, à mort outragez.

The foreign guard will betray the fortress,
Hope and shadow of a higher marriage:
Guard deceived, fort seized in the press,
Loire, Saone, Rhone, Garonne, mortal outrage.

II 26
Pour la faueur que la cité fera,
Au grand qui tost perdra champ de bataille
Puis le rang Pau, Thesin versera
De sang, feux, morts, noyez, de coups de taille.

Because of the favor that the city will show
To the great one who will soon lose the field of battle,

Fleeing the Po position, the Ticino will overflow
With blood, fires, deaths, drowned by the long-edged blow.

II 27
Le diuin verbe sera du ciel frappé
Qui ne pourra proceder plus auant,
Du reserant le secret estoupé
Qu'on marchera par dessus & deuant.

The divine word will be struck from the sky,
One who cannot proceed any further:
The secret closed up with the revelation,
Such that they will march over and ahead.

II 28
Le penultiéme du ſurnom du Prophete
Prendra Diane pour ſon iour & repos.
LOIN vaguera par ferentique teſte,
En deliurant vn grand peuple d'impos.

Le penultine du surnom de prophete
Prendra Diane pour son iour & repos,
Loing vaguera par frenetique teste,
Et deliurant vn grand peuple d'imposts.

Le penultieme du ſurnom du Prophete,
Prendra Diane pour ſon iour & repos :
Loing vaguera par frenetique teſte,
Et deliurant vn grand peuple d'impos.

The penultimate of the surname of the Prophet
Will take Diana [Thursday] for his day and rest:
He will wander far because of a frantic head,
And delivering a great people from subjection.

II 29
L'oriental sortira de son siege,
Passer les monts Apennins, voir la Gaule,
Transpercera du ciel les eaux & neiges
En vn chacun frappera de sa gaule.

The Easterner will leave his seat,
To pass the Apennine mountains to see Gaul:

He will transpire the sky, the waters and the snow,
And everyone will be struck with his rod.

II 30
Vn qui les dieux d'Annibal infernaux
Fera renaistre effrayeur des humains
Oncq plus d'horreur, ne plus pire iournaux
Qu'aduint viendra par Babel aux Romains.

One who the infernal gods of Hannibal
Will cause to be reborn, terror of mankind
Never more horror nor worse of days
In the past than will come to the Romans through Babel.

II 31
En campagne Cassilin fera tant
Qu'on ne verra que d'eau les champs couuerts
Deuant, apres, la pluye de long temps
Hors mis les arbres rien l'on verra de vert.

In Campania the Capuan [river] will do so much
That one will see only fields covered by waters:
Before and after the long rain
One will see nothing green except the trees.

II 32
Laict, sang, grenoüilles escondre en Dalmatie
Conflit donné, peste preste, de baleine
Cry sera grand par toute Esclauonie,
Lors naistra monstre pres & dedans

Lors naistra monstre pres & dedans Rauenne.

Milk, frog's blood prepared in Dalmatia.
Conflict given, plague near Treglia:
A great cry will sound through all Slavonia,
Then a monster will be born near and within Ravenna.

II 33
Par le torrent qui descend de Veronne,
Par lors qu'au Pol guindera son entree,
Vn grand naufrage, & non moins en Garonne
Quand ceux de Gennes marcheront leur contree,

42

Through the torrent which descends from Verona
Its entry will then be guided to the Po,
A great wreck, and no less in the Garonne,
When those of Genoa march against their country.

II 34
L'ire insensée du combat furieux,
Fera à table par freres le fer luyre,
Les departir mort blesse curieux,
Le fier duelle viendra en France nuyre.

The senseless ire of the furious combat
Will cause steel to be flashed at the table by brothers:
To part them death, wound, and curiously,
The proud duel will come to harm France.

II 35
Dans deux logis de nuict le feu prendra,
Plusieurs dedans estouffez & rostis,
Pres de deux fleuues pour seur il aduiendra
Sol, l'Arc & Caper, tous seront amortis.

Dans deux logis de nui¢t le feu prendra,
Plu*f*ieurs dedans e*f*touffez & ro*f*tis.
Pres de deux fleuues pour *f*eur il aduiendra :
Soll' Arq, Caper tous *f*eront amortis.

Dans deux logis de nuit le feu prendra,
Plu*f*ieurs dedans e*f*touffez & ro*f*tis :
Pres de deux fluues pour *f*eur il aduiendra
Sol Arc, Caper. tous *f*eront amortis.

The fire by night will take hold in two lodgings,
Several within suffocated and roasted.
It will happen near two rivers as one:
Sun, Sagittarius and Capricorn all will be reduced.

II 36
Du grand Prophete les lettres seront prinses
Entre les mains du tyran deuiendront,
Frauder son Roy seront les entreprinses,
Mais ses rapines bien tost le troubleront.

43

Du grand Prophete les lettres ſeront prinſes,
Entre les mains du Tyran deuiendront :
Frauder ſon Roy feront ſes entreprinſes,
Mais ſes rapines bien-toſt le troubleront.

Du grand Prophete les lettres ſeront priſes,
Entre les mains du Tyran deuiendront.
Frauder ſon Roy feront ſes entrepriſes :
Mais ſes rapines bien toſt le troubleront.

The letters of the great Prophet will be seized,
They will come to fall into the hands of the tyrant:
His enterprise will be to deceive his King,
But his extortions will very soon trouble him.

II 37
De ce grand nombre que l'on enuoyera
Pour secourir dans le fort assiegez,
Peste & famine tous les deux deuorera,
Hors mis septante qui seront profligez.

Of that great number that one will send
To relieve those besieged in the fort,
Plague and famine will devour them all,
Except seventy who will be destroyed.

II 38
Des condamnez sera fait vn grand nombre.
Quand les Monarques seront conciliez :
Mais l'vn d'eux viendra si mal encombre,
Que guerre ensemle ne seront raliez.

II. 38.
Des condannez ſera fait vn grand nombre,
Quand les Monarques ſeront conciliez.
Mais à l'vn d'eux viendra tel malencombre,
Que guere enſemle ne ſeront ralliez.

Des condamnez ſera fait vn grand nombre,
Quand les Monarques ſeront conciliez :
Mais à l'vn d'eux viendra ſi malencombre,
Que gueres enſemle ne ſeront raliez.

44

A great number will be condemned
When the monarchs will be reconciled:
But for one of them such a bad impediment will arise
That they will be joined together but loosely.

II 39
Vn an deuant le conflit Italique
Germain, Gaulois, Espagnols pour le fort,
Cherra l'escolle maison de republique,
Ou, hors mis peu, seront suffoquez morts.

One year before the Italian conflict,
Germans, Gauls, Spaniards for the fort:
The republican schoolhouse will fall,
There, except for a few, they will be choked dead.

II 40
Vn peu apres non point longue interualle
Par mer & terre sera fait grand tumulte,
Beaucoup plus grande sera pugne naualle,
Feux, animaux, qui plus feront d'insulte.

Shortly afterwards, without a very long interval,
By sea and land a great uproar will be raised:
Naval battle will be very much greater,
Fires, animals, those who will cause greater insult.

II 41
La grand, estoille par sept iours bruslera.
Nuë fera deux Soleils apparoir,
Le gros mastin toute nuict hurlera,
Quand grand pontife changera de terroir.

The great star will burn for seven days,
The cloud will cause two suns to appear:
The big mastiff will howl all night
When the great pontiff will change country.

II 42
Coq, chiens, & chats, de sang seront repeus,
Et de la playe du tyrant trouué mort :
Au lict d'vn autre iambes & bras rompus,

Qui n'auoit peu mourir de cruelle mort.

Cock, dogs and cats will be satiated with blood
And from the wound of the tyrant found dead,
At the bed of another legs and arms broken,
He who was not afraid to die a cruel death.

II 43
Durant l'estoille cheueluë apparente,
Les trois grands Princes seront faits ennemys,
Frappez du ciel paix terre trembulente,
pau, Tymbre, vndans, serpens sur le bord mis.

During the appearance of the bearded star.
The three great princes will be made enemies:
Struck from the sky, peace earth quaking,
Po, Tiber overflowing, serpent placed upon the shore.

II 44
L'aigle posee entour des pauillons,
Par autres oyseaux d'entour sera chassee,
Quand bruit des cymbres, tubes et sonnaillons
Rendront le sens de la Dame insensee.

The Eagle driven back around the tents
Will be chased from there by other birds:
When the noise of cymbals, trumpets and bells
Will restore the senses of the senseless lady.

II 45
Trop le ciel pleure l'androgin procreé
Pres de ce ciel sang humain respandu,
Par mort trop tarde grand peuple recreé,
Tard & tost vient le secours attendu.

Trop le ciel pleure. Androgyn procrée.
Pres de ce ciel ƒang humain reƒpandu.
Par mort trop tarde grand peuple recrée.
Tard & toƒt vient le ƒecours attendu.

Trop du ciel pleurel' Androgin procrée,
Pres de ce ciel ƒang humain reƒpandu :
Par mort trop tard grand peuple recrée,

46

Tard & to*ſt* vient le *ſ*ecours attendu.

Too much the heavens weep for the Androgyne begotten,
Near the heavens human blood shed:
Because of death too late a great people re-created,
Late and soon the awaited relief comes.

II 46
Apres grâd trouble humain plus grâd s'appreste,
Le grand moteur les siecles renouuelle,
Pluye, sang, laict, famine, feu & peste :
Au ciel veu feu, courant longue estincelle.

After great trouble for humanity, a greater one is prepared
The Great Mover renews the ages:
Rain, blood, milk, famine, steel and plague,
Is the heavens fire seen, a long spark running.

II 47
L'ennemy grand vieil dueil meurt de poison
Les souuerains par infinis subiuguez,
Pierres plouuoir cachez soubs la toyson,
Par mort articles en vain sont alleguez

The great old enemy mourning dies of poison,
The sovereigns subjugated in infinite numbers:
Stones raining, hidden under the fleece,
Through death articles are cited in vain.

II 48
La grand coppie qui passera les monts,
Saturne en l'Arc tournant du poisson Mars,
Venins chachez soubs testes de Saulmons,
Leurs chefs pendus à fil de polemars.

The great force which will pass the mountains.
Saturn in Sagittarius Mars turning from the fish:
Poison hidden under the heads of salmon,
Their war-chief hung with cord.

II 49
Les conseillers du premier monopole,
Les conquerans seduits par le Melite,

Rhodes, Bisance pour leur exposant pole,
Terre faudra les poursuiuants de fuitte.

The advisers of the first monopoly,
The conquerors seduced for Malta:
Rhodes, Byzantium for them exposing their pole:
Land will fail the pursuers in flight.

II 50
Quand ceux d'Hinault, Do, Gand & de Bruxelles
Verront à Langres le siege deuant mis,
Derriere leurs flancs seront guerres cruelles,
La pluye antique, fera pis qu'ennemys.

When those of Hainault, of Ghent and of Brussels
Will see the siege laid before Langres:
Behind their flanks there will be cruel wars,
The ancient wound will do worse than enemies.

II 51
Le sang du iuste à Londres fera faute,
Bruslez par foudres de vingt trois les six,
La dame antique cherra de place haute,
De mesme secte plusieurs seront occis.

II 52
Dans plusieurs nuicts la terre tremblera,
Sur le printemps deux efforts feront suitte,
Corinthe, Ephese aux deux mers nagera,
Guerre s'esmeut par deux vailants de luitte.

For several nights the earth will tremble:
In the spring two efforts in succession:
Corinth, Ephesus will swim in the two seas:
War stirred up by two valiant in combat.

The blood of the just will commit a fault at London,
Burnt through lightning of twenty threes the six:
The ancient lady will fall from her high place,
Several of the same sect will be killed.

II 53
La grande peste de cité maritime

Ne cessera que mort ne soit vengee :
Du iuste sang par pris damne sans crime,
De la grand' dame par fainte n'outragee.

The great plague of the maritime city
Will not cease until there be avenged the death
Of the just blood, condemned for a price without crime,
Of the great lady outraged by pretense.

II 54

Par gent estrange, & de Romains loingtaine,
Leur grand cité apres eau fort troublee :
Fille sans main, trop different domaine,
Prins, chef terreure n'auoit este riblee.

Because of people strange, and distant from the Romans
Their great city much troubled after water:
Daughter handless, domain too different,
Chief taken, lock not having been picked.

II 55

Dans le conflit le grand qui peu valloit
A son dernier fera cas merueilleux :
Pendant qu'Hadrie verra ce qu'il falloit,
Dans le banquet pongnale l'orgueilleux.

In the conflict the great one who was worth little
At his end will perform a marvelous deed:
While Adria will see what he was lacking,
During the banquet the proud one stabbed.

II 56

Que peste & glaiue n'a peu s'en definer,
Mort dans le puys sommet du ciel frappé,
L'abbé mourra quand verra ruyner
Ceux du naufrage, l'escueil voulant grapper.

One whom neither plague nor steel knew how to finish,
Death on the summit of the hills struck from the sky:
The abbot will die when he will see ruined
Those of the wreck wishing to seize the rock.

II 57

Auant conflit le grand mur tombera,
Le grand à mort, mort trop subite & plainte
Nef imparfaict : la plus part nagera,
Aupres du fleuue de sang la terre tainte.

Before the conflict the great wall will fall,
The great one to death, death too sudden and lamented,
Born imperfect: the greater part will swim:
Near the river the land stained with blood.

II 58
Sans pied ne main dent ayguë & forte
Par globe au fort de porc & l'aisné nay,
Pres du portail desloyal se transporte,
Silene luyt petit grand emmené.

With neither foot nor hand because of sharp and strong tooth
Through the crowd to the fort of the pork and the elder born:
Near the portal treacherous proceeds,
Moon shining, little great one led off.

II 59
Classe Gauloise par appuy de grand'garde,
Du grand Neptune, & ses tridens soldats,
Rongee prouence pour soustenir grand'bande,
Plus Mars Narbon par iauelots & dards.

Gallic fleet through support of the great guard
Of the great Neptune, and his trident soldiers,
Provence reddened to sustain a great band:
More at Narbonne, because of javelins and darts.

II 60
La foy Punique en Orient rompuë,
Gang, lud. & Rosne, Loyre & Tag. changeront,
Quand du mulet la faim sera repuë,
Classe espargie sang & corps nageront.

The Punic faith broken in the East,
Ganges, Jordan, and Rhone, Loire, and Tagus will change:
When the hunger of the mule will be satiated,
Fleet sprinkles, blood and bodies will swim.

II 61

Euge, Tamins, Gironde & la Rochelle,
Osang Troien mort au port de la flesche,
Derriere le fleuue au fort mise l'eschelle,
Pointes feu grand meurtre sus la breche.

Bravo, ye of Tamins, Gironde and La Rochelle:
O Trojan blood! Mars at the port of the arrow
Behind the river the ladder put to the fort,
Points to fire great murder on the breach.

II 62

Mabus puis tost alors mourra viendra,
De gens & bestes vne horrible deffaite,
Puis tout à coup la vengeance on verra,
Cent, main, soif, faim, quand courra la comette.

Mabus then will soon die, there will come
Of people and beasts a horrible rout:
Then suddenly one will see vengeance,
Hundred, hand, thirst, hunger when the comet will run.

II 63

Gaulois, Ausone, bien peu subiuguera,
Pau, Marne, & Seine fera Perme l'vrie :
Qui le grand mur contre eux dressera,
Du moindre au mur le grand perdra la vie.

II 64

Seicher de faim, de soif gent Geneuoise,
Espoir prochain viendra au defaillir,
Sur point tremblant sera loy Gebenoise,
Classe au grand port ne se peut accueillir.

The people of Geneva drying up with hunger, with thirst,
Hope at hand will come to fail:
On the point of trembling will be the law of him of the
Cevennes,
Fleet at the great port cannot be received.

The Gauls Ausonia will subjugate very little,
Po, Marne and Seine Parma will make drunk:
He who will prepare the great wall against them,

He will lose his life from the least at the wall.

II 65
Le parc enclin grande calamité,
Par l'Hesperie & Insubre fera,
Le feu en nef, peste & captiuité,
Mercure en l'arc, Saturne fenera.

The sloping park great calamity
To be done through Hesperia and Insubria:
The fire in the ship, plague and captivity,
Mercury in Sagittarius Saturn will fade.

II 66
Par grands dangers le captif eschappé,
Peu de temps grand la fortune changee.
Dans le palais le peuple est attrapé,
Par bon augure la Cité assiegee.

Through great dangers the captive escaped:
In a short time great his fortune changed.
In the palace the people are trapped,
Through good omen the city besieged.

II 67
La blonde au nez forché viendra commettre
Par le duelle & chassera dehors,
Les exilez dedans fera remettre
Aux lieux marins commettant les plus forts.

The blond one will come to compromise the fork-nosed one
Through the duel and will chase him out:
The exiles within he will have restored,
Committing the strongest to the marine places.

II 68
De l'Aquilon les efforts seront grands,
Sur l'Ocean sera la porte ouuerte,
Le regne en l'isle sera reintegrand,
Tremblera Londres par voille descouuerte.

The efforts of Aquilon will be great:
The gate on the Ocean will be opened,

The kingdom on the Isle will be restored:
London will tremble discovered by sail.

II 69
Le Roy Gaulois par la Celtique dextre
Voyant discorde de la grand Monarchie,
Sur les trois parts fera fleurir son sceptre,
Contre la cappe de la grand Hierarchie.

The Gallic King through his Celtic right arm
Seeing the discord of the great Monarchy:
He will cause his scepter to flourish over the three parts,
Against the cope of the great Hierarchy.

II 70
Le dard du Ciel fera son estenduë,
Morts en parlant grande execution,
La pierre en l'arbre la fiere gent renduë,
Bruit humain monstre, purge expiration.

The dart from the sky will make its extension,
Deaths speaking: great execution.
The stone in the tree, the proud nation restored,
Noise, human monster, purge expiation.

II 71
Les exilez en Sicile viendront,
Pour deliurer la gent estrange :
Au point du iour les Celtes luy faudront,
La vie demeure à raison Roy se range.

The exiles will come into Sicily
To deliver form hunger the strange nation:
At daybreak the Celts will fail them:
Life remains by reason: the King joins.

II 72
Armee Celtique en Italie vexee,
De toutes parts conflit & grande perte,
Romains fuis, ô Gaule repoussee,
Pres du Thesin, Rubicon pugne incerte.

Celtic army vexed in Italy

53

On all sides conflict and great loss:
Romans fled, O Gaul repelled!
Near the Ticino, Rubicon uncertain battle.

II 73
Au lac Fucin de Benac le riuage,
Prins du Leman ou port de l'Origuion.
Nay de trois bras predict belliq' image.
Par trois couronnes au grand Endymion.

The shore of Lake Garda to Lake Fucino,
Taken from the Lake of Geneva to the port of L'Orguion:
Born with three arms the predicted warlike image,
Through three crowns to the great Endymion.

II 74
De Sens, d'Autun viendront iusques au Rosne
Pour passer outre vers les monts Pyrennees
La gent sortir de la marque d'Auconne,
Par terre & mer le suyura à grands trainnées.

From Sens, from Autun they will come as far as the Rhone
To pass beyond towards the Pyrenees mountains:
The nation to leave the March of Ancona:
By land and sea it will be followed by great suites.

II 75
La voix ouye de l'insolit oyseau,
Sur le canon du respiral estage :
Si haut viendra de froment le boisseau,
Que l'homme d'homme sera Antropophage.

The voice of the rare bird heard,
On the pipe of the air-vent floor:
So high will the bushel of wheat rise,
That man will be eating his fellow man.

II 76
Foudre en Bourgogne fera cas portenteux,
Que par engin homme ne pourroit faire :
De leur senat sacrifiste fait boyteux,
Fera sçauoir aux ennemis l'affaire,

Lightning in Burgundy will perform a portentous deed,
One which could never have been done by skill,
Sexton made lame by their senate
Will make the affair known to the enemies.

II 77
Par arcs, feux, poix & par feu repoussez,
Crys, hurlemens sur la minuict ouys :
Dedans sont mis par les ramparts cassez,
Par cunicule les traditeurs fuis.

Hurled back through bows, fires, pitch and by fires:
Cries, howls heard at midnight:
Within they are place on the broken ramparts,
The traitors fled by the underground passages.

II 78
Le grand Neptune du profond de la mer,
De gent bunique & sang Gaulois meslé :
Les isles à sang, pour le tardif ramer,
Plus luy nuyra que l'occult mal celé.

The great Neptune of the deep of the sea
With Punic race and Gallic blood mixed.
The Isles bled, because of the tardy rowing:
More harm will it do him than the ill-concealed secret.

II 79
La barbe crespe & noire par engin,
Subiuguera la gent cruelle & fiere :
Vn grand Chyren ostera du longin,
Tous les captifs par Seline baniere.

The beard frizzled and black through skill
Will subjugate the cruel and proud people:
The great Chyren will remove from far away
All those captured by the banner of Selin

II 80
Apres conflit du Ieffé l'éloquence,
Par peu de temps se tramme faim, repos,
Point on n'admet les grands à deliurance,
Des ennemis sont remis à propos.

After the conflict by the eloquence of the wounded one
For a short time a soft rest is contrived:
The great ones are not to be allowed deliverance at all:
They are restored by the enemies at the proper time.

II 81
Par feu du Ciel la cité pres qu'aduste,
Vrna menasse encor Ceucalion,
Vexee Sardagne par la punique fuste,
Apres que Libra lairra son Phaeton.

Through fire from the sky the city almost burned:
The Urn threatens Deucalion again:
Sardinia vexed by the Punic foist,
After Libra will leave her Phaethon.

II 82
Par faim la proye sera loup prisonnier,
L'assaillant hors en extreme detresse :
Vn nay ayant au deuant le dernier,
Le grand n'eschappe au milieu de la presse.

Through hunger the prey will make the wolf prisoner,
The aggressor then in extreme distress.
The heir having the last one before him,
The great one does not escape in the middle of the crowd.

II 83
Par le traffic du grand Lyon changé
Et la plus-part tourné en pristine ruine.
Proye aux soldats par pille vendangé,
Par Iura mont & Sueue bruine.

The large trade of a great Lyons changed,
The greater part turns to pristine ruin
Prey to the soldiers swept away by pillage:
Through the Jura mountain and Suevia drizzle.

II 84
Entre Champagne, Sienne, Flora, Tustie,
Six mois neuf iours ne pleuuera vne goutte :
Estrange langue en terre d'Almatie,

56

Courira sus, gastant la terre toute,

Between Campania, Siena, Florence, Tuscany,
Six months nine days without a drop of rain:
The strange tongue in the Dalmatian land,
It will overrun, devastating the entire land.

II 85
Vieux plains de barbe sous le statut seuere
A Lyon fait dessus l'Aigle Celtique :
Le petit grand trop outre perseuere,
Bruit d'armes au ciel, mer rouge Lygustique.

The old full beard under the severe statute
Made at Lyon over the Celtic Eagle:
The little great one perseveres too far:
Noise of arms in the sky: Ligurian sea red.

II 86
Naufrage à classe pres d'onde Hadriatique,
La terre esmeuë sus lair en terre mis :
Egypte tremble augment Mahommetique,
Heraut se rendre à crier est commis.

Wreck for the fleet near the Adriatic Sea:
The land trembles stirred up upon the air placed on land:
Egypt trembles Mahometan increase,
The Herald surrendering himself is appointed to cry out.

II 87
Apres viendra des extremes contrees
Prince Germain sur le throsne doré :
En seruitude & par eaux rencontrees
La dame serue, son temps plus n'a duré.

After there will come from the outermost countries
A German Prince, upon the golden throne:
The servitude and waters met,
The lady serves, her time no longer adored.

II 88
Le circuit du grand fait ruyneux,
Au nom septiesme le cinquiesme sera :

57

D'vn tiers plus grand l'estrange belliqueux
Mouton, Lutece, Aix garantira.

The circuit of the great ruinous deed,
The seventh name of the fifth will be:
Of a third greater the stranger warlike:
Sheep, Paris, Aix will not guarantee.

II 89
Vn iour seront damis les deux grands maistres
Leur grand pouuoir se verra augmenté :
La terre neufue sera en ses hauts estres,
Au sanguinaire, le nombre racompté.

Du ioug feront demis les deux grands maiƒtres,
Leur grand pouuoir se verra augmenté :
La terre-neufue ƒera en ƒes hauts eƒtres,
Au ƒanguinaire le nombre raconté.

Du ioug feront demis les deux grands Maiƒtres :
Leur grand pouuoir ƒe verra augmenté.
La Terre-neuue ƒera en ƒes hauts eƒtres.
Au Sanguinaire le nombre racompté.

One day the two great masters will be friends,
Their great power will be seen increased:
The new land will be at its high peak,
To the bloody one the number recounted.

II 90
Par vie & mort changé regne d'Hongrie,
La loy sera plus aspre que seruice :
Leur grand cité d'vrlemens, plaints & cris,
Castor & Pollux ennemis dans la lice.

Though life and death the realm of Hungary changed:
The law will be more harsh than service:
Their great city cries out with howls and laments,
Castor and Pollux enemies in the arena.

II 91
Soleil leuant vn grand feu on verra,
Bruit & clarté vers Aquilon tendant :

Dedans le rond mort & cris on orra,
Par glaiue, feu, faim mort les attendans.

At sunrise one will see a great fire,
Noise and light extending towards Aquilon:
Within the circle death and one will hear cries,
Through steel, fire, famine, death awaiting them.

II 92
Feu, couleur d'or du ciel en terre veu,
Frappé du haut n'ay, fait cas merueilleux :
Grand meurtre humain, prinse du grand neueu,
Morts d'expectacles, eschappé l'orgueilleux.

Fire color of gold from the sky seen on earth:
Heir struck from on high, marvelous deed done:
Great human murder: the nephew of the great one taken,
Deaths spectacular the proud one escaped.

II 93
Bien pres du Tymbre presse la Lybitine,
Vn peu deuant grand inondation :
Le chef du nef prins, mis en la sentine,
Chasteau, palais en conflagration.

Very near the Tiber presses Death:
Shortly before great inundation:
The chief of the ship taken, thrown into the bilge:
Castle, palace in conflagration.

II 94
Gran, Po, grand mal pour Gaulois receura,
Vaine terreur au maritin Lyon :
Peuple infiny par la mer passera,
Sans eschapper vn quart d'vn million.

Great Po, great evil will be received through Gauls,
Vain terror to the maritime Lion:
People will pass by the sea in infinite numbers,
Without a quarter of a million escaping.

II 95
Les lieux peuplez seront inhabitables,

Pour champs auoir grande diuision :
Regnes liurez à prudens incapables,
Entre les freres mort & dissention.

The populous places will be uninhabitable:
Great discord to obtain fields:
Realms delivered to prudent incapable ones:
Then for the great brothers dissension and death.

II 96
Flambeau ardant au ciel sera veu,
Pres de la fin & principe du Rosne,
Famine, glaiue, tard le secours pourueu,
La Perse tourne enuahit Macedoine.

Burning torch will be seen in the sky at night
Near the end and beginning of the Rhone:
Famine, steel: the relief provided late,
Persia turns to invade Macedonia.

II 97
Romain Pontife garde de t'aprocher,
De la cité qui deux fleuues arrouse :
Ton sang viendras aupres de là cracher
Toy & les tiens quand fleurira la rose,

Roman Pontiff beware of approaching
The city that two rivers flow through,
Near there your blood will come to spurt,
You and yours when the rose will flourish.

II 98
Celuy du sang resperse le visage,
De la victime proche sacrifice,
Tonant en leo augure presage,
Mais estre à mort lors pour la fiancee.

The one whose face is splattered with the blood
Of the victim nearly sacrificed:
Jupiter in Leon, omen through presage:
To be put to death then for the bride.

II 99

Terroir Romain qu'interpretoit augure,
Par gent Gauloise par trop sera vexee
Mais nation Celtique craindra l'heure,
Boreas, classe trop loing l'auoir poussee.

Roman land as the omen interpreted
Will be vexed too much by the Gallic people:
But the Celtic nation will fear the hour,
The fleet has been pushed too far by the north wind.

II 100
Dedans les isles si horrible tumulte,
Rien on n'orra qu'vne bellique brigue,
Tant grand sera des prediteurs l'insulte,
Qu'on se viendra ranger à la grand ligue.

Within the isles a very horrible uproar,
One will hear only a party of war,
So great will be the insult of the plunderers
That they will come to be joined in the great league.

Century 3

III 1
A Pres combat & bataille nauale,
Le grand Neptun à son plus haut beffroy.
Rouge aduersaire de peur deuiendra pasle
Mettât le grâd Ocean en effroy.

After combat and naval battle,
The great Neptune in his highest belfry:
Red adversary will become pale with fear,
Putting the great Ocean in dread.

III 2
Le diuin verbe pourra à la substance,
Comprins ciel, terre, or occult au fait mystique
Corps, ame, esprit ayant toute puissance,
Tant soubs ses pieds comme au siege Celique.

The divine word will give to the sustenance,
Including heaven, earth, gold hidden in the mystic milk:

Body, soul, spirit having all power,
As much under its feet as the Heavenly see.

III 3
Mars & Mercure & l'argent ioint ensemble
Vers le midy extréme siccité,
Au fond d'Asie on dit à terre tremble,
Corinthe, Ephese lors en perplexité.

Mars and Mercury, and the silver joined together,
Towards the south extreme drought:
In the depths of Asia one will say the earth trembles,
Corinth, Ephesus then in perplexity.

III 4
Quand seront proches le deffaut des lunaires,
De l'vn à l'autre ne distant grandement :
Froid, siccité, danger vers les frontieres,
Mesme où l'oracle a prins commencement.

When they will be close the lunar ones will fail,
From one another not greatly distant,
Cold, dryness, danger towards the frontiers,
Even where the oracle has had its beginning.

III 5
Pres loing defaut de deux grands lumi-
Qui suruiendra entre Auril & Mars,
O quel cherté ! mais deux grands debonnaires,
Par terre & mer secourront toutes parts.

Near, far the failure of the two great luminaries
Which will occur between April and March.
Oh, what a loss! but two great good-natured ones
By land and sea will relieve all parts.

III 6
Dans temples clos le foudre y entrera,
Les citadins dedans leurs forts greuez :
Cheuaux, bœufs, hommes, l'onde leur touchera
Par faim, soif soubs les plus foibles armez,

Within the closed temple the lightning will enter,

The citizens within their fort injured:
Horses, cattle, men, the wave will touch the wall,
Through famine, drought, under the weakest armed.

III 7
Les fugitifs feu du ciel sus les piques,
Conflit prochain des corbeaux s'esbatans :
De terre on crie aide secours celiques,
Quand pres des murs seront combatans.

The fugitives, fire from the sky on the pikes:
Conflict near the ravens frolicking,
From land they cry for aid and heavenly relief,
When the combatants will be near the walls.

III 8
Les Cimbres ioints auec leurs voisins,
Depopuler viendront pres de l'Espagne :
Gens amaffez Guienne & Limousins
Seront en ligue & leur feront compagne.

The Cimbri joined with their neighbors
Will come to ravage almost Spain:
Peoples gathered in Guienne and Limousin
Will be in league, and will bear them company.

III 9
Bordeaux, Roüen, & la Rochelle ioints,
Tiendront autour de la grand mer Occeane :
Anglois, Bretons, & les Flamans conioints,
Les chasseront iusques aupres de Rouane.

Bordeaux, Rouen and La Rochelle joined
Will hold around the great Ocean sea,
English, Bretons and the Flemings allied
Will chase them as far as Roanne.

III 10
De sang & faim plus grand calamité,
Sept fois s'appreste à la marine plage :
Monech de faim, lieu pris captiuité,
Le grand mené croc enferree cage.

Greater calamity of blood and famine,
Seven times it approaches the marine shore:
Monaco from hunger, place captured, captivity,
The great one led crunching in a metaled cage.

III 11
Les armes battre au ciel longue saison,
L'arbre au milieu de la cité tombé :
Vermine, rongne, glaiue en face tyfon,
Lors le Monarque d'Hadrie succombé.

The arms to fight in the sky a long time,
The tree in the middle of the city fallen:
Sacred bough clipped, steel, in the face of the firebrand,
Then the monarch of Adria fallen.

III 12
Par la tumeur de Heb. Po, Tag. Tymb. & Rome,
Et par l'estang Geman & Aretin :
Les deux grands chefs & citez de Garonne,
Prins, morts, noyez, partir humain butin.

Because of the swelling of the Ebro, Po, Tagus, Tiber and Rhône
And because of the pond of Geneva and Arezzo,
The two great chiefs and cities of the Garonne,
Taken, dead, drowned: human booty divided.

III 13
Par foudre en l'arche or & argent fondu.
Des deux captifs l'vn l'autre mangera,
De la cité le plus grand estendu,
Quand submergee la classe nagera.

Through lightning in the arch gold and silver melted,
Of two captives one will eat the other:
The greatest one of the city stretched out,
When submerged the fleet will swim.

III 14
Par le rameau du vaillant personnage,
De France infime par le pere infelice :
Honneurs, richesses, trauail en son vieil aage,

Pour auoir creu le conseil d'homme nice.

Through the branch of the valiant personage
Of lowest France: because of the unhappy father
Honors, riches, travail in his old age,
For having believed the advice of a simple man.

III 15
Cœur, vigueur, gloire, le regne changera,
De tous points, contre ayant son aduersaire :
Lors France enfance par mort subiugera,
Le grand regent sera lors plus contraire.

The realm, will change in heart, vigor and glory,
In all points having its adversary opposed:
Then through death France an infancy will subjugate,
A great Regent will then be more contrary.

III 16
Le prince Anglois Mars à son cœur de ciel,
Voudra pour suyure sa fortune prospere :
Des deux duels l'vn percera le fiel,
Hay de luy, bien aymé de sa mere.

An English prince Marc in his heavenly heart
Will want to pursue his prosperous fortune,
Of the two duels one will pierce his gall:
Hated by him well loved by his mother.

III 17
Mont Auentine brusler nuict sera veu,
Le ciel obscur tout à vn coup en Flandres :
Quand le Monarque chassera son neueu,
Les gens d'Eglise commettront les esclandres.

Mount Aventine will be seen to burn at night:
The sky very suddenly dark in Flanders:
When the monarch will chase his nephew,
Then Church people will commit scandals.

III 18
Apres la pluye laict, assez longuette,
En plusieurs lieux de Reims le ciel touché,

O quel conflit de sang pres d'eux s'appreste!
Peres & fils, Roys n'oseront approché.

After the rather long rain milk,
In several places in Reims the sky touched:
Alas, what a bloody murder is prepared near them,
Fathers and sons Kings will not dare approach.

III 19
En Luques sang & laict viendra pleuuoir,
Vn peu deuant changement de preteur,
Grand peste & guerre, faim & soif fera voir,
Loing ou mourra prince & grand recteur

In Lucca it will come to rain blood and milk,
Shortly before a change of praetor:
Great plague and war, famine and drought will be made
visible
Far away where their prince and rector will die.

III 20
Par les contrees du grand fleuve Bethique
Loing d'Ibere au royaume de Grenade,
Croix repoussees par gens Mahometiques,
Vn de Cordube trahyra la contrade.

Through the regions of the great river Guadalquivir
Deep in Iberia to the Kingdom of Grenada
Crosses beaten back by the Mahometan peoples
One of Cordova will betray his country

III 21
Au crustamin par mer Hadriatique,
Apparoistra vn horribe poisson,
De face humaine & la fin aquatique,
Qui se prendra dehors de l'hameçon.

In the Conca by the Adriatic Sea
There will appear a horrible fish,
With face human and its end aquatic,
Which will be taken without the hook.

III 22

Six iours l'assaut deuant cité donné,
Liuree sera forte & aspre bataille,
Trois la rendront & à eux pardonné,
Le reste à feu & à sang tranche taille.

Six days the attack made before the city:
Battle will be given strong and harsh:
Three will surrender it, and to them pardon:
The rest to fire and to bloody slicing and cutting.

III 23
Si, France, passe outre mer Lygustique,
Tu te verra en isles & mers enclos,
Mahommet contraire plus mer Hadriatique
Cheuaux & d'asnes tu rongeras les os.

If, France, you pass beyond the Ligurian Sea,
You will see yourself shut up in islands and seas:
Mahomet contrary, more so the Adriatic Sea:
You will gnaw the bones of horses and asses.

III 24
De l'entreprinse grande confusion,
Perte de gens, tresor innumerables :
Tu ny dois faire encores tension,
France, à mon dire fais que sois recordable.

Great confusion in the enterprise,
Loss of people, countless treasure:
You ought not to extend further there.
France, let what I say be remembered.

III 25
Qui au royaume Nauarrois paruiendra,
Quand le Sicile & Naples seront ioints :
Bigorre & landes par fois larron tiendra,
D'vn qui d'Espagne sera par trop conioints.

He who will attain to the kingdom of Navarre
When Sicily and Naples will be joined:
He will hold Bigorre and Landes through Foix and Oloron
From one who will be too closely allied with Spain.

III 26

Des Roys & princes dresseront simulachres
Augures creuz, escleuez arus ices :
Corne victime doree, & d'azur d'acres,
Interpretez seront les extipices.

They will prepare idols of Kings and Princes,
Soothsayers and empty prophets elevated:
Horn, victim of gold, and azure, dazzling,
The soothsayers will be interpreted.

III 27

Prince lybinique puissant en Occident,
François d'Arabe viendra tant enflammer :
Sçauans aux lettres sera condescendent,
La langue Arabe en François translater.

Libyan Prince powerful in the West
Will come to inflame very much French with Arabian.
Learned in letters condescending he will
Translate the Arabian language into French.

III 28

De terre foible & pauure parentelle
Par bout & paix paruiendra dans l'Empire,
Long temps regner vne ieune femelle,
Qu'oncq' en regne n'en furuint vn si pire.

Of land weak and parentage poor,
Through piece and peace he will attain to the empire.
For a long time a young female to reign,
Never has one so bad come upon the kingdom.

III 29

Les deux ne pueux en diuers lieux nour ris,
Nauale pugne, terre pierres tombees
Viendront si haut esleué enguerris,
Venger l'iniure ennemys succombez.

The two nephews brought up in diverse places:
Naval battle, land, fathers fallen:
They will come to be elevated very high in making war
To avenge the injury, enemies succumbed.

III 30

Celuy qu'en luitte & fer au fait bellique,
Aura porté plus grand que luy le pris :
De nuit au lit fix luy feront la pique,
Nud sans harnois subit sera surprins.

Celuy qu en luite & fer au fait bellique,
Aura porté plus grand que luy le pris :
De nuiçt au liçt fix luy feront la pique,
Nud ƒans harnois ƒubit ƒera ƒurpris.

Celuy qu'en luite & fer au fait bellique
Aura porté plus grand que luy le pris,
De nuit au lit fix luy feront la pique :
Nud ƒans harnois ƒubit ƒera ƒurpris.

He who during the struggle with steel in the deed of war
Will have carried off the prize from on greater than he:
By night six will carry the grudge to his bed,
Without armor he will surprised suddenly.

III 31

Aux champs de Mede, d'Arabe & d'armenie
Deux grands copies trois fois s'assembleront :
Prcs du riuage d'Araxes la mesnie,
Du grand Soliman en terre tomberont.

On the field of Media, of Arabia and of Armenia
Two great armies will assemble thrice:
The host near the bank of the Araxes,
They will fall in the land of the great Suleiman.

III 32

Le grand sepulchre du peuple Aquitanique
S'approchera aupres de la Toscane :
Quand Mars sera pres du coing Germanique,
Et au terroir de la gent Mantuane.

The great tomb of the people of Aquitaine
Will approach near to Tuscany,
When Mars will be in the corner of Germany
And in the land of the Mantuan people.

III 33

En la cité où le loup entrera,
Bien pres de là les ennemis seront :
Copie estrange grand pays gastera,
Aux monts & Alpes les amis passeront.

En la cité où le loup entrera,
Bien pres de là les ennemis feront :
Copie eſtrange grand pays gaſtera.
Aux murs & Alpes les amis paſſeront.

En la cité ou le loup entrera,
Bien prés de là les ennemis feront.
Copie eſtrange grand pays gaſtera.
Aux monts & Alpes les amis paſſeront.

In the city where the wolf will enter,
Very near there will the enemies be:
Foreign army will spoil a great country.
The friends will pass at the wall and Alps.

III 34

Quand le deffaut du Soleil lors sera,
Sur le plein iour le monstre sera veu;
Tout autrement on l'interpretera,
Cherté n'a garde, nul n'y aura pourueu.

When the eclipse of the Sun will then be,
The monster will be seen in full day:
Quite otherwise will one interpret it,
High price unguarded: none will have foreseen it.

III 35

Du plus profond de l'Occident d'Europe,
De pauures gens vn ieune enfant naistra :
Qui par sa langue seduira grande trouppe,
Son bruit au regne d'Orient plus croistra,

From the very depths of the West of Europe,
A young child will be born of poor people,
He who by his tongue will seduce a great troop:
His fame will increase towards the realm of the East.

70

III 36
Enseuely non mort apopletique,
Sera trouué auoir les mains mangées
Quand la cité damnera l'heretique,
Qu'auoit leurs loix ce ieur sembloit changées.

Buried apoplectic not dead,
He will be found to have his hands eaten:
When the city will condemn the heretic,
He who it seemed to them had changed their laws.

III 37
Auant l'assaut oraison prononçee,
Milan prins d'Aigle par embusches deceus :
Muraille antique par canons enfoncee,
Par feu & sang à mercy peu receus.

The speech delivered before the attack,
Milan taken by the Eagle through deceptive ambushes:
Ancient wall driven in by cannons,
Through fire and blood few given quarter.

III 38
La gent Gauloise & nation estrange,
Outre les monts morts, prins & profligez :
Au moys contraire & proche de vendange
Par les Seigneurs en accord redigez.

The Gallic people and a foreign nation
Beyond the mountains, dead, captured and killed:
In the contrary month and near vintage time,
Through the Lords drawn up in accord.

III 39
Les sept en trois mis en concorde,
Pour subiuguer les Alphes Apennines :
Mais la tempeste & ligure coüarde,
Les profigent en subiets ruynes.

The seven in three months in agreement
To subjugate the Apennine Alps:
But the tempest and cowardly Ligurian,

Destroys them in sudden ruins.

III 40
Le grand theatre se viendra redresser,
Le dez ietté, & les rets ia tendus :
Trop le premier en glaz viendra lasser,
Par arcs prostraits de long temps ia fendus.

The great theater will come to be set up again:
The dice cast and the snares already laid.
Too much the first one will come to tire in the death knell,
Prostrated by arches already a long time split.

III 41
Bossu sera esleu par le conseil,
Plus hydeux monstre en terre n'aperceu;
le coup volant Prelat creuera l'œil,
Le traistre au Roy pour fidelle receu,

Hunchback will be elected by the council,
A more hideous monster not seen on earth,
The willing blow will put out his eye:
The traitor to the King received as faithful.

III 42
L'enfant naistra à deux dents en la gorge,
Pierre en Tulcie par pluye tomberont :
Peu d'ans apres ne sera bled ne orge,
Pour faouller ceux qui de faim failliront.

The child will be born with two teeth in his mouth,
Stones will fall during the rain in Tuscany:
A few years after there will be neither wheat nor barley,
To satiate those who will faint from hunger.

III 43
Gens d'alentour de Tarn, Loth, & Garonne
Gardez les monts Appennines passer,
Vostre tombeau pres de Rome & d'Anconne
Le noir poil crespe fera trophee dresser.

People from around the Tarn, Lot and Garonne
Beware of passing the Apennine mountains:

Your tomb near Rome and Ancona,
The black frizzled beard will have a trophy set up.

III 44
Quand l'animal à l'homme domestique
Apres grand peine & sauts viendra parler :
Le foudre à vierge sera si malefique
De terre prinse & suspenduë en l'air.

When the animal domesticated by man
After great pains and leaps will come to speak:
The lightning to the virgin will be very harmful,
Taken from earth and suspended in the air.

III 45
Les cinq estrangers entrez dedans le temple
Leur sang viendra la terre prophaner;
Aux Thoulouseins sera bien dure exemple
D'vn qui viendra les loix exterminer.

The five strangers entered in the temple,
Their blood will come to pollute the land:
To the Toulousans it will be a very hard example
Of one who will come to exterminate their laws.

III 46
Le ciel (Plancus lacité) nous preſage
Par clairs inſignes & par eſtoilles fixes,
Que de ſon change ſubit s'approche l'age,
Ni pour ſon bien, ni pour ſes malefices.

Le Ciel (de Plancus la cité) nous presage
Par clairs insignes & par estoilles fixes,
Que de son change subit s'approche l'aage
Ne pour son bien ne pour les malefices.

Le ciel (de Plancus a cité) nous preſage,
Par clairs inſignes & par eſtoilles fixes,
Que de ſon change ſubit s'approche l'aage,
Ne pour ſon bien, ne pour ſes malefices.

The sky (of Plancus' city) forebodes to us
Through clear signs and fixed stars,

73

That the time of its sudden change is approaching,
Neither for its good, nor for its evils.

III 47
Le vieux monarque dechassé de son regne
Aux Oriens son secours ira querre,
Pour peur de croix ployera son enseigne,
En Mitilene ira par port & par terre.

The old monarch chased out of his realm
Will go to the East asking for its help:
For fear of the crosses he will fold his banner:
To Mitylene he will go through port and by land.

III 48
Sept cens captifs attachez rudement,
Pour la moitié meurdrir, donne le fort :
Le proche espoir viendra si promptement,
Mais non si tost qu'vne quinziesme mort.

Seven hundred captives bound roughly.
Lots drawn for the half to be murdered:
The hope at hand will come very promptly
But not as soon as the fifteenth death.

III 49
Regne Gaulois tu seras bien changé,
En lieu estenge l'Empire translaté,
En autres loix & mœurs seras rangé,
Roüen & Chartres te fera bien du pire.

Gallic realm, you will be much changed:
To a foreign place is the empire transferred:
You will be set up amidst other customs and laws:
Rouen and Chartres will do much of the worst to you.

III 50
La republique de la grande Cité
A grand rigueur ne voudra consentir :
Roy sortir hors par trompette cité,
L'eschelle au mur la cité repentir.

The republic of the great city

Will not want to consent to the great severity:
King summoned by trumpet to go out,
The ladder at the wall, the city will repent.

III 51
Paris coniure vn grand murtre commettre,
Blois le fera venir à plein effe¢t.
Ceux d'Orleans voudront leur Chef remettre.
Tours, Langre, Angiers leur feront grand forfait.

Paris coniure vn grand meurtre commettre,
Bloys le fera ſortir en plein effet :
Ceux d'Orleans voudront leur chef remettre,
Angers, Troye, Langres leur feront grand forfait.

Paris coniure vn grand meurtre commettre
Blois le fera sortir en plain effect :
Ceux d'Orleans voudront leur chef remettre,
Angiers, Troye, Langres : leur feront grâd forfait.

Paris conspires to commit a great murder
Blois will cause it to be fully carried out:
Those of Orléans will want to replace their chief,
Angers, Troyes, Langres will commit a misdeed against
them.

III 52
En la campagne #&131;era #&131;i longue pluye,
Et en la Pouille #&131;i grande siccité,
Coq verra l'Aigle l'esle mal accomplie,
Par Lyon miſe ſera en extremité.

In Campania there will be a very long rain,
In Apulia very great drought.
The Cock will see the Eagle, its wing poorly finished,
By the Lion will it be put into extremity.

III 53
Quand le plus grand emportera le pris
De Nuremberg, d'Auspurg, & ceux de Basle,
Par Agripine chef Frank fort repris,
Trauerseront par Flamans iusqu'en Gale.

75

When the greatest one will carry off the prize
Of Nuremberg, of Augsburg, and those of Bâle
Through Cologne the chief Frankfort retaken
They will cross through Flanders right into Gaul.

III 54
L'vn des plus grands fuyra aux Espagnes,
Qu'en longue playe apres viendra seigner
Passant copies par les hautes montaignes,
Deuastant tout & puis en paix regner.

One of the greatest ones will flee to Spain
Which will thereafter come to bleed in a long wound:
Armies passing over the high mountains,
Devastating all, and then to reign in peace.

III 55
En l'an qu'vn œil en France regnera,
La cour *f*era à vn bien fa*f*cheux trouble :
Le grand de Bloys *f*on amy tuera :
Le regne mis en mal & doute double.

En l'an qu'vn œil en France regnera
La Cour *f*era en vn bien facheux trouble.
Le grand de BLOYS *f*on amy tuera.
Le regne mis en mal & doubte double.

En l'an qu'vn œil en France regnera,
La court sera en vn bien fascheux trouble :
Le grand de Bloys son amy tuëra,
Le regne mis en mal & doute double.

In the year that one eye will reign in France,
The court will be in very unpleasant trouble:
The great one of Blois will kill his friend:
The realm placed in harm and double doubt.

III 56
Montauban, Nismes, Auignon, & Besiers,
Peste, tonnerre, & gresle à fin de Mars :
De Paris pont Lyon mur, Montpellier,
Depuis six cens et sept xxiii. parts.

76

Montauban, Nîmes, Avignon and Béziers,
Plague, thunder and hail in the wake of Mars:
Of Paris bridge, Lyons wall, Montpellier,
After six hundreds and seven score three pairs.

III 57
Sept fois changer verrez gent Britannique
Taints en sang en deux cents nonante an :
France, non, point par appuy Germanique,
Ariez doubte son pole Bastarnan.

Seven times will you see the British nation change,
Steeped in blood in 290 years:
Free not at all its support Germanic.
Aries doubt his Bastarnian pole.

III 58
Aupres du Rin des montagnes Moriques
Naistra vn grand de gens trop tard venu.
Qui deffendra Saurome & Pannoniques,
Qu'on ne sçaura qu'il sera deuenu.

Near the Rhine from the Noric mountains
Will be born a great one of people come too late,
One who will defend Sarmatia and the Pannonians,
One will not know what will have become of him.

III 59
Barbare Empire par le tiers vsurpé,
La plus part de son sang mettre à mort,
Par mort senile, par luy, le quart frappé,
Par peur que sang par la sang en soit mort.

Barbarian empire usurped by the third,
The greater part of his blood he will put to death:
Through senile death the fourth struck by him,
For fear that the blood through the blood be not dead.

III 60
Par toute Asie grande proscription,
Mesme en Mysie, Lysie, & Pamphylie :
Sang versera par absolution,
D'vn ieune noir remply de felonnie.

Throughout all Asia (Minor) great proscription,
Even in Mysia, Lycia and Pamphilia.
Blood will be shed because of the absolution
Of a young black one filled with felony.

III 61
La grande bande & secte crucigere
Se dressera en Mesopotamie,
Du proche fleuue compagnie legere,
Que telle loy tiendra pour ennemie.

The great band and sect of crusaders
Will be arrayed in Mesopotamia:
Light company of the nearby river,
That such law will hold for an enemy.

III 62
Proche del duero par mer Cire ne close,
Viendra percer les grands monts Pyrenées.
La main plus courte & sa perçée glose
A Carcassonne conduira ses menées.

Near the Douro by the closed Tyrian sea,
He will come to pierce the great Pyrenees mountains.
One hand shorter his opening glosses,
He will lead his traces to Carcassone.

III 63
Romain pouuoir sera du tout à bas
Son grand voisin imiter ses vestiges :
Occultes haines ciuiles & debats
Retarderont aux bouffons leurs follies.

The Roman power will be thoroughly abased,
Following in the footsteps of its great neighbor:
Hidden civil hatreds and debates
Will delay their follies for the buffoons.

III 64
Le chef de Perse remplira grands Olchades
Classe trireme contre gent Mahometique,
De Parthe & Mede, & pilliers les Cyclades,

Repos long temps au grand port Ionique.

The chief of Persia will occupy great Olchades,
The trireme fleet against the Mahometan people
From Parthia, and Media: and the Cyclades pillaged:
Long rest at the great Ionian port.

III 65
Quand le sepulcre du grand Romain trouué
Le iour apres sera esleu pontife :
Du senat gueres il ne sera prouué,
Emprisonné son sang au sacré scyphe.

When the sepulcher of the great Roman is found,
The day after a Pontiff will be elected:
Scarcely will he be approved by the Senate
Poisoned, his blood in the sacred chalice.

III 66
Le grand Baillif d'Orleans mis à mort,
Sera par vn de sang vindicatif :
De mort merite ne mourra ne par fort,
Des pieds & mains mal le faisoit captif.

Le grand Baillif d'Orleans mis à mort
Sera par vn de ſang vindicatif :
De mort merite ne mourra, ne par fort :
Des pieds & mains mal le faiſoit captif.

Le grand Baillif d'Orleans mis à mort
Sera par vn de ſang vindicatif.
De mort merite ne mourra, ni par fort.
Des pieds & mains mal le faiſoit captif.

The great Bailiff of Orléans put to death
Will be by one of blood revengeful:
Of death deserved he will not die, nor by chance:
He made captive poorly by his feet and hands.

III 67
Vne nouuelle fe#te de Philoſophes
Meſpriſant mort, or, honneurs & richeſſes :
Des monts Germains ils ſeront limitrophes :

A les enſuiure auront appuis & preſſes.

Vne nouuelle fecte de Philosophes,
Mesprisant mort, or, honneurs & richesses,
Des monts Germains ne seront limitrophes,
A les ensuyure auront appuy & presses.

Vne nouuelle fecte de Philosophes,
Mesprisant mort, or, honneurs & richesses,
Des monts Germains ne ſeront limitrophes :
A les ensuyure auront appuy & preſſes.

A new sect of Philosophers
Despising death, gold, honors and riches
Will not be bordering upon the German mountains:
To follow them they will have power and crowds.

III 68
Peuple sans chef d'Espagne & d'Italie,
Morts profligez dedans la Cherrenosse :
Leur duict trahy par legere folie,
Le sang nager par tout à la trauerse.

Leaderless people of Spain and Italy
Dead, overcome within the Peninsula:
Their dictator betrayed by irresponsible folly,
Swimming in blood everywhere in the latitude.

III 69
Grand exercice conduit par iouuenceau,
Se viendra rendre aux mains des ennemis :
Mais le vieillard nay au demy pourceau,
Fera Chalon & Mascon estre amis.

The great army led by a young man,
It will come to surrender itself into the hands of the enemies:
But the old one born to the half-pig,
He will cause Châlon and Mâcon to be friends.

III 70
La grand Bretagne comprinse d'Angleterre.
Viendra par eaux si fort à inonder :
La ligue neufue d'Ausonne fera guerre,

Que contre eux il se viendra bander.

The great Britain including England
Will come to be flooded very high by waters
The new League of Ausonia will make war,
So that they will come to strive against them.

III 71

Ceux dans les Isles de long temps assiegez,
Prendront vigueur force contre ennemis,
Ceux par dehors morts de faim profliegez
En plus grand faim que jamais seront mis.

Those in the isles long besieged
Will take vigor and force against their enemies:
Those outside dead overcome by hunger,
They will be put in greater hunger than ever before.

III 72

Le bon vieillard tout enseuely,
Pres du grand fleuue par faute soupçon,
Le nouueau vieux de richesse ennobly :
Prins à chemin tout l'or de la rançon.

The good old man buried quite alive,
Near the great river through false suspicion:
The new old man ennobled by riches,
Captured on the road all his gold for ransom.

III 73

Quand dans le regne paruiendra la boiteux,
Compediteur aura proche bastard,
Luy & le regne viendront si fort rogneux
Qu'ains qu'il guerisse son fait sera bien tard.

When the cripple will attain to the realm,
For his competitor he will have a near bastard:
He and the realm will become so very mangy
That before he recovers, it will be too late.

III 74

Naples, Florence, Fauence, & Imole,
Seront en termes de telles fascherie,

Que pour complaire aux malheureux de Noll
Plaint d'auoir fait à son chef moquerie.

Naples, Florence, Faenza and Imola,
They will be on terms of such disagreement
As to delight in the wretches of Nola
Complaining of having mocked its chief.

III 75
Pau, Veronne, Vincence, Saragousse,
De glaiues loings, terroirs de sang humides :
Peste si grande viendra à la grande gousse
Proches secours & bien loings les remedes.

Pau, Verona, Vicenza, Saragossa,
From distant swords lands wet with blood:
Very great plague will come with the great shell,
Relief near, and the remedies very far.

III 76
En Germanie naistront diuerses feçtes,
S'approchans fort de l'heureux Paganiƒme :
Le cœur captif & petites receptes
Feront retour à payer le vray diƒme.

En Germanie naistront diuerses fectes,
S'approchant fort de l'heureux paganisme,
Le cœur captif, & petites receptes
Feront retour à payer le vray dixme.

En Germanie naiƒtront diuerƒes feçtes,
Approchans fort de l'heureux paganiƒme.
Le cueur captif, & petites recettes
Feront retour à payer le vray diƒme.

In Germany will be born diverse sects,
Coming very near happy paganism,
The heart captive and returns small,
They will return to paying the true tithe.

III 77
Le tiers climat sous Aries comprins,
L'an mil sept cens vingt & sept en Octobre,

Le Roy de Perse par ceus d'Egypte prins,
Conflit, mort, perte, à la croix grand opprobre.

The third climate included under Aries
The year 1727 in October,
The King of Persia captured by those of Egypt:
Conflict, death, loss: to the cross great shame.

III 78
Le chef d'Escosse, auec six d'Alemagne,
Par gens de mer Orientaux captifs,
Trauerseront le Calpre & Espagne,
Present en Perse au nouueau Roy craintif.

The chief of Scotland, with six of Germany,
Captive of the Eastern seamen:
They will pass Gibraltar and Spain,
Present in Persia for the fearful new King.

III 79
L'ordre fatal sempiternel par chaine,
Viendra tourner par ordre consequent :
Du port Phocen sera rompuë la chaine,
La cité prinse l'ennemy quant & quant.

The fatal everlasting order through the chain
Will come to turn through consistent order:
The chain of Marseilles will be broken:
The city taken, the enemy at the same time.

III 80
Du regne Anglois l'indigne dechasser,
Le conseiller, par ire mis à feu :
Ses adherants iront si bas trasser,
Que le bastard sera demy receu.

The worthy one chased out of the English realm,
The adviser through anger put to the fire:
His adherents will go so low to efface themselves
That the bastard will be half received.

III 81
Le grand criard ſans honte audacieux,

Sera e∫le gouuerneur del' armée :
La hardie∫∫e de ∫on contentieux.
Le pontrompu, cité de peur pa∫mée.

Le grand Criard ∫ans honte audacieux
E∫leu ∫era Gouuerneur de l'armée.
La hardie∫∫e de ∫on contentieux.
Le Pont rompu, cité de pœur pa∫mee.

Le grand criard sans honte audacieux,
Sera esle gouuerneur de l'armee,
La hardiesse de son contentieux
Le pont rompu, Cité de peur pasmee.

The great shameless, audacious bawler,
He will be elected governor of the army:
The boldness of his contention,
The bridge broken, the city faint from fear.

III 82
Freins, Antibol, villes autour de Nice,
Seront vastees fort, par mer & par terre,
Les sauterelles terre & mer vent propice,
Prins, morts, trossez, pillez sans loy de guerre.

Fréjus, Antibes, towns around Nice,
They will be thoroughly devastated by sea and by land:
The locusts by land and by sea the wind propitious,
Captured, dead, bound, pillaged without law of war.

III 83
Les longs cheueux de la Gaule Celtique,
Accompagnez d'estranges nations,
Mettront captif la gent Aquitanique,
Pour succomber à leurs intentions.

The long hairs of Celtic Gaul
Accompanied by foreign nations,
They will make captive the people of Aquitaine,
For succumbing to their designs.

III 84
La grand cité sera bien desolee,

Des habitans vn seul ny demourra,
Mur, sexe, temple, & vierge violee,
Par fer, feu, peste, canon, peuple mourra.

The great city will be thoroughly desolated,
Of the inhabitants not a single one will remain there:
Wall, sex, temple and virgin violated,
Through sword, fire, plague, cannon people will die.

III 85
La Cité prinse par tromperie & fraude,
Par le moyen d'vn beau ieune attrappé,
L'assaut donné, Raubine pres de Laude,
Luy & tous morts pour auoir bien trompé.

The city taken through deceit and guile,
Taken in by means of a handsome youth:
Assault given by the Robine near the Aude,
He and all dead for having thoroughly deceived.

III 86
Vn chef d'Ausonne aux Espagnesira,
Par mer fera arrest dedans Marseille,
Auant sa mort vn long temps languira,
Apres sa mort l'on verra grand merueille.

A chief of Ausonia will go to Spain
By sea, he will make a stop in Marseilles:
Before his death he will linger a long time:
After his death one will see a great marvel.

III 87
Classe Gauloise n'approches de Corsegne,
Moins de Sardaigne tu t'en repentiras,
Trestous mourrez frustrez de l'aide grogne.
Sang nagera captif ne me croiras.

Gallic fleet, do not approach Corsica,
Less Sardinia, you will rue it:
Every one of you will die frustrated of the help of the cape:
You will swim in blood, captive you will not believe me.

III 88

De Barcelone par mer si grande armee
Toute Marseille de frayeur tremblera,
Isles saisies, de mer ayde fermee,
Ton traditeur en terre nagera.

From Barcelona a very great army by sea,
All Marseilles will tremble with terror:
Isles seized help shut off by sea,
Your traitor will swim on land.

III 89
En ce temps là sera frustré Cypres,
De son secours de ceux de mer Egee,
Vieux trucidez, mais par masles & liphres,
Seduict leur Roy, Royne plus outragee.

At that time Cyprus will be frustrated
Of its relief by those of the Aegean Sea:
Old ones slaughtered: but by speeches and supplications
Their King seduced, Queen outraged more.

III 90
Le grand satyre & Tygre d'Hycarnie,
Don présenté à ceux de l'Ocean :
Vn chef de classe ystra de Carmanie,
Qui prendra terre au Tyrran Phocean.

The great Satyr and Tiger of Hyrcania,
Gift presented to those of the Ocean:
A fleet's chief will set out from Carmania,
One who will take land at the Tyrren Phocaean.

III 91
L'arbre qu'auoit par long temps mort feché,
Dans vne nuit viendra à reuerdir.
Chron. Roy malade. Prince pied ettaché,
Craint d'ennemis fera voiles bondir.

L'arbre qu'auoit par long-temps mort feiché,
Dans vne nuiςt viendra à reuerdir :
Cron, Roy malade, Prince pied eftaché
Craint d'ennemis fera voile bondir.

L'arbre qu'estoit par si long temps seché,
Dans vne nuict viendra à reuerdir :
Cron, Roy malade, prince pied estaché,
Craint d'ennemis fera voile bondir.

The tree which had long been dead and withered,
In one night it will come to grow green again:
The Cronian King sick, Prince with club foot,
Feared by his enemies he will make his sail bound.

III 92
Le monde proche du dernier periode,
Saturne encor tard sera de retour :
Translat empire nation Brodde :
L'œil arraché à Narbon par autour.

The world near the last period,
Saturn will come back again late:
Empire transferred towards the Dusky nation,
The eye plucked out by the Goshawk at Narbonne.

III 93
Dans Auignon tout le chef de l'empire,
Fera apprest pour Paris desolé :
Tricast tiendra l'Annibalique ire,
Luon par change sera mal consolé.

In Avignon the chief of the whole empire
Will make a stop on the way to desolated Paris:
Tricast will hold the anger of Hannibal:
Lyons will be poorly consoled for the change.

III 94
De cinq cens ans plus compte l'on tiendra,
Celuy qu'estoit l'ornement de son temps :
Puis à vn coup grande clarté donrra,
Que par ce siecle les rendra trescontens.

For five hundred years more one will keep count of him
Who was the ornament of his time:
Then suddenly great light will he give,
He who for this century will render them very satisfied.

87

III 95

La loy Moricque on verra deffaillir,
Apres vne autre beaucoup plus seductiue,
Boristhenes premier viendra faillir,
Par dons & Langues vne plus attractiue.

The law of More will be seen to decline:
After another much more seductive:
Dnieper first will come to give way:
Through gifts and tongue another more attractive.

III 96

Chef de Fossan aura gorge couppee,
Par le ducteur du limier & leurier :
La fait paré par ceux du mont Tarpee,
Saturne en leo treziesme Feurier.

The Chief of Fossano will have his throat cut
By the leader of the bloodhound and greyhound:
The deed executed by those of the Tarpeian Rock,
Saturn in Leo February 13.

III 97

Nouuelle loy terre neuue occuper,
Vers la Syrie, Iudee, & Palestine,
Le grand Empire Barbare corruer,
Auant que Pheses son siecle determeine.

New law to occupy the new land
Towards Syria, Judea and Palestine:
The great barbarian empire to decay,
Before the Moon completes it cycle.

III 98

Deux royaus freres ſi fort guerroyeront,
Entre eux ſera la guerre ſi mortelle,
Qu'vn chacun places fortes occuperont.
De regne & vie ſera leur grand querelle.

Deux Royals freres si fort guerroyeront,
Qu'entr'eux sera la guerre si mortelle,
Qu'vn chacun places fortes occuperont,
De regne & vie sera leur grand querelle.

Deux royals freres ʃi forr guerroyeront,
Qu'entre eux ʃera la guerre ʃi mortelle,
Qu'vn chacun place-fortes occuperont :
De regne & vie ʃera leur grand querelle.

Two royal brothers will wage war so fiercely
That between them the war will be so mortal
That both will occupy the strong places:
Their great quarrel will fill realm and life.

III 99
Aux champs herbeux d'alein & du Varneigne,
Dumont Lebron proche de la Durance
Camp des deux parts conflit sera si aigre,
Mesopotamie deffaillira en la France.

In the grassy fields of Alleins and Vernègues
Of the Lubéron range near the Durance,
The conflict will be very sharp for both armies,
Mesopotamia will fail in France.

III 100
Entre Gaulois le dernier honoré,
D'homme ennemy sera victorieux,
Force & terroir en moment exploré,
D'vn coup de trait quand mourra l'enuieux.

The last one honored amongst the Gauls,
Over the enemy man will he be victorious:
Force and land in a moment explored,
When the envious one will die from an arrow shot.

Century IV

IV 1
CEla du reste de sang non espandu,
Venise quiert secours estre donné,
Apres quoir bien long temps attendu,
Cite liuree au premier cornet sonné.

That of the remainder of blood unshed:

89

Venice demands that relief be given:
After having waited a very long time,
City delivered up at the first sound of the horn.

IV 2
Par mort la France prendra voyage à faire,
Classe par mer, marcher monts Pyrenees,
Espagne en trouble, marcher gent militaire,
Des plus grand; dames en France emmenees.

Because of death France will take to making a journey,
Fleet by sea, marching over the Pyrenees Mountains,
Spain in trouble, military people marching:
Some of the greatest Ladies carried off to France.

IV 3
D'Arras & Bourges de Brodes grands enseignes
Vn plus grand nombre de Gascons battre à pied,
Ceux long du Rosne saigneront les Espagnes,
Proche du mont ou Sagonte s'assied.

From Arras and Bourges many banners of Dusky Ones,
A greater number of Gascons to fight on foot,
Those along the Rhône will bleed the Spanish:
Near the mountain where Sagunto sits.

IV 4
L'impotent prince fasché, plaines & querelles
De raps & pillés par coqs & par lybiques
Grand est par terre, par mer infinies voilles,
Seure Italie sera chassant Celtiques.

The impotent Prince angry, complaints and quarrels,
Rape and pillage, by cocks and Africans:
Great it is by land, by sea infinite sails,
Italy alone will be chasing Celts.

IV 5
Croix, paix ſous vn accomply diuin verbe,
L'Eſpagne & Gaules ſeront vnis enſemble,
Grand clade proche, & combat tresacerbe,
Cœur ſi hardy ne ſera qui ne tremble.

Croix, paix ſoubs vn, accompli diuin verbe :
L'Eſpagne & Gaule vnis feront enſemble.
Grand clade proche & combat tresacerbe,
Cueur ſi hardi ne ſera qui ne tremble.

Croix paix soubs vn, accomply diuin verbe,
Espaigne & Gaule seront vnis ensemble,
Grand clade proche, & combat tresacerbe,
Cœur si hardy ne sera qui ne tremble.

Cross, peace, under one the divine word accomplished,
Spain and Gaul will be united together:
Great disaster near, and combat very bitter:
No heart will be so hardy as not to tremble.

IV 6
D'habits nouueaux apres fait la treuue,
Malice tramme & machination :
Premier mourra qui en sera la preuue,
Couleur Venise insidiation.

By the new clothes after the find is made,
Malicious plot and machination:
First will die he who will prove it,
Color Venetian trap.

IV 7
Le fils mineur du grand & aimé Prince
De lepre aura à vint ans grande tache.
De deul ſa mere mourra bien triſte & mince :
Et il mourra là ou tombe chair lache.

Le mineur fils du grand, & hay Prince,
De lepre aura à vingt ans grande tache :
De dueil ſa mere mourra bien triſte & mince,
Et il mourra là où tombe chef laſche.

Le mineur fils du grand & hay prince,
De lepre aura à vingt ans grande tache :
De dueil sa mere mourra bien triste & mince,
Et il mourra là où tombe chef lasche.

The minor son of the great and hated Prince,

91

He will have a great touch of leprosy at the age of twenty:
Of grief his mother will die very sad and emaciated,
And he will die where the loose flesh falls.

IV 8

La grand cité d'assaut pront & repentin,
Surprins de nuict, gardes interrompus :
Les excubies & veilles saint Quintin,
Trucidez gardes & les portails rompus.

The great city by prompt and sudden assault
Surprised at night, guards interrupted:
The guards and watches of Saint-Quentin
Slaughtered, guards and the portals broken.

IV 9

Le chef du camp au milieu de la presse,
D'vn coup de flesche sera blessé aux cuisses.
Lors que Geneue en larmes & en detresse
Sera trahy par Lozan & Souysses.

The chief of the army in the middle of the crowd
Will be wounded by an arrow shot in the thighs,
When Geneva in tears and distress
Will be betrayed by Lausanne and the Swiss.

IV 10

Le ieune Prince accusé faucement,
Mettra en trouble le camp & en querelles;
Meurtry le chef pour le soustenement,
Sceptre appaiser, puis guerir escroüelles.

The young Prince falsely accused
Will plunge the army into trouble and quarrels:
The chief murdered for his support,
Scepter to pacify: then to cure scrofula.

IV 11

Celuy qu'aura couuert de la grand cappe,
Sera induit à quelque cas patrer :
Le douze rouges viendront souiller la nape,
Soubs meurtre, meurtre se viendra perpetrer.

He who will have the government of the great cope
Will be prevailed upon to perform several deeds:
The twelve red one who will come to soil the cloth,
Under murder, murder will come to be perpetrated.

IV 12
Le camp plus grand de route mis en fuite,
Gueres plus outre ne sera pourchassé :
Ost recampé & region reduicte,
Puis hors de Gaule du tout sera chassé.

The greater army put to flight in disorder,
Scarcely further will it be pursued:
Army reassembled and the legion reduced,
Then it will be chased out completely from the Gauls.

IV 13
De plus grand perte nouuelles rapportees,
Le rapport fait le camp s'eslongnera :
Bendes vnies encontre reuoltees,
Double phalange grand abandonnera.

News of the greater loss reported,
The report will astonish the army:
Troops united against the revolted:
The double phalanx will abandon the great one.

IV 14
La mort subiette du premier personnage,
Aura changé & mis vn autre au regne :
Tost, tard venu a si haut & bas aage,
Que terre & mer faudra qu'on le craingne.

The sudden death of the first personage
Will have caused a change and put another in the
sovereignty:
Soon, late come so high and of low age,
Such by land and sea that it will be necessary to fear him.

IV 15
D'où pensera faire venir famine,
De là viendra le rassasiement :
L'œil de la mer par auare canine,

Pour de l'vn l'autre donra huille froment.

From where they will think to make famine come,
From there will come the surfeit:
The eye of the sea through canine greed
For the one the other will give oil and wheat.

IV 16
La Cité franche de liberté fait serue,
Des profligez & resueurs fait azyle :
Le Roy changé, à eux non si proterue,
De cent seront deuenus plus de mille.

The city of liberty made servile:
Made the asylum of profligates and dreamers.
The King changed to them not so violent:
From one hundred become more than a thousand.

IV 17
Changer à Beaune, Nuy, Chaalon, Dijon
Le duc voulant amender la Barree,
Marchant pres fleuue, Poisson bec de Plongeon,
Verra la queuë porte sera serree.

To change at Beaune, Nuits, Châlon and Dijon,
The duke wishing to improve the Carmelite [nun]
Marching near the river, fish, diver's beak
Will see the tail: the gate will be locked.

IV 18
Des plus lettrez dessus les faits celestes
Seront par princes ignorans reprouuez,
Punis d'edit, chassez comme celestes,
Et mis à mort là où seront trouuez.

Some of those most lettered in the celestial facts
Will be condemned by illiterate princes:
Punished by Edict, hunted, like criminals,
And put to death wherever they will be found.

IV 19
Devant Roüan d'insubres mis le siege,
Par terre & mer enfermez les passages,

D'Haynaut : & Flâdres de Gand & ceux de Liege,
Par dons leuees rauiront les riuages.

Before Rouen the siege laid by the Insubrians,
By land and sea the passages shut up:
By Hainaut and Flanders, by Ghent and those of Liége
Through cloaked gifts they will ravage the shores.

IV 20
Paix vbertré long temps Dieu loüera
Par tout son regne desert la fleur de lis,
Corps morts d'eau, terre là l'on apporter,
Sperant vain heur d'estre là enseuelis.

Peace and plenty for a long time the place will praise:
Throughout his realm the fleur-de-lis deserted:
Bodies dead by water, land one will bring there,
Vainly awaiting the good fortune to be buried there.

IV 21
Le changement sera fort difficile,
Cité prouince au change gain sera,
Cœur haut, prudent mis, chassé luy habile
Mer; terre, peuple, son estat changera.

The change will be very difficult:
City and province will gain by the change:
Heart high, prudent established, chased out one cunning,
Sea, land, people will change their state.

IV 22
La grand copie qui *f*era de*f*cha*ff*ée,
Dans vn moment fera be*f*oin au Roy :
La foy promi*f*e de loing *f*era fau*ff*ee,
Nud *f*e verra en piteux de*f*arroy.

La grand copie qui *f*era decha*ff*ée,
Dans vn moment fera be*f*oin au Roy.
La foy promi*f*e de LOIN *f*era fau*ff*ée.

Nud *f*e verra en piteux de*f*arroy.
La grand copie qui sera dechassee
Dans vn moment fera besoin au Roy,

La foy promise de loing sera faussee,

The great army will be chased out,
In one moment it will be needed by the King:
The faith promised from afar will be broken,
He will be seen naked in pitiful disorder.

IV 23
La legion dans la marine classe
Calcine, Magne, souphre & poix bruslera,
Le long repos de l'asseuree place,
Port Selin, Herc le feu les consumera.

The legion in the marine fleet
Will burn lime, lodestone sulfur and pitch:
The long rest in the secure place:
Port Selyn and Monaco, fire will consume them.

IV 24
Quy sous terre saincte d'ame voix fainte
Humaine flemme pour diuin veoir luire,
Fera des seuls de leur sang terre tainte,
Et les saints temples pour les impurs destruire.

Beneath the holy earth of a soul the faint voice heard,
Human flame seen to shine as divine:
It will cause the earth to be stained with the blood of the
monks,
And to destroy the holy temples for the impure ones.

IV 25
Corps sublimes sans fin à l'œil visibles,
Obnubiler viendra par ses raisons,
Corps, front comprins, sens, chef & inuisibles,
Diminuant les sacrees oraisons.

Lofty bodies endlessly visible to the eye,
Through these reasons they will come to obscure:
Body, forehead included, sense and head invisible,
Diminishing the sacred prayers.

IV 26
Lou grand cyssame le leuera d'albelhos,

Que non sauran don, te signen venguddos,
Denech l'embousq, sou gach sous las tail hos,
Ciutat traihdo per cinq leugos non nudos.

The great swarm of bees will arise,
Such that one will not know whence they have come;
By night the ambush, the sentinel under the vines
City delivered by five babblers not naked.

IV 27
Salon, Mansol, Tarascon de Sex l'arc,
Où est debout encor la pyramide :
Viendront liurer le prince d'Annemarc,
Rachapt honny au prince d'Artamide.

Salon, Tarascon, Mausol, the arch of SEX.,
Where the pyramid is still standing:
They will come to deliver the Prince of Annemark,
Redemption reviled in the temple of Artemis.

IV 28
Lors que Venus du Sol ſera couuert,
Sous l'eſplendeur ſera forme occulte,
Mercure au feu les aura deſcouuert,
Par bruit bellique ſera mis à l'inſulte.

Lors que Venus du Sol sera couuert :
Soubs l'esplendeur sera forme occulte :
Mercure au feu les aura descouuert,
Par bruit bellique sera mis à l'insulte.

Lors que Venus du Sol ſera couuert,
Soubs la ſplendeur ſera forme occulte.
Mercure au feu les aura decouuert :
Par bruit bellique ſera mis à l'inſulte.

When Venus will be covered by the Sun,
Under the splendor will be a hidden form:
Mercury will have exposed them to the fire,
Through warlike noise it will be insulted.

IV 29
Le Sol caché ecclipsé par Mercure,

97

Ne sera mis que pour le ciel fecond :
De Vulcan Hermes sera faite pasture,
Slo sera veu pur rutilant & blond.

The Sun hidden eclipsed by Mercury
Will be placed only second in the sky:
Of Vulcan Hermes will be made into food,
The Sun will be seen pure, glowing red and golden.

IV 30
Plus vnze fois Luna Sol ne voudra,
Tous augmentez & baissez de degré :
Et si bas mis que peu or on coudra,
Qu'apres faim, peste, decouuert le secret.

Eleven more times the Moon the Sun will not want,
All raised and lowered by degree:
And put so low that one will stitch little gold:
Such that after famine plague, the secret uncovered.

IV 31
La lune au plain de nuict sur le haut mont
Le nouueau sophe d'vn seul cerueau l'a veu,
Par ses disciples estre immortel semond,
Yeux au midy, en sens mains corps au feu.

The Moon in the full of night over the high mountain,
The new sage with a lone brain sees it:
By his disciples invited to be immortal,
Eyes to the south. Hands in bosoms, bodies in the fire.

IV 32
Es lieux & temps chair au poiff. donra lieu.
La loy commune $f$era faite au contraire.
Vieil tiendra fort, puis o$f$té du milieu.
.... mis fort arriere.

Es lieux & temps chair au poisson dorna lieu,
La loy commune sera faite au contraire
Vieux tiendra fort, puis osté du milieu,
Le Panta choina philon mis fort arriere.

Es lieux & temps chair au poiff. donra lieu :

98

La loy commune *f*era faite au contraire :
Vieux tiendra fort, puis o*f*té du milieu
Le Panta coina philôn mis fort arriere.

In the places and times of flesh giving way to fish,
The communal law will be made in opposition:
It will hold strongly the old ones, then removed from the
midst,
Loving of Everything in Common put far behind.

IV 33
Iupiter ioint plus Venus qu'à la Lune
Appatoi*ff*ant de plenitude blanche :
Venus cachée *f*ous la blancheur Neptune,
De Mars frappé par la granée blanche.

Iupiter ioint plus Venus qu'a la Lune,
Apparoissant de plenitude blanche :
Venus cachee sous la blancheur Neptune,
De Mars frappee par la grande branche.

Iupiter ioint plus Venus qu'à la Lune
Apparoi*ff*ant de plenitude blanche.
Venus cachée *f*oubs la blancheur. Neptune
De Mars frapé par la granée branche.

Jupiter joined more to Venus than to the Moon
Appearing with white fullness:
Venus hidden under the whiteness of Neptune
Struck by Mars through the white stew.

IV 34
Le grand mené captif d'estrange terre,
D'or enchainé au Roy Chyren offert :
Qui dans Ausone, Milan perdra la guerre,
Et tout son ost mis à feu & à fer.

The great one of the foreign land led captive,
Chained in gold offered to King Chyren:
He who in Ausonia, Milan will lose the war,
And all his army put to fire and sword.

IV 35

Le feu estaint les vierges trahyront,
La plus grand part de la bande nouuelle;
Foudre à fer, lance les seuls Roy garderont,
Etrusque & Corse de nuict gorge allumelle.

The fire put out the virgins will betray
The greater part of the new band:
Lightning in sword and lance the lone Kings will guard
Etruria and Corsica, by night throat cut.

IV 36
Les ieux nouueax en Gaule redressez.
Apres victoire de l'Insubre champaigne,
Monts d'Esperie, les grand liez troussez,
De peur trembler la Romaine & l'Espagne.

The new sports set up again in Gaul,
After victory in the Insubrian campaign:
Mountains of Hesperia, the great ones tied and trussed up:
Romania and Spain to tremble with fear.

IV 37
Gaulois par sauts, monts viendra penetrer,
Occupera le grand lieu de l'Insubre :
Au plus profond son ost fera entrer,
Gennes, Monech pousseront classe rubre.

The Gaul will come to penetrate the mountains by leaps:
He will occupy the great place of Insubria:
His army to enter to the greatest depth,
Genoa and Monaco will drive back the red fleet.

IV 38
Pedant que Duc, Roy, Royne occupera,
Chef bizantin captif en Samothrace :
Auant l'assaut l'vn l'autre mangera,
Rebours ferré suyura de sang la trace.

While he will engross the Duke, King and Queen
With the captive Byzantine chief in Samothrace:
Before the assault one will eat the order:
Reverse side metaled will follow the trail of the blood.

IV 39
Les Rodiens demanderont secours,
Par le neglet de ses hoirs deaissée,
L'empire Arabe reualera son cours,
Par Hesperies la cause radressee.

The Rhodians will demand relief,
Through the neglect of its heirs abandoned.
The Arab empire will reveal its course,
The cause set right again by Hesperia.

IV 40
Les forteresses des assiegez ferrez,
Par poudre à feu profondes en abysme :
Les proditeurs seront tous vifs serrez,
Onc aux Sacrifices n'aduint si piteux scisme.

The fortresses of the besieged shut up,
Through gunpowder sunk into the abyss:
The traitors will all be stowed away alive,
Never did such a pitiful schism happen to the sextons.

IV 41
Cymnique sexe captiue par hostage,
Viendra de nuict custodes deceuoir :
Le chef du camp deceu par son lignage,
Lairra le genre, fera piteux auoir.

Female sex captive as a hostage
Will come by night to deceive the guards:
The chief of the army deceived by her language
Will abandon her to the people, it will be pitiful to see.

IV 42
Geneue & Lâgres par ceux de Chartre & Dolle,
Et par Grenoble captif au Montlimart
Seysset, Losanne par fraudulente dole,
Les trahyront par or soixante marc.

Geneva and Langres through those of Chartres and Dôle
And through Grenoble captive at Montélimar
Seyssel, Lausanne, through fraudulent deceit,
They will betray them for sixty marks of gold.

IV 43
Seront ouye au ciel armes battre,
Celuy an me∫me les diuins ennemis :
Voudront loix fain¢tes iniu∫tement debattre :
Par fraude & guerre bien croyans à mort mis.

Seront ouys au Ciel les armes battre,
Celuy an mesme les diuins ennemis,
Voudront loix sainctes iniustement debatre,
Par foudre & guerre bien croyants à mort mis.

Ouis feront au ciel les armes batre.
Celuy an me∫me les diuins ennemis
Voudront loy fainte iniu∫tement debatre.
Par foudre & guerre bien croyants à mort mis.

Arms will be heard clashing in the sky:
That very same year the divine ones enemies:
They will want unjustly to discuss the holy laws:
Through lightning and war the complacent one put to death.

IV 44
Ious gros de Mende, de Roudês, & Milhau,
Cahours, Lymoges, Ca∫tres malo fapmano
De nuech l'intrado, de Bordeaux vn calihau,
Par Perigort toc de la campano.

Lous gros de Mende, de Rhodez & Millau,
Cahors, Limoges, Ca∫tres malo fapmano :
De nuech l'intrado. de Bordeaux vn caillau
Par Perigort au toc de la campano.

Deux gros de Mende de Rhodes & Milhau,
Cahors, Limoges, Castre malo sapmano,
De nuech l'intrado, de Bordeaux vncailhau,
Par Perigort au toc de la Campano.

Two large ones of Mende, of Rodez and Milhau
Cahors, Limoges, Castres bad week
By night the entry, from Bordeaux an insult
Through Périgord at the peal of the bell.

IV 45
Pa conflit Roy, regne abandonnera,
Le plus grand chef faillira au besoing,
Morts profligez, peu en rechappera,
Tous destranchez, vn en sera tesmoing.

Through conflict a King will abandon his realm:
The greatest chief will fail in time of need:
Dead, ruined few will escape it,
All cut up, one will be a witness to it.

IV 46
Bien defendu le fait par excellence,
Garde toy Tours de ta proche ruyne :
Londres & Nantes par Reims fera deffence
Ne paſſez outre au temps de la bruine.

Bien defendu le fait par excellence.
Garde toy Tours de ta proche ruine.
Londres & Nantes par Rheins ſeront defenſe.
Ne paſſez outre au temps de la bruine.

Bien deffendu le fait par excellence,
Garde toy Tours de ta proche ruyne :
Londres & Nantes par Reims fera deffence,
Ne passez outre au temps de la bruyne.

The fact well defended by excellence,
Guard yourself Tours from your near ruin:
London and Nantes will make a defense through Reims
Not passing further in the time of the drizzle.

IV 47
Le noir farouche quand aura essayé,
Sa main sanguine par feu, fer, arcs tendus,
Trestout le peuple sera tant effrayé,
Voir les plus grands par col & pieds pendus.
Le noir farouche quand aura eſſayé

Sa main ſanguine par feu fer, arcs tendus,
Treſtous le peuple ſera tant effrayé
Voir les plus grands par col, & pieds pendus.
Le Noir farouche quand aura eſſayé

Sa main ſanguine par feu, fer, arcs tendus :
Treſtout le peuple ſera tant effrayé,
Voir des plus Grands par col & pieds pendus.

The savage black one when he will have tried
His bloody hand at fire, sword and drawn bows:
All of his people will be terribly frightened,
Seeing the greatest ones hung by neck and feet.

IV 48
Plannure, Ausonne fertille, spacieuse,
Produira tahons si tant de sauterelles,
Clarté solaire viendra nubileuse,
Reger le tout, grand peste venir d'elles.

The fertile, spacious Ausonian plain
Will produce so many gadflies and locusts,
The solar brightness will become clouded,
All devoured, great plague to come from them.

IV 49
Deuant le peuple sang sera respandu,
Que du haut ciel ne viendra eslongner :
Mais d'vn long-temps ne sera entendu,
L'esprit d'vn seul le viendra tesmoigner.

Before the people blood will be shed,
Only from the high heavens will it come far:
But for a long time of one nothing will be heard,
The spirit of a lone one will come to bear witness against it.

IV 50
Libra verra regner les Hesperies,
De ciel & terre tenir la Monarchie,
D'Asie forces nul ne verra peries.
Que sept ne tiennent par rang la Hierarchie.

Libra will see the Hesperias govern,
Holding the monarchy of heaven and earth:
No one will see the forces of Asia perished,
Only seven hold the hierarchy in order.

IV 51
Ve Duc cupide son ennemy ensuyure,
Dans entrera empeschant la phalange,
Hastez à pied si pres viendront poursuyure,
Que la iournee conflite pres de Gange.

A Duke eager to follow his enemy
Will enter within impeding the phalanx:
Hurried on foot they will come to pursue so closely
That the day will see a conflict near Ganges.

IV 52
En cité obsesse aux murs hommes & femmes
Ennemys hors le chef prest à soy rendre :
Vent sera fort encotre les gens-d'armes,
Chassez seront par chaux, poussiere & cendre.

In the besieged city men and woman to the walls,
Enemies outside the chief ready to surrender:
The wind will be strongly against the troops,
They will be driven away through lime, dust and ashes.

IV 53
Les fugitifs & bannis reuoquez,
Peres & fils grand garnissant les haut puits :
Le cruel pere & les siens suffoquez,
Son fils plus pire submergé dans le puis.

Les fugitifs & bannis reuoquez,
Pere & fils grand garni*ff*ant les haut puis.
Le cruel pere, & les *f*iens *f*uffoquez,
Son fils plus pire *f*ubmergé dans le puits.

Les fugitifs & bannis reuoquez.
Pere & fils Grand garni*ff*ants les hauts puits.
Le cruel pere & les *f*iens *f*uffoquez.
Le fils plus pire *f*ubmergé dans le puis.

The fugitives and exiles recalled:
Fathers and sons great garnishing of the deep wells:
The cruel father and his people choked:
His far worse son submerged in the well.

IV 54

Du nom qui oncques ne fut au Roy Gaulois,
Iamais ne fust vn fouldre si craintif,
Tremblant l'Italie l'Espagne & les Anglois,
De femme estrangers grandement attentif.

Of the name which no Gallic King ever had
Never was there so fearful a thunderbolt,
Italy, Spain and the English trembling,
Very attentive to a woman and foreigners.

IV 55

Quand la Corneille sur tour de brique iointe,
Durant sept heures ne fera que crier,
Mort presagee de sang statuë tainte,
Tyran meurtry aux Dieux peuple prier.

When the crow on the tower made of brick
For seven hours will continue to scream:
Death foretold, the statue stained with blood,
Tyrant murdered, people praying to their Gods.

IV 56

Apres victoire de raibeuse langue,
L'esprit tempté en tranquil & repos :
Victeur sanguin par conflit fait harengue,
Rostir la langue & la chair & les os.

After the victory of the raving tongue,
The spirit tempered in tranquillity and repose:
Throughout the conflict the bloody victor makes orations,
Roasting the tongue and the flesh and the bones.

IV 57

Ignare enuie du grand ROy supportee,
Tiendra propos deffendre les escrits :
Sa femme non femme par vn autre tentee,
Plus double deux ne feront ne cris.

Ignorant envy upheld before the great King,
He will propose forbidding the writings:
His wife not his wife tempted by another,
Twice two more neither skill nor cries.

106

IV 58
Soleil ardant dans le gosier coller,
De sang humain arroser terre Etrusque :
Chef seille d'eau mener son fils filer,
Captiue dame conduite en terre Turque.

To swallow the burning Sun in the throat,
The Etruscan land washed by human blood:
The chief pail of water, to lead his son away,
Captive lady conducted into Turkish land.

IV 59
Deux assiegez en ardante fureur,
De soir estaints pour deux plaines tasses,
Le fort limé, & vn vieillard resueur,
Aux ganeuois de Nira monstra trasse.

Two beset in burning fervor:
By thirst for two full cups extinguished,
The fort filed, and an old dreamer,
To the Genevans he will show the track from Nira.

IV 60
Les sept enfans en hostage laissez,
Le tiers viendra son enfant trucider :
Deux par son fils seront d'estoc percez,
Gennes, Florence, lors viendra enconder.

The seven children left in hostage,
The third will come to slaughter his child:
Because of his son two will be pierced by the point,
Genoa, Florence, he will come to confuse them.

IV 61
Le vieux mocqué, & priué de sa place,
Par l'estranger qui le subornera :
Mains de soon fils mangees duant sa face
Les freres à Chartres, Orleans, Rouen trahyra,

The old one mocked and deprived of his place,
By the foreigner who will suborn him:
Hands of his son eaten before his face,

His brother to Chartres, Orléans Rouen will betray.

IV 62
Vn coronel machine ambition,
Se saisira de la plus grande armée :
Contre son prince feinte inuentinon,
Et descouuert sera sous sa ramée.

A colonel with ambition plots,
He will seize the greatest army,
Against his Prince false invention,
And he will be discovered under his arbor.

IV 63
L'armée Celtique contre les montagnars,
Qui seront sceus & prins à la lipée :
Paysans fresz pouseront tost faugnars,
Precipitez tous au fil de l'espée.

Celtique armée contre les montagnars,
Qui feront fceus & pris à la lipée
Payfans frefes poufferont toft faugnars,
Precipitez tous au fil de l'efpée.

L'Armée Celtique contre les montagnars,
Qui feront fceus, & pris à la lippée :
Payfans frefes pouferont toft faognars,
Precipitez tous au fil de l'efpée.

The Celtic army against the mountaineers,
Those who will be learned and able in bird-calling:
Peasants will soon work fresh presses,
All hurled on the sword's edge.

IV 64
Le deffaillant en habit de bourgeois,
Viendra le Roy tempter de son offence :
Quinze soldats la plus part Vstagois,
Vie derniere & chef de sa cheuance.

The transgressor in bourgeois garb,
He will come to try the King with his offense:
Fifteen soldiers for the most part bandits,

108

Last of life and chief of his fortune.

IV 65
Au deserteur de la grand forteresse,
Apres qu'aura son lieu abandonné :
Son aduersaire fera si grand proüesse,
L'Empereur tost mort sera condamné.

Towards the deserter of the great fortress,
After he will have abandoned his place,
His adversary will exhibit very great prowess,
The Emperor soon dead will be condemned.

IV 66
Soubs couleur fainte de sept testes rasées,
Seront semez diuers explorateurs :
Puys & fontaines de poyson arrousées
Au fort de Gennes humains deuorateurs.

Under the feigned color of seven shaven heads
Diverse spies will be scattered:
Wells and fountains sprinkled with poisons,
At the fort of Genoa devourers of men.

IV 67
L'an que Saturne & Mars esgaux combust,
L'air fort sieché, longue traiection :
Par feux secrets, d'ardeur grand lieu adust
Peu pluye, vent, chaud, guerres, incursions,

The year that Saturn and Mars are equal fiery,
The air very dry parched long meteor:
Through secret fires a great place blazing from burning heat,
Little rain, warm wind, wars, incursions.

IV 68
En l'an bien proche eslongné de Venus,
Les deux plus grands de l'Asie & d'Affrique :
Du Rin & Hyster, qu'on dira sont venus,
Cris, pleurs à Malte & costé à Lygustique.

The two greatest ones of Asia and of Africa,
From the Rhine and Lower Danube they will be said to have

come,
    Cries, tears at Malta and the Ligurian side.

IV 69
La cité grande les exilez tiendront,
Les citadins morts meurtris & chassez :
Ceux d'Aquilée à Parme promettront,
Monstrer l'entrée par les lieux non trassez.

The exiles will hold the great city,
The citizens dead, murdered and driven out:
Those of Aquileia will promise Parma
To show them the entry through the untracked places.

IV 70
Bien contiguë des grands monts Pyrenées,
Vn contre l'aigle grand copie addresser :
Ouuertes vaines, forces exterminées,
Que iusque à Pau, le chef viendra chasser.

Quite contiguous to the great Pyrenees mountains,
One to direct a great army against the Eagle:
Veins opened, forces exterminated,
As far as Pau will he come to chase the chief.

IV 71
En lieu d'espouse les filles trucidées,
Meurtre à grand faute ne sera superstile :
Dedans le puys vestules inondées,
L'espouse estainte par hauste d'Aconile.

In place of the bride the daughters slaughtered,
Murder with great error no survivor to be:
Within the well vestals inundated,
The bride extinguished by a drink of Aconite.

IV 72
Les Artomiques par Agen & l'Estore,
A saint Felix feront le parlement,
Ceux de Basas viendront à la malheure,
Saisir Condon & Marsan promptement,

Those of Nîmes through Agen and Lectoure

At Saint-Félix will hold their parliament:
Those of Bazas will come at the unhappy hour
To seize Condom and Marsan promptly.

IV 73
Le nepueu grand par forces prouuera,
Le pache fait du cœur pusillanime :
Ferrare & Ast le Duc esprouuera,
Par lors qu'au soir fera la pantomine,

The great nephew by force will test
The treaty made by the pusillanimous heart:
The Duke will try Ferrara and Asti,
When the pantomime will take place in the evening.

IV 74
Du lac lyman & ceux de Brannonices,
Tous assemblez contre ceux d'Aquitaine,
Germains beaucoup encor plus Souysses,
Seront deffaicts auec ceux d'Humaine.

Those of lake Geneva and of Mâcon:
All assembled against those of Aquitaine:
Many Germans many more Swiss,
They will be routed along with those of the Humane.

IV 75
Prest à combattre fera defection,
Chef aduersaire obtiendra la victoire :
L'arriere garde fera defention
Les deffaillans mort au blanc territoire.

Ready to fight one will desert,
The chief adversary will obtain the victory:
The rear guard will make a defense,
The faltering ones dead in the white territory.

IV 76
Les Nictobriges par ceux de Perigort,
Seront vexez tenant iusques au Rosne :
L'associé de Gascons & Begorn
Trahir le temple, le prestre estant au prosne.

The people of Agen by those of Périgord
Will be vexed, holding as far as the Rhône:
The union of Gascons and Bigorre
To betray the temple, the priest giving his sermon.

IV 77
Selin maonarque, l'Italie pacifique,
Regnes vnis Roy chrestien du monde :
Mourant voudra coucher en terre belsique
Apres pyrates auoir chassé de l'onde.

Selin monarch Italy peaceful,
Realms united by the Christian King of the World:
Dying he will want to lie in Blois soil,
After having chased the pirates from the sea.

IV 78
La grand armee de la pugne ciuille,
Pour de nuict Parme à l'estrange trouuee
Septante neuf meurtris dedans la ville,
Les estrangers passez tous à l'espee,

The great army of the civil struggle,
By night Parma to the foreign one discovered,
Seventy-nine murdered in the town,
The foreigners all put to the sword.

IV 79
Sang Royal fuis Monthurt, Mas, Eguillon,
Remplis seront de Bourdelois les Landes,
Nauarre, Bygorre, pointes & eguillons,
Profonds de faim vorer de Liege glandes.

Blood Royal flee, Monheurt, Mas, Aiguillon,
The Landes will be filled by Bordelais,
Navarre, Bigorre points and spurs,
Deep in hunger to devour acorns of the cork oak.

IV 80
Pres du grand fleuue grand fosse terre egeste
En quinze part sera l'eau diuisee :
La cité prinse, feu, sang cris, conflit mestre,
Et la plus part concerne au collisee.

Near the great river, great ditch, earth drawn out,
In fifteen parts will the water be divided:
The city taken, fire, blood, cries, sad conflict,
And the greatest part involving the coliseum.

IV 81
Pont on fera promptement de nacelles,
Passer l'armee du grand prince Belgique :
Dans profondrées & non loing de Bruxelles
Outre passez, destrenchez sept à picque.

Promptly will one build a bridge of boats,
To pass the army of the great Belgian Prince:
Poured forth inside and not far from Brussels,
Passed beyond, seven cut up by pike.

IV 82
Amas s'approche venant d'Esclauonie,
L'Olestant vieux cité ruynera :
Fort desolee verra sa Romanie,
Puis la grand flamme estaindre ne sçaura,

A throng approaches coming from Slavonia,
The old Destroyer the city will ruin:
He will see his Romania quite desolated,
Then he will not know how to put out the great flame.

IV 83
Combat nocturne le vaillant capitaine
Vaincu fuyra, peu de gens profligé :
Son peuple esmeu sedition non vaine,
Son propre fils le tiendra assiegé.

Combat by night the valiant captain
Conquered will flee few people conquered:
His people stirred up, sedition not in vain,
His own son will hold him besieged.

IV 84
Vn grand d'Auserre mourra bien miserable
Chassé de ceux qui soubs luy ont esté,
Serré de chaisnes, apres d'vn rude cable,

En l'an que Mars Venus, Sol mis en esté.

A great one of Auxerre will die very miserable,
Driven out by those who had been under him:
Put in chains, behind a strong cable,
In the year that Mars, Venus and Sun are in conjunction in summer.

IV 85
Le charbon blanc du noir sera chassé,
Prisonnier fait mené au tumbereau,
Moré Chameau sus pieds entrelassez,
Lors le puisné filera l'aubereau.

The white coal will be chased by the black one,
Made prisoner led to the dung cart,
Moor Camel on twisted feet,
Then the younger one will blind the hobby falcon.

IV 86
L'an que Saturne en eau sera conioinct,
Auec Sol, le Roy fort & puissant,
A Reims & Aix sera receu & oingt,
Apres conquestes meurtrira innocens,

The year that Saturn will be conjoined in Aquarius
With the Sun, the very powerful King
Will be received and anointed at Reims and Aix,
After conquests he will murder the innocent.

IV 87
Vn fils du Roy tant de langues appris,
A ſon aiſné au regne differant :
Son pere beau au plus grand fils compris
Fera perir principal adherant.

Vn fils du Roy tant de langues apris,
A ſon aiſné au regne different.
Son pere beau au plus Grand fils compris,
Fera perir principal adherent.

Vn fils du Roy tant de langues aprins
A son aisné au regne different,

114

Son pere beau au plus beau filz comprins,
Fera perir principe adherent.

A King's son learned in many languages,
Different from his senior in the realm:
His handsome father understood by the greater son,
He will cause his principal adherent to perish.

IV 88
Le grand Anthoine du moindre fait sordide
De Phytriase à son dernier rongé,
Vn qui de plomb voudra estre cupide,
Passant le port d'esleu sera plongé.

Anthony by name great by the filthy fact
Of Lousiness wasted to his end:
One who will want to be desirous of lead,
Passing the port he will be immersed by the elected one.

IV 89
Trente de Londres secret coniureront,
Contre leur Roy sur le pont l'entreprinse,
Luy, satalites la mort degousteront.
Vn Roy esleu blonde, natif de Frize.

Thirty of London will conspire secretly
Against their King, the enterprise on the bridge:
He and his satellites will have a distaste for death,
A fair King elected, native of Frisia.

IV 90
Les deux copis aux murs ne pourront ioindre
Dans cest instant trembler Milan, Ticin :
Faim, soif, doutance si fort les viendra poindre
Chair, pain, ne viures, n'auront vn seul boucin.

The two armies will be unable to unite at the walls,
In that instant Milan and Pavia to tremble:
Hunger, thirst, doubt will come to plague them very strongly
  They will not have a single morsel of meat, bread or
victuals.

IV 91

Au Duc Gaulois contrainct battre au duelle,
La nef Meselle monech n'approchera.
Tort accusé prison perpetuelle,
Son fils regner auant mort taschera.

For the Gallic Duke compelled to fight in the duel,
The ship of Melilla will not approach Monaco,
Wrongly accused, perpetual prison,
His son will strive to reign before his death.

IV 92
Teste trenchee du vaillant Capitaine,
Ser ietté deuant son aduersaire,
Son corps pendu de sa classe à l'antenne,
Confus fuira par rames à vent contraire.

The head of the valiant captain cut off,
It will be thrown before his adversary:
His body hung on the sail-yard of the ship,
Confused it will flee by oars against the wind.

IV 93
Vn serpent veu proche du lit Royal,
Sera par dame, nuict chiens n'abbayeront :
Lors naistre en France vn Prince tant Royal
Du Ciel venu tous les princes verront.

A serpent seen near the royal bed,
It will be by the lady at night the dogs will not bark:
Then to be born in France a Prince so royal,
Come from heaven all the Princes will see him.

IV 94
Deux grands freres seront chassez d'Espaigne
L'aisné vaincu soubs les monts Pyrennees :
Rougir mer, Rosne sang leman d'alemagne,
Narbon, Blyterres, d'Ath, contaminees.

Two great brothers will be chased out of Spain,
The elder conquered under the Pyrenees mountains:
The sea to redden, Rhône, bloody Lake Geneva from
Germany,
Narbonne, Béziers contaminated by Agde.

116

IV 95

Le regne à deux laissé bien peu tiendront,
Trois ans sept mois passez feront la guerre :
Les deux vestales contre rebelleront,
Victor puis nay en Armonique terre.

The realm left to two they will hold it very briefly,
Three years and seven months passed by they will make war:
The two Vestals will rebel in opposition,
Victor the younger in the land of Brittany.

IV 96

La sœur aisnee de l'Isle Britannique,
Quinze ans deuant le frere aura naissance,
Par son promis moyennant verrifique,
Succedera au regne de Balance.

The elder sister of the British Isle
Will be born fifteen years before her brother,
Because of her promise procuring verification,
She will succeed to the kingdom of the balance.

IV 97

L'an que Mercure, Mars, Venus retrograde,
Du grand Monarque la ligne ne faillir,
Esleu du peuple l'vsitant pres de Gagdole,
Qu'en paix & regne viendra fort enuiellir.

The year that Mercury, Mars, Venus in retrogression,
The line of the great Monarch will not fail:
Elected by the Portuguese people near Cadiz,
One who will come to grow very old in peace and reign.

IV 98

Les Albanois passeront dedans Rome,
Moyennant Langres demiples affublez,
Marquis & Duc ne pardonner à homme,
Feu, sang morbile, point d'eau, faillir les bleds.

Those of Alba will pass into Rome,
By means of Langres the multitude muffled up,
Marquis and Duke will pardon no man,

Fire, blood, smallpox no water the crops to fail.

IV 99
L'aisné vaillant de la fille du Roy,
Repoussera si auant les Celtiques,
Qu'il mettra foudres, combien en tel arroy,
Peu & loing puis profondes Hesperiques.

The valiant elder son of the King's daughter,
He will hurl back the Celts very far,
Such that he will cast thunderbolts, so many in such an array
Few and distant, then deep into the Hesperias.

IV 100
De feu celeste au Royal edifice,
Quand la lumiere du Mars deffaillira,
Sept mois grand' guerre, mort gent de malefice,
Rouen Eureux, au Roy ne faillira.

From the celestial fire on the Royal edifice,
When the light of Mars will go out,
Seven months great war, people dead through evil
Rouen, Evreux the King will not fail.

Century V

V 1
A Vant venuë de ruyne Celtique,
Dedans le temple deux parlementerôt,
Poignar cœur, d'vn monté au coursier & pique
Sans faire bruit le grand enterreront.

Before the coming of Celtic ruin,
In the temple two will parley
Pike and dagger to the heart of one mounted on the steed,
They will bury the great one without making any noise.

V 2
Sept coniurez au banquet feront luyre,
Contre les trois le fer hors de nauire,
L'vn les deux classes au grand fera conduire,

Quand par le mail denier au front luy tire.

Seven conspirators at the banquet will cause to flash
The iron out of the ship against the three:
One will have the two fleets brought to the great one,
When through the evil the latter shoots him in the forehead.

V 3
Le successeur de la Duché viendra,
Beaucoup plus outre que la mer de Toscane,
Gauloise branche la Florence tiendra,
Dans son giron d'accord nautique Rane.

The successor to the Duchy will come,
Very far beyond the Tuscan Sea:
A Gallic branch will hold Florence,
The nautical Frog in its bosom be agreement.

V 4
Le gros mastin de cité dechassé
Sera fasché de l'estrange alliance,
Apres aux champs auoir le chef chassé,
Le Loup & l'ours se donneront defiance.

The large mastiff expelled from the city
Will be vexed by the strange alliance,
After having chased the stag to the fields
The wolf and the Bear will defy each other.

V 5
Sous ombre saincte d'oster de seruitude,
Peuple & cité l'vsurpera luy-mesmes,
Pire fera par faux de ieune pute,
Liuré au champ lisant le faux proesme.

Under the shadowy pretense of removing servitude,
He will himself usurp the people and city:
He will do worse because of the deceit of the young prostitute,
Delivered in the field reading the false poem.

V 6
Au Roy l'augure sus le chef la main mettre

119

Viendra prier pour la paix Italique;
A la main gauche viendra changer se Sceptre,
De Roy viendra Empereur pacifique.

The Augur putting his hand upon the head of the King
Will come to pray for the peace of Italy:
He will come to move the scepter to his left hand,
From King he will become pacific Emperor.

V 7

Du trium vir seront trouuez les os,
Cerchant profond tresor enigmatique :
Ceux d'alentour ne seront en repos,
De concauer marbre & plomb metalique.

The bones of the Triumvir will be found,
Looking for a deep enigmatic treasure:
Those from thereabouts will not be at rest,
Digging for this thing of marble and metallic lead.

V 8

Sera laissé le feu mort vif caché,
Dedans les globes horribles espouuentable
De nuict à classé cité en poudre laché,
Ls cité à feu, l'ennemy fauorable.

There will be unleashed live fire, hidden death,
Horrible and frightful within the globes,
By night the city reduced to dust by the fleet,
The city afire, the enemy amenable.

V 9

Iusques au fond la grand arq demoluë,
Par chef captif l'amy anticipé,
Naistra de dame front face cheueluë,
Puis par astuce Duc à mort attrappé.

The great arch demolished down to its base,
By the chief captive his friend forestalled,
He will be born of the lady with hairy forehead and face,
Then through cunning the Duke overtaken by death.

V 10

Vn chef Celtique dans le conflit blessé,
Aupres de caue voyant siens mort abbatre :
De sang & playes & d'ennemis pressé,
Et secours par incogneuz de quatre.

A Celtic chief wounded in the conflict
Seeing death overtaking his men near a cellar:
Pressed by blood and wounds and enemies,
And relief by four unknown ones.

V 11
Mer par solaires seure ne passera,
Ceux de Venus tiendront toute l'Affrique :
Leur regne plus Sol, Saturne n'occupera,
Et changera la mort Asiatique.

The sea will not be passed over safely by those of the Sun,
Those of Venus will hold all Africa:
Saturn will no longer occupy their realm,
And the Asiatic part will change.

V 12
Aupres du Lac Leman sera conduite,
Par garse estrange cité voulant trahir,
Auant son meurtre à Aspurg la grand fuitte,
Et ceux du Rhin la viendront inuahir.

To near the Lake of Geneva will it be conducted,
By the foreign maiden wishing to betray the city:
Before its murder at Augsburg the great suite,
And those of the Rhine will come to invade it.

V 13
Par grand fureur le Roy Romain Belgique,
Vexer voudra par phalange barbare :
Fureur grinçant chassera gent Lybique,
Depuis Pannons iusques Hercules la hare.

With great fury the Roman Belgian King
Will want to vex the barbarian with his phalanx:
Fury gnashing, he will chase the African people
From the Pannonias to the pillars of Hercules.

121

V 14

Saturne & Mars en Leo Espagne captiue,
Par chef Libique au conflit attrapé :
Proche de Malte, Heredde prinse viue,
Et Romain sceptre sera par coq frappé.

Saturn and Mars in Leo Spain captive,
By the African chief trapped in the conflict,
Near Malta, Herod taken alive,
And the Roman scepter will be struck down by the Cock.

V 15

En nauigant captif prins grand pontife;
Grands apprestez saillir les clercs tumultuez :
Second esleu absent son bien debise,
Son fauory bastard à mort tué.

The great Pontiff taken captive while navigating,
The great one thereafter to fail the clergy in tumult:
Second one elected absent his estate declines,
His favorite bastard to death broken on the wheel.

V 16

A son haut prix la lerme Sabee,
D'humaine chair pour mort en cendre mettre,
A l'isle Pharos croisars perturbee,
Alors qu'a Rodes paroistra dure espectre.

The Sabaean tear no longer at its high price,
Turning human flesh into ashes through death,
At the isle of Pharos disturbed by the Crusaders,
When at Rhodes will appear a hard phantom.

V 17

De nuict passant le Roy pres d'vne Andronne
Celuy de Cypres & principal guette,
Le Roy failly la main fuit long du Rosne,
Les coniurez l'iront à mort mettre.

By night the King passing near an Alley,
He of Cyprus and the principal guard:
The King mistaken, the hand flees the length of the Rhône,
The conspirators will set out to put him to death.

V 18
De dueil mourra l'infelix profligé,
Celebrera son vitrix l'heccatombe :
Pristine loy, franc Edit redigé,
Le mur & Prince au septieme iour tombe.

The unhappy abandoned one will die of grief,
His conqueress will celebrate the hecatomb:
Pristine law, free edict drawn up,
The wall and the Prince falls on the seventh day.

V 19
Le grand Royal d'or, d'airain augmenté,
Rompu la pache, par ieune ouuerte guerre,
Peuple affligé par vn chef lamenté,
De sang barbare sera couuert de terre.

The great Royal one of gold, augmented by brass,
The agreement broken, war opened by a young man:
People afflicted because of a lamented chief,
The land will be covered with barbarian blood.

V 20
Delà les Alpes grand armee passera,
Vn peu deuant naistra monstre vapin :
Prodigieux & subit tournera,
Le grand Toscan à son lieu plus propin.

The great army will pass beyond the Alps,
Shortly before will be born a monster scoundrel:
Prodigious and sudden he will turn
The great Tuscan to his nearest place.

V 21
Par le trespas du Monarque latin,
Ceux qu'il aura par regne secourus :
Le feu luyra, diuisé le butin,
La mort publique aux hardis incorus,

By the death of the Latin Monarch,
Those whom he will have assisted through his reign:
The fire will light up again the booty divided,

123

Public death for the bold ones who incurred it.

V 22
Auant qu'a Rome grand ait rendu l'ame,
Effrayeur grande à l'armee estrangere :
Par escadrons l'embusche pres de Parme,
Puis les deux rouges ensemble feront chere.

Before the great one has given up the ghost at Rome,
Great terror for the foreign army:
The ambush by squadrons near Parma,
Then the two red ones will celebrate together.

V 23
Les deux contents seront vnis ensemble
Quant la pluspart à Mars sera conioinct :
Le grand d'Affrique en effrayeur & tremble,
Duumuirat par la classe desioint.

The two contented ones will be united together,
When for the most part they will be conjoined with Mars:
The great one of Africa trembles in terror,
Duumvirate disjoined by the fleet.

V 24
Le regne & loy soubs Venus esleué,
Saturne aura sus Iupiter empire :
La Loy & regne par le Soleil leué,
Par Saturnius endurera le pire :

The realm and law raised under Venus,
Saturn will have dominion over Jupiter:
The law and realm raised by the Sun,
Through those of Saturn it will suffer the worst.

V 25
Le prince Arabe, Mars, Sol, Venus, Lyon,
Regne d'Eglise par mer succombera :
Deuers la Perse bien pres d'vn million,
Bisance, Egypte, ver. serp. inuadera.

The Arab Prince Mars, Sun, Venus, Leo,
The rule of the Church will succumb by sea:

124

Towards Persia very nearly a million men,
The true serpent will invade Byzantium and Egypt.

V 26
La gent esclaue par vn heur martiel,
Viendra en haut degré tant esleué :
Changeront prince, naistra vn prouincial,
Passer la mer copie aux monts leué.

The slavish people through luck in war
Will become elevated to a very high degree:
They will change their Prince, one born a provincial,
An army raised in the mountains to pass over the sea.

V 27
Par feu & armes non loing de la marnegro,
Viendra de Perse occuper Trebisonde :
Trembler Pharos Methelin, Solalegro,
De sang Arabe d'Hadrie couuert onde.

Through fire and arms not far from the Black Sea,
He will come from Persia to occupy Trebizond:
Pharos, Mytilene to tremble, the Sun joyful,
The Adriatic Sea covered with Arab blood.

V 28
Le bras pendu & la iambe liée,
Visage pasle au sein poignard caché :
Trois qui seront iurez de la meslée,
Au grand de Gennes sera le fer lasché.

His arm hung and leg bound,
Face pale, dagger hidden in his bosom,
Three who will be sworn in the fray
Against the great one of Genoa will the steel be unleashed.

V 29
La liberté ne sera recouurée,
L'occupera noir fier vilain inique :
Quant la matiere du pont sera ouurée,
D'Hister, Venise faschée la republique.

Liberty will not be recovered,

A proud, villainous, wicked black one will occupy it,
When the matter of the bridge will be opened,
The republic of Venice vexed by the Danube.

V 30
Tout à l'entour de la grande cité,
Seront soldats logez par champs & ville,
Donner l'assaut Paris, Rome incité,
Sur le pont lors sera faite grand pille,

All around the great city
Soldiers will be lodged throughout the fields and towns:
To give the assault Paris, Rome incited,
Then upon the bridge great pillage will be carried out.

V 31
Ou tout bon est tout bien Soleil & Lune,
Est abondant sa ruyne s'approche,
Du ciel s'aduance vaner ta fortune,
En mesme que la septiesme roche.

Through the Attic land fountain of wisdom,
At present the rose of the world:
The bridge ruined, and its great pre-eminence
Will be subjected, a wreck amidst the waves.

V 32
Where all is good, the Sun all beneficial and the Moon
Is abundant, its ruin approaches:
From the sky it advances to change your fortune.
In the same state as the seventh rock.

V 33
Des principaux de cité rebelée
Qui tiendront fort pour liberté rauoir :
Detrencher masses infelice meslée,
Cris vrlemens a Nante; piteux voir.

Of the principal ones of the city in rebellion
Who will strive mightily to recover their liberty:
The males cut up, unhappy fray,
Cries, groans at Nantes pitiful to see.

V 34

Du plus profond de l'occident Anglois.
Ou est le chef de l'isle Britannique :
Entrera classe dans Gyronde par Blois,
Par vin & feux cachez aux barriques.

From the deepest part of the English West
Where the head of the British isle is
A fleet will enter the Gironde through Blois,
Through wine and salt, fires hidden in the casks.

V 35

Par cité franche de la grand mer Seline,
Qui porte encore à l'estomach la pierre :
Angloise classe viendra sous la bruine,
Vn rameau prendre du grand ouuerte guerre.

Par cité franche de la grand mer Seline,
Qui porte encores à l'e∫tomach la pierre,
Angloi∫e cla∫∫e viendra ∫ous la bruine
Vn rameau prendre, du grand ouuerte guerre.

Par cité franche de la grand mer Seline,
Qui porte encore à l'e∫tomac la pierre :
Angloi∫e cla∫∫e viendra ∫oubs la bruine
Vn rameau prendre de grande ouuerte guerre.

For the free city of the great Crescent sea,
Which still carries the stone in its stomach,
The English fleet will come under the drizzle
To seize a branch, war opened by the great one.

V 36

De sœur le frere par simulte faintise,
Viendra mesler rosee en myneral :
Sur la placente donne à vieille tardiue,
Meurt le goustant sera simple & rural.

The sister's brother through the quarrel and deceit
Will come to mix dew in the mineral:
On the cake given to the slow old woman,
She dies tasting it she will be simple and rustic.

V 37

Trois cens seront d'vn vouloir & accord,
Que pour venir au bout de leur attainte :
Vingt mois apres tous & records,
Leur Roy trahir simulant haine fainte.

Three hundred will be in accord with one will
To come to the execution of their blow,
Twenty months after all memory
Their king betrayed simulating feigned hate.

V 38

Ce grand Monarque qu'au mort ſuccedera,
Donnera vie illicite & lubrique :
Par nonchalance à tous concedera,
Qu'à la parfin faudra la loy Salique.

Ce grand monarque qu'au mort succedera,
Donnera vie illicite & lubrique :
Par nonchalance à tous concedera,
Qu'a la parfin faudra la loy Salique.

Ce grand Monarque qu'au mort ſuccedera,
Donnera vie illicite & lubrique,
Par nonchalance à tous concedera,
Qu'à la parfin faudra la loy Salique.

He who will succeed the great monarch on his death
Will lead an illicit and wanton life:
Through nonchalance he will give way to all,
So that in the end the Salic law will fail.

V 39

Du vray rameau des fleurs de lys yssu,
Mis & logé heritier d'Herutrie :
Son sang antique de longue main yssu,
Fera Florence florir en l'ermoirie.

Issued from the true branch of the fleur-de-lis,
Placed and lodged as heir of Etruria:
His ancient blood woven by long hand,
He will cause the escutcheon of Florence to bloom.

V 40

Le sang royal sera si tresmeslé,
Contrainct seront Gaulois de l'Hesperie :
On attendra que terme soit coulé,
Et que memoire de la voix soit perie.

The blood royal will be so very mixed,
Gauls will be constrained by Hesperia:
One will wait until his term has expired,
And until the memory of his voice has perished.

V 41

Nay sous les vmbres & iournée nocturne
Sera en regne & bonté souueraine,
Fera renaistre son sang de l'antique verné,
Renouuellant siecle d'or pour l'airain.

Born in the shadows and during a dark day,
He will be sovereign in realm and goodness:
He will cause his blood to rise again in the ancient urn,
Renewing the age of gold for that of brass.

V 42

Mars esleué en son plus haut beffroy,
Fera retraire les Allobrox de France :
La gent Lombarde fera si grand effroy,
A ceux de l'Aigle compris sous la Balance.

Mars raised to his highest belfry
Will cause the Savoyards to withdraw from France:
The Lombard people will cause very great terror
To those of the Eagle included under the Balance.

V 43

La grand ruyne des sacrees ne s'eslongne,
Prouence, Naples, Sicile Seez & Ponce :
En Germanie, au Rin & à Cologne,
Vexez à mort par tous ceux de Magonce.

The great ruin of the holy things is not far off,
Provence, Naples, Sicily, Sées and Pons:
In Germany, at the Rhine and Cologne,
Vexed to death by all those of Mainz.

129

V 44
Par mer le rouge sera prins des pyrates,
La paix sera par son moyen troublee :
L'ire & l'auare commettra par sainct acte,
Au grand Pontife sera l'armee doublee.

On sea the red one will be taken by pirates,
Because of him peace will be troubled:
Anger and greed will he expose through a false act,
The army doubled by the great Pontiff.

V 45
Le grand Empire sera tost desolé,
Et translaté pres d'arduenne silue :
Les deux bastards pres l'aisné decollé,
Et regnera Aeneodarb, nez de milue.

The great Empire will soon be desolated
And transferred to near the Ardennes:
The two bastards beheaded by the oldest one,
And Bronzebeard the hawk-nose will reign.

V 46
Par chappeaux rouges querelles & nouueaux scismes,
Quand on aura esleu le Sabinois,
On produira contre luy grands sophismes,
Et sera Rome lesee par Albanois.

Quarrels and new schism by the red hats
When the Sabine will have been elected:
They will produce great sophism against him,
And Rome will be injured by those of Alba.

V 47
Le grand Arabe marchera bien auant,
Trahy sera par les Bisantinois,
L'antique Rodes luy viendra au deuant,
Et plus grand mal par austre Pannonois.

The great Arab will march far forward,
He will be betrayed by the Byzantians:
Ancient Rhodes will come to meet him,

And greater harm through the Austrian Hungarians.

V 48
Apres la grande affliction du sceptre,
Deux ennemis par eux seront daffaits,
Classe d'Affrique aux Pannonois viedra naistre,
Par mer & terre seront horribles faits.

After the great affliction of the scepter,
Two enemies will be defeated by them:
A fleet from Africa will appear before the Hungarians,
By land and sea horrible deeds will take place.

V 49
Nul de l'Espagne mais de l'antique France,
Ne sera esleu pour le tremblant nacelle :
A l'ennemy sera faicte fiance,
Qui dans son regne sera peste cruelle.

Not from Spain but from ancient France
Will one be elected for the trembling bark,
To the enemy will a promise be made,
He who will cause a cruel plague in his realm.

V 50
L'an que les freres du lys seront en aage,
Lvn d'eux tiendra la grande Romanie,
Trembler les monts, ouuert Latin passage,
Pache marcher contre fort d'Armenie.

The year that the brothers of the lily come of age,
One of them will hold the great Romania:
The mountains to tremble, Latin passage opened,
Agreement to march against the fort of Armenia.

V 51
La gent de Dace, d'Angleterre & Polonne,
Et de Bohesme feront nouuelle ligue :
Pour passer ourre d'Hercules la colonne,
Barcyns, Tyrrens dresser cruelle brigue.

The people of Dacia, England, Poland
And of Bohemia will make a new league:

To pass beyond the pillars of Hercules,
The Barcelonians and Tuscans will prepare a cruel plot.

V 52
Vn Roy sera qui donrra l'opposite,
Les exilez esleuez sur le regne :
De sang nager la gent caste hypolite,
Et florira long temps soubs telle enseigne.

There will be a King who will give opposition,
The exiles raised over the realm:
The pure poor people to swim in blood,
And for a long time will he flourish under such a device.

V 53
La loy de Sol, & Venus contendans,
Appropriant l'esprit de prophetie :
Ne l'vn ne l'autre ne seront entendans,
Par Sol tiendra la loy du grand Messie.

The law of the Sun and of Venus in strife,
Appropriating the spirit of prophecy:
Neither the one nor the other will be understood,
The law of the great Messiah will hold through the Sun.

V 54
Du pont Eunixe & la grand Tartarie,
Vn Roy sera qui viendra voir la Gaule,
Transpercera Alane & l'Armenie,
Et dans Bisance lairra sanglante Gaule.

From beyond the Black Sea and great Tartary,
There will be a King who will come to see Gaul,
He will pierce through Alania and Armenia,
And within Byzantium will he leave his bloody rod.

V 55
De la felice Arabie contrade,
Naistre puissant de loy Mahometique :
Vexer l'Espagne, conquester la Grenade,
Et plus par mer a la gent Lygustique.

In the country of Arabia Felix

There will be born one powerful in the law of Mahomet:
To vex Spain, to conquer Grenada,
And more by sea against the Ligurian people.

V 56
Par le trespas du tres vieillard pontife,
Sera esleu Romain de bon aage :
Qu'il sera dit que le Siege debiffe
Et long tiendra & de picquant ouurage.

Through the death of the very old Pontiff
A Roman of good age will be elected,
Of him it will be said that he weakens his see,
But long will he sit and in biting activity.

V 57
Istra du mont Gaulsier & Auentin,
Qui par le trou aduertira l'armee :
Entre deux rocs sera prins le butin,
De Sext. mansol faillir la renommee.

There will go from Mont and Aventin,
One who through the hole will warn the army:
Between two rocks will the booty be taken,
Of Sectus' mausoleum the renown to fail.

V 58
De l'archeduc d'Vticense, Gardoing,
Par la forest & mont inaccessible.
En my du pont sera tasché au poing,
Le chef Nemans qui tant sera terrible.

By the aqueduct of Uzès over the Gard,
Through the forest and inaccessible mountain,
In the middle of the bridge there will be cut in the fist
The chief of Nîmes who will be very terrible.

V 59
Au chef Anglois à Nimes trop feiour,
Deuers l'Espagne au secours Areobarbe,
Plusieurs mourront par Mars ouuert ce iour,
Quand en Artois faillir estoille en barbe.

Too long a stay for the English chief at Nîmes,
Towards Spain Redbeard to the rescue:
Many will die by war opened that day,
When a bearded star will fall in Artois.

V 60
Par teste rase viendra bien mal eslire,
Plus que sa charge ne porte passera :
Si grand fureur & rage fera dire,
Qu'à feu & sang tout sexe tranchera.

By the shaven head a very bad choice will come to be made,
Overburdened he will not pass the gate:
He will speak with such great fury and rage,
That to fire and blood he will consign the entire sex.

V 61
L'enfant du grand n'estant à sa naissance,
Subiuguera les hauts monts Appennins,
Fera trembler tous ceux de la Balance,
Et des monts feux iusques à mont Cenis.

The child of the great one not by his birth,
He will subjugate the high Apennine mountains:
He will cause all those of the balance to tremble,
And from the Pyrenees to Mont Cenis.

V 62
Sur les rochers sang on verra plouuoir,
Sol, Orient, Saturne Occidental,
Pres Orgon guerre, à Rome grand mal voir,
Nefs parfondrées & prins le Tridental,

One will see blood to rain on the rocks,
Sun in the East, Saturn in the West:
Near Orgon war, at Rome great evil to be seen,
Ships sunk to the bottom, taken by Trident.

V 63
De vaine emprinse l'honneur indeuë plainte,
Gallots errants, par latins froid, faim vagues :
Non loing du Tymbre de sang terre tainte
Et sur humains seront diuerses plagues.

From the vain enterprise honor and undue complaint,
Boats tossed about among the Latins, cold, hunger, waves
Not far from the Tiber the land stained with blood,
And diverse plagues will be upon mankind.

V 64
Les assemblez par repos du grand nombre,
Par terre & mer, conseil contremandé :
Pres de l'Automne, Gennes, Nice de l'ombre,
Par champs & villes le chef contrebandé.

Those assembled by the tranquillity of the great number,
By land and sea counsel countermanded:
Near Antonne Genoa, Nice in the shadow
Through fields and towns in revolt against the chief.

V 65
Subit venu l'effrayeur sera grande,
Des principaux de l'affaire cachez :
Et dame en braise plus ne sera veuë,
De peu à peu seront les grands faschez.

Come suddenly the terror will be great,
Hidden by the principal ones of the affair:
And the lady on the charcoal will no longer be in sight,
Thus little by little will the great ones be angered.

V 66
Soubs les antiques edifices estaux,
Non eslongnez d'aqueduct ruyne,
De Sol & Luna sont les luysants mataux,
Ardante lampe Trayan d'or buriné.

Under the ancient vestal edifices,
Not far from the ruined aqueduct:
The glittering metals are of the Sun and Moon,
The lamp of Trajan engraved with gold burning.

V 67
Quand chef Perousse n'osera sa tunique,
Sens au couuert tout nud s'expolier,
Seront print sept faict Aristocratique,

Le pere & fils morts par pointe au collier.

When the chief of Perugia will not venture his tunic
Sense under cover to strip himself quite naked:
Seven will be taken Aristocratic deed,
Father and son dead through a point in the collar.

V 68
Dans le Danube & du Rin viendra boire,
Le grand Chameau, ne s'en repentira :
Trembler du Rosne & plus fort ceux de Loire,
Et pres des Alpes coq les ruynera.

In the Danube and of the Rhine will come to drink
The great Camel, not repenting it:
Those of the Rhône to tremble, and much more so those of
the Loire,
and near the Alps the Cock will ruin him.

V 69
Plus ne sera le grand en faux sommeil,
L'inquiétude viendra prendre repos :
Dresser phalange d'or, azur & vermeil,
Subiuger Affrique la ronger iusque aux os.

No longer will the great one be in his false sleep,
Uneasiness will come to replace tranquillity:
A phalanx of gold, azure and vermilion arrayed
To subjugate Africa and gnaw it to the bone,

V 70
Des regions subiettes à la Balance,
Feront troubler les monts par grande guerre :
Captif tout sexe deu & toute bisance,
Qu'on criera à l'aube terre à terre.

Of the regions subject to the Balance,
They will trouble the mountains with great war,
Captives the entire sex enthralled and all Byzantium,
So that at dawn they will spread the news from land to land.

V 71
Par la fureur d'vn qui attandra l'eau,

Par la grand rage tout l'exercice esmeu,
Chargé de nobles à dix-sept batteaux,
Au long du Rosne tard messager venu.

By the fury of one who will wait for the water,
By his great rage the entire army moved:
Seventeen boats loaded with the noble,
The messenger come late along the Rhône.

V 72
Pour le plaifir d'edi¢t voluptueux,
On meflera la poifon dans la loy.
Venus fera en cours fi vertueux,
Qu'obfufquera du Soleil tout aloy.

Pour le plaisir d'edict voluptueux,
On meslera la poison dans l'aloy :
Venus sera en cours si vertueux,
Qu'offusquera du Soleil tout aloy.

Pour le plaifir d'edi¢t voluptueux,
On meflera la poifon dans la loy :
Venus fera en cours fi vertueux,
Qu'offufquera du Soleil tout à loy.

For the pleasure of the voluptuous edict,
One will mix poison in the faith:
Venus will be in a course so virtuous
As to becloud the whole quality of the Sun.

V 73
Persecutee de Dieu sera l'Eglise,
Et les saints temples seront expoliez :
L'enfant la mere mettra nud en chemise,
Seront Arabes aux Polons raliez.

The Church of God will be persecuted,
And the holy Temples will be plundered,
The child will put his mother out in her shift,
Arabs will be allied with the Poles.

V 74
De sang Troy en naistra cœur Germanique,

137

Qui deuiendra en si haute puissance,
Hors chassera gent estrange Arabique,
Tournant l'Eglise en pristine preeminence.

Of Trojan blood will be born a Germanic heart
Who will rise to very high power:
He will drive out the foreign Arabic people,
Returning the Church to its pristine pre-eminence.

V 75
Montera haut sur le bien plus à dextre,
Demourra assis sur la pierre carree :
Vers le midy posé à sa fenestre,
Baston tortu en main bouche serree.

He will rise high over the estate more to the right,
He will remain seated on the square stone,
Towards the south facing to his left,
The crooked staff in his hand his mouth sealed.

V 76
En lieu libere tendra son pauillon,
Et ne voudra en citez prendre place :
Aix, Carpen, l'Isle volce mont Cauaillon
Par tout les lieux abolira la trasse.

In a free place will he pitch his tent,
And he will not want to lodge in the cities:
Aix, Carpentras, L'Isle, Vaucluse Mont, Cavaillon,
Throughout all these places will he abolish his trace.

V 77
Tous les degrez d'honneur Ecclesiastique,
Seront changez en dial quirinal :
En Martial quirinal flaminique,
Vn Roy de France le rendra vulcanal.

All degrees of Ecclesiastical honor
Will be changed to that of Jupiter and Quirinus:
The priest of Quirinus to one of Mars,
Then a King of France will make him one of Vulcan.

V 78

138

Les deux vnis ne tiendront longuement,
Et dans treze ans au barbare s'attrappe :
Aux deux costez feront tel perdement,
Qu'vn benira la barque & sa cappe.

The two will not be united for very long,
And in thirteen years to the Barbarian Satrap:
On both sides they will cause such loss
That one will bless the Bark and its cope.

V 79
La sacree pompe viendra baisser les aisles
Par la venuë du grand Legislateur :
Humble haussera, vexera les rebelles,
Naistra sur terre aucun aemulateur.

The sacred pomp will come to lower its wings,
Through the coming of the great legislator:
He will raise the humble, he will vex the rebels,
His like will not appear on this earth.

V 80
Logmion grande Bisance approchera,
Chassée sera la barbarique ligue,
Des deux loix l'vne l'aethinique laschera,
Barbare & franche en perpetuelle brigue.

Ogmios will approach great Byzantium,
The Barbaric League will be driven out:
Of the two laws the heathen one will give way,
Barbarian and Frank in perpetual strife.

V 81
L'oyseau Royal sur la Cité solaire,
Sept mois deuant fera nocturne augure :
Mur d'Orient cherra tonnerre esclaire,
Sept iours aux portes les ennemis à l'heure.

The royal bird over the city of the Sun,
Seven months in advance it will deliver a nocturnal omen:
The Eastern wall will fall lightning thunder,
Seven days the enemies directly to the gates.

V 82

Au conclud pache hors de la forteresse,
Ne sortira celuy en desespoir mis :
Quand ceux d'Albois, de Langres contre Bresse,
Auront monts Dolle bouscade d'ennemis.

At the conclusion of the treaty outside the fortress
Will not go he who is placed in despair:
When those of Arbois, of Langres against Bresse
Will have the mountains of Dôle an enemy ambush.

V 83

Ceux qui auront entrepris subuertir
Nompareil regne puissant & inuincible,
Feront par fraude, nuicts trois aduertir,
Quand le plus grand à table lira Bible.

Those who will have undertaken to subvert,
An unparalleled realm, powerful and invincible:
They will act through deceit, nights three to warn,
When the greatest one will read his Bible at the table.

V 84

Naistra du gouphre & cité immesuree,
Nay de parens obscurs & tenebreux :
Quand la puissance du grand Roy reueree,
Voudra destruire par Rouan & Eureux.

He will be born of the gulf and unmeasured city,
Born of obscure and dark family:
He who the revered power of the great King
Will want to destroy through Rouen and Evreux.

V 85

Par les Sueues & lieux circonuoisins,
Seront en guerres pour cause des nuees,
Gamp marins locustes & cousins,
Du Leman fautes seront bien desnuees.

Through the Suevi and neighboring places,
They will be at war over the clouds:
Swarm of marine locusts and gnats,
The faults of Geneva will be laid quite bare.

V 86

Par les deux te*f*tes, & trois bras *f*eparez,
La cité grande par eaux *f*era vexee :
Des grands d'entr'eux par exil e*f*garez,
Par te*f*te Per*f*e Bi*f*ance fort pre*ff*ée.

Par les deux te*f*tes & trois bras *f*eparez
La grand cité *f*era par eux vexée.
Des Grands d'entr'eux par exil e*f*garez.
Par te*f*te Per*f*e Bysance fort pre*ff*ée.

Par les deux testes & trois bras separez,
La cité grande par eau sera vexee,
Des grands d'entr'eux par exil esgarez,
Par teste perse, Bisance fort pressee.

Divided by the two heads and three arms,
The great city will be vexed by waters:
Some great ones among them led astray in exile,
Byzantium hard pressed by the head of Persia.

V 87

L'an que Saturne sera hors de seruage,
Au franc terroir sera d'eau inondé :
De sang Troyen sera son mariage,
Et sera seur d'Espagnol circonder.

The year that Saturn is out of bondage,
In the Frank land he will be inundated by water:
Of Trojan blood will his marriage be,
And he will be confined safely be the Spaniards.

V 88

Sur le sablon par vn hydeux deluge,
Des autres mers trouué monstre marin :
Proche du lieu sera fait vn refuge,
Tenant Sauone esclaue de Turin.

Through a frightful flood upon the sand,
A marine monster from other seas found:
Near the place will be made a refuge,
Holding Savona the slave of Turin.

V 89

Dedans Hongrie par Boheme, Nauarre,
Et par banniere feintes seditions :
Par fleurs de lys pays portant la barre,
Contre Orleans fera esmotions.

Into Hungary through Bohemia, Navarre,
and under that banner holy insurrections:
By the fleur-de-lis legion carrying the bar,
Against Orléans they will cause disturbances.

V 90

Dans les cyclades en Perinthe & Larisse,
Dedans Sparte tout le Pelloponesse;
Si grand famine, peste, par faux connisse,
Neuf mois tiendra & tout le cherrouesse.

In the Cyclades, in Perinthus and Larissa,
In Sparta and the entire Pelopennesus:
Very great famine, plague through false dust,
Nine months will it last and throughout the entire peninsula.

V 91

Au grand marché qu'on dit des mensongers,
Du bout Torrent & camp Athenien :
Seront surprins par les cheuaux legers,
Par Albanois Mars, Leo, Sat. vn versien.

At the market that they call that of liars,
Of the entire Torrent and field of Athens:
They will be surprised by the light horses,
By those of Alba when Mars is in Leo and Saturn in
Aquarius.

V 92

Apres le siege tenu dix sept ans,
Cinq changeront en tel reuolu terme :
Puis sera l'vn esleu de mesme temps,
Qui des Romains ne sera trop conforme.

After the see has been held seventeen years,
Five will change within the same period of time:

142

Then one will be elected at the same time,
One who will not be too comfortable to the Romans.

V 93
Sous le terroir du rond globe lunaire,
Lors que sera dominateur Mercure :
L'isle d'Escosse sera vn luminaire,
Qui les Anglois mettra à deconfiture.

Under the land of the round lunar globe,
When Mercury will be dominating:
The isle of Scotland will produce a luminary,
One who will put the English into confusion.

V 94
Translatera en la grand Germanie,
Brabant & Flandres, Gand, Burges & Bologne :
La treue sainte le grand duc d'Armenie,
Assaillira Vienne & la Cologne.

He will transfer into great Germany
Brabant and Flanders, Ghent, Bruges and Boulogne:
The truce feigned, the great Duke of Armenia
Will assail Vienna and Cologne.

V 95
Nautique rame inuitera les vmbres,
Du grand Empire, lors viendra conciter :
La mer Egee des lignes les encombres,
Empeschant l'onde Tyrrene de floter.

The nautical oar will tempt the shadows,
Then it will come to stir up the great Empire:
In the Aegean Sea the impediments of wood
Obstructing the diverted Tyrrhenian Sea.

V 96
Sur le milieu du grand monde la rose,
Pour nouueaux faits sang public espandu,
A dire vray on aura bouche close,
Lors au besoin viendra tard l'attendu.

Sur le milieu du grand monde la ro*f*e,

Pour nouueaux faits ſang public eſpandu;
A dire vray on aura bouche cloſe,
Lors au beſoin viendra tard l'attendu.

Sur le milieu du grand monde la roſe
Pour nouueaux faits ſang public eſpandu.
A dire vray, on aura bouche cloſe.
Lors au beſoin viendra tard l'attendu.

The rose upon the middle of the great world,
For new deeds public shedding of blood:
To speak the truth, one will have a closed mouth,
Then at the time of need the awaited one will come late.

V 97
Le nay difforme par horreur ſuffoqué
Dans la cité du grand Roy habitable :
L'ediçt ſeuere des captifs reuoqué,
Greſle & tonnerre, Condon ineſtimable.

Le né difforme par horreur ſuffoqué
Dans la cité du grand Roy habitable.
L'ediçt ſeuere des captifs reuoqué.
Greſle & tonnerre Condom ineſtimable.

Le nay difforme par horreur suffoqué,
Dans la cité du grand Roy habitable :
L'edit seuere des captifs reuoque,
Gresle & tonnerre Coudom inestimable.

The one born deformed suffocated in horror,
In the habitable city of the great King:
The severe edict of the captives revoked,
Hail and thunder, Condom inestimable.

V 98
A quarante-huict degré climatterique,
Afin de Cancer si grande secheresse,
Poisson en mer fleuue, lac cuit hectique
Bearn, Bigorre par feu ciel en detresse.

At the forty-eighth climacteric degree,
At the end of Cancer very great dryness:

Fish in sea, river, lake boiled hectic,
Béarn, Bigorre in distress through fire from the sky.

V 99
Milan, Ferrare, Turin & Aquilleye,
Capne Brundis vexez par gent Celtique,
Par le Lyon & phalange aquilee,
Quand Rome aura le chef vieux Britannique.

Milan, Ferrara, Turin and Aquileia,
Capua, Brindisi vexed by the Celtic nation:
By the Lion and his Eagle's phalanx,
When the old British chief Rome will have.

V 100
Le boute-feu par son feu attrapé,
De feu du ciel par Carcas & Cominge,
Foix, aux, Mazeres, haut vieillard eschappé,
Par ceux de Hasse, des Saxons & Turinge.

The incendiary trapped in his own fire,
Of fire from the sky at Carcassonne and the Comminges:
Foix, Auch, Mazères, the high old man escaped,
Through those of Hesse and Thuringia, and some Saxons.

Century VI

VI 1
AV tour des monts Pyrennees grand amas,
De gent estrange, secourir Roy nouueau :
Pres de Garonne du grand temple du Mas,
Vn Romain chef le craindra dedans l'eau.

Around the Pyrenees mountains a great throng
Of foreign people to aid the new King:
Near the great temple of Le Mas by the Garonne,
A Roman chief will fear him in the water.

VI 2
En l'an cinq cens o¢tante plus & moins
On attendra le ſiecle bien eſtrange.

En l'an ſept cens & trois (cieux en teſmoins)
Regnes pluſieurs, vn à cinq, feront change.

En l'an cinq cents o¢tante plus & moins,
On attendra le ſiecle bien eſtrange :
En l'an ſept cens, & trois cieux en teſmoins
Aue pluſieurs regnes vn à cinq feront change.

En l'an cinq cens octante plus & moins
On attend le siecle bien estrange :
En l'an sept cens & trois (cieux en tesmoins)
Aue plusieurs regnes vn à cinq feront change.

In the year five hundred eighty more or less,
One will await a very strange century:
In the year seven hundred and three the heavens witness thereof,
That several kingdoms one to five will make a change.

VI 3
Fleuue qu'esprouue le nouueau nay Celtique,
Sera en grande de l'Empire discorde :
Le ieune prince par gent Ecclesiastique,
Ostera le sceptre coronal de concorde.

Fleuue qu'eſpreuue le nouueau nay Celtique
Sera grande de l'Empire diſcorde :
Le ieune Prince par gent Eccleſiaſtique,
Oſtera le ſceptre coronal de concorde.

Fleuue qu'eſprouue le nouueau né Celtique,
Sera en grande de l'empire diſcorde :
Au ieune Prince par gent eccleſiaſtique,
Le ſceptre oſter coronal de concorde.

The river that tries the new Celtic heir
Will be in great discord with the Empire:
The young Prince through the ecclesiastical people
Will remove the scepter of the crown of concord.

VI 4
Le Celtique fleuue changera de riuage,
Plus ne tiendra la cité d'Aripine :

Tout trasmué ormis le vieil langage,
Saturne, Leo, Mars, Cancer en rapine.

The Celtic river will change its course,
No longer will it include the city of Agrippina:
All changed except the old language,
Saturn, Leo, Mars, Cancer in plunder.

VI 5
Si grand famine par vnde pestifere,
Par pluye longue le long du pole arctique :
Samarobryn cent lieux de l'hemispere,
Viuront sans loy, exempt de politique.

Very great famine through pestiferous wave,
Through long rain the length of the arctic pole:
Samarobryn one hundred leagues from the hemisphere,
The will live without law exempt from politics.

VI 6
Apparoistra vers Septentrion,
Non loing de Cancer l'Estoille cheueluë :
Suse, Sienne, Boece, Eretrion
Mourra de Rome grand, la nuit disperuë.

There will appear towards the North
Not far from Cancer the bearded star:
Susa, Siena, Boeotia, Eretria,
The great one of Rome will die, the night over.

VI 7
Norneigre & Dace, & l'isle Britanique,
Par les vnis freres seront vexees :
Le chef Romain issu du sang Gallique,
Et les copies aux forests repoulsees.

Norway and Dacia and the British Isle
Will be vexed by the united brothers:
The Roman chief sprung from Gallic blood
And his forces hurled back into the forests.

VI 8
Ceux qui estoient en regne pour sçauoir

147

Au Royal change deuiendront appouuris :
Vns exilez sans appuy, or n'auoir,
Lettres & lettres ne seront à grand pris.

Those who were in the realm for knowledge
Will become impoverished at the change of King:
Some exiled without support, having no gold,
The lettered and letters will not be at a high premium.

VI 9
Aux ſacrez temples ſeront fait eſcandales,
Comptez ſeront par honneurs, & loüanges,
D'vn qu'on graue d'argent d'or les medailles,
La fin ſera en tourmens bien eſtranges.

Aux temples saints seront faits grâds scandales,
Comptez seront par honneur & loüanges
D'vin que l'on graué d'argent, d'or les medalles,
La fin sera en tourmens bien estranges.

Aux teples ſaints ſeront faits grands ſcandales.
Côptez ſeront pour honneurs & louanges.
D'vn que lon graue d'argent d'or les medales,
La fin ſera en tourments bien eſtranges.

In the sacred temples scandals will be perpetrated,
They will be reckoned as honors and commendations:
Of one of whom they engrave medals of silver and of gold,
The end will be in very strange torments.

VI 10
Vn peu de temps les temples de couleurs,
De blanc & noir les deux entremeslee :
Rouges & iaunes leur embleront les leurs,
Sang, terre, peste, faim, feu, d'eau affolce.

In a short time the temples with colors
Of white and black of the two intermixed:
Red and yellow ones will carry off theirs from them,
Blood, land, plague, famine, fire extinguished by water.

VI 11
Des ſept rameaux à trois ſeront reduits.

148

Les plus ai∫nez feront ∫urpris par mort.
Fratricider les deux feront ∫eduits.
Les coniurez en dormant feront morts.

Des ∫ept rameaux à trois feront reduits,
Les plus ai∫nez feront ∫urpris par mort,
Fratricider les deux feront ∫eduits,
Les coniurez en dormans feront morts.

Des sept rameaux à trois seront reduits,
Les plus aisnez seront surprins par mort.
Fratricider les deux seront seduits,
Les coniurez en dormant seront morts.

The seven branches will be reduced to three,
The elder ones will be surprised by death,
The two will be seduced to fratricide,
The conspirators will be dead while sleeping.

VI 12
Dresser copies pour monter à l'Empire,
Du Vatican le sang Royal tiendra :
Flamans, Anglois, Espaigne auec Aspire,
Contre l'Italie & France contendra.

To raise forces to ascend to the empire
In the Vatican the Royal blood will hold fast:
Flemings, English, Spain with Aspire
Against Italy and France will he contend.

VI 13
Vn dubiteux ne viendra loing du regne,
La plus grand part le voudra soustenir
Vn capitole ne voudra point qu'il regne,
Sa grande charge ne pourra maintenir.

A doubtful one will not come far from the realm,
The greater part will want to uphold him:
A Capitol will not want him to reign at all,
He will be unable to bear his great burden.

VI 14
Loing de sa terre Roy perdra la bataille,

Prompt eschappé poursuiuy suyuant prins,
Ignare prins soubs la dorée maille,
Soubs faint habit & l'ennemy surprins.

Far from his land a King will lose the battle,
At once escaped, pursued, then captured,
Ignorant one taken under the golden mail,
Under false garb, and the enemy surprised.

VI 15
Dessous la tombe sera trouué le prince,
Qu'aura le prix par dessus Nuremberg :
L'Espagnol Roy en Capricorne mince,
Faint & trahy par le grand Vitemberg.

Under the tomb will be found a Prince
Who will be valued above Nuremberg:
The Spanish King in Capricorn thin,
Deceived and betrayed by the great Wittenberg.

VI 16
Ce que rauy sera du ieune Milue,
Par les Normans de France & Picardie :
Les noirs du temple du lieu Negrisiluc,
Feront aulberge & feu de Lombardie.

That which will be carried off by the young Hawk,
By the Normans of France and Picardy:
The black ones of the temple of the Black Forest place
Will make an inn and fire of Lombardy.

VI 17
Apres les limes bruslez les asiniers,
Contraints seront changer habits diuers :
Les Saturnins bruslez par les musniers,
Hors la pluspart qui ne sera musniers,

After the files the ass-drivers burned,
They will be obliged to change diverse garbs:
Those of Saturn burned by the millers,
Except the greater part which will not be covered.

VI 18

Par les phisiques le grand Roy delaissé,
Par sort non art ne l'Ebrieu est en vie :
Luy & son genre au regne haut poussé,
Grace donne à gent qui Christ enuie.

The great King abandoned by the Physicians,
By fate not the Jew's art he remains alive,
He and his kindred pushed high in the realm,
Pardon given to the race which denies Christ.

VI 19
La vray flamme engloutira la dame,
Que voudra mettre les innocens à feu,
Pres de l'assaut l'exercite s'enflamme,
Quand dans Seuille monstre en bœuf sera veu.

The true flame will devour the lady
Who will want to put the Innocent Ones to the fire:
Before the assault the army is inflamed,
When in Seville a monster in beef will be seen.

VI 20
L'vnion fainste sera peu de duree
Des vns changes reformez la pluspart :
Dans les vaisseaux sera gent enduree,
Lors aura Rome vn nouueau Liepart.

The feigned union will be of short duration,
Some changed most reformed:
In the vessels people will be in suffering,
Then Rome will have a new Leopard.

VI 21
Quand ceux de polle artique vnis ensemble,
En Orient grand effrayeur & crainte,
Esleu nouueau soustenu le grand temple,
Rodes, Bisance de sang barbare tainte,

When those of the arctic pole are united together,
Great terror and fear in the East:
Newly elected, the great trembling supported,
Rhodes, Byzantium stained with Barbarian blood.

VI 22
Dedans la terre du grand temple celique,
Nepueu à Londres par paix faincte meurtry,
La barque alors deuiendra scismatique,
Liberté faincte sera au corn. & cry.

Within the land of the great heavenly temple,
Nephew murdered at London through feigned peace:
The bark will then become schismatic,
Sham liberty will be proclaimed everywhere.

VI 23
D'esprit de regne munisememens descriees,
Et seront peuples esmeus contre leur Roy,
Paix, fait nouueau, sainctes loix empirees,
Rapis onc fut en si tresdur arroy.

Defpit de regne numifmes decriez,
Peuples feront efmeus contre leur Roy.
Paix. fait nouueau. faintes loix empirées.
RAPIS onq fut en fi tres dur arroy.

D'efprit de regne munifmes defcriez.
Et feront peuples efmeus contre leur Roy,
Paix, fainçt nouueau fainçtes loix empirées,
Rapis onc fut en fi tres-dur arroy.

Coins depreciated by the spirit of the realm,
And people will be stirred up against their King:
New peace made, holy laws become worse,
Paris was never in so severe an array.

VI 24
Mars & le sceptre se trouuera conioint,
Dessous Cancer calamiteuse guerre :
Vn peu apres sera nouueau Riy oingt,
Qui par long temps pacifiera la terre,

Mars and the scepter will be found conjoined
Under Cancer calamitous war:
Shortly afterwards a new King will be anointed,
One who for a long time will pacify the earth.

VI 25
Par Mars contraire sera la Monarchie,
Du grand pescheur en trouble ruyneux :
Ieune noir rouge prendra la hierarchie,
Les proditeurs iront iour bruyneux.

Through adverse Mars will the monarchy
Of the great fisherman be in ruinous trouble:
The young red black one will seize the hierarchy,
The traitors will act on a day of drizzle.

VI 26
Quatre ans le siege quelque peu bien tiendra,
Vn suruiendra libidineux de vie :
Rauenne & Pise, Veronne soustiendront,
Por esleuer la croix du Pape enuie.

For four years the see will be held with some little good,
One libidinous in life will succeed to it:
Ravenna, Pisa and Verona will give support,
Longing to elevate the Papal cross.

VI 27
Dedans les isles de cinq fleuues à vn,
Par le croissant du grand Chyren Selin :
Par les bruynes de l'air fureur de l'vn,
Six eschappez, cachez fardeaux de lyn.

Within the Isles of five rivers to one,
Through the expansion of the great Chyren Selin:
Through the drizzles in the air the fury of one,
Six escaped, hidden bundles of flax.

VI 28
Le grand celtique entrera dedans Rome,
Menant amas d'exilez & bannis :
Le grand pasteur mettra à mort tout homme
Qui pour le coq estoit aux Alpes vnis.

The great Celt will enter Rome,
Leading a throng of the exiled and banished:
The great Pastor will put to death every man
Who was united at the Alps for the cock.

153

VI 29

La vefue ſainte entendant les nouuelles
De ſes rameaux mis en perplex & trouble :
Qui ſera duit appaiſer les querelles,
Par ſon pourchas des Razes fera comble.

La vefue ſain¢te entendant les nouuelles,
De ſes rameaux mis en perplex & trouble :
Qui ſera dui¢t appaiſer les querelles,
Par ſon pourchas de razes fera comble.

La vefue saincte entendant les nouuelles,
De ses rameaux mis en perplex & trouble,
Qui sera duict appaiser les querelles,
Par son pourchas des razes fera comble.

The saintly widow hearing the news,
Of her offspring placed in perplexity and trouble:
He who will be instructed to appease the quarrels,
He will pile them up by his pursuit of the shaven heads.

VI 30

Par l'apparence de saincte saincteté,
Sera trahy aux ennemis le siege,
Nuict qu'on cuidoit dormir en seureté,
Pres de Braban marcheront ceux du Liege.

Through the appearance of the feigned sanctity,
The siege will be betrayed to the enemies:
In the night when they trusted to sleep in safety,
Near Brabant will march those of Liège.

VI 31

Roy trouuera ce qu'il desiroit tant,
Quand le Prelat sera reprins à tort :
Responce au duc le rendra mal content,
Qui dans Milan mettra plusieurs à mort.

Roy trouuera ce qu'il de ſiroit tant,
Quand le Prelat ſera reprins à tort :
Reſponce au Duc le rendra mal content,
Qui dans Milan mettra pluſieurs à mort.

Roy trouuera ce qu'il defiroit tant,
Quand le Prelat fera repris à tort.
Refponfe au Duc le rendra malcontent,
Qui dans Milan mettra plufieurs à mort.

The King will find that which he desired so much
When the Prelate will be blamed unjustly:
His reply to the Duke will leave him dissatisfied,
He who in Milan will put several to death.

VI 32
Par trahisons de verges à mort battu,
Puis surmonté sera par son desordre :
Conseil friuole au grand captif sentu,
Naz par fureur quand Begich viendra mordre.

Beaten to death by rods for treason,
Captured he will be overcome through his disorder:
Frivolous counsel held out to the great captive,
When Berich will come to bite his nose in fury.

VI 33
Sa main derniere par Alus sanguinaire,
Ne se pourra plus la mer garentir;
Entre deux fleuues craindre main militaire,
Le noir l'ireux le fera repentir.

His last hand through sanguinary,
He will be unable to protect himself by sea:
Between two rivers he will fear the military hand,
The black and irate one will make him rue it.

VI 34
De feu volant la machination,
Viendra troubler au grand chef assiegez :
Dedans sera telle sedition,
Qu'en desespoir seront les profligez.

The device of flying fire
Will come to trouble the great besieged chief:
Within there will be such sedition
That the profligate ones will be in despair.

VI 35
Pres de Rion, & proche à blanche laine,
Aries, Taurus, Cancer, Leo, la Vierge :
Mars, Iupiter, le Sol ardra grand plaine
Bloys & cités lettres cachez au cierge.

Near the Bear and close to the white wool,
Aries, Taurus, Cancer, Leo, Virgo,
Mars, Jupiter, the Sun will burn a great plain,
Woods and cities letters hidden in the candle.

VI 36
Ne bien ne mal par bataille terrestre,
Ne paruiendra aux confins de Perouse,
Rebeller Pise, Florence voir mal estre,
Roy nuict blessé sur mulet à noire housse.

Neither good nor evil through terrestrial battle
Will reach the confines of Perugia,
Pisa to rebel, Florence to see an evil existence,
King by night wounded on a mule with black housing.

VI 37
L'œuure ancienne se paracheuera,
Du toict cherra sur le grand mal ruyne,
Innocent faict mort on accusera,
Nocent caché, taillis à la bruyne.

The ancient work will be finished,
Evil ruin will fall upon the great one from the roof:
Dead they will accuse an innocent one of the deed,
The guilty one hidden in the copse in the drizzle.

VI 38
Aux profligez de paix les ennemis,
Apres auoir l'Italie supperee :
Noir sanguinaire, rouge sera commis,
Feu, sang verser, eau de sang coloree.

The enemies of peace to the profligates,
After having conquered Italy:
The bloodthirsty black one, red, will be exposed,

156

Fire, blood shed, water colored by blood.

VI 39
L'enfant du regne part paternelle prince,
Expolié sera pour deliurer :
Aupres du lac Trasimen l'azur prinse,
La trope hostage pour trop fort s'enyurer.

The child of the realm through the capture of his father
Will be plundered to deliver him:
Near the Lake of Perugia the azure captive,
The hostage troop to become far too drunk.

VI 40
Grand de Magonce pour grande soif estaindre
Sera priué de la grand dignité :
Ceux de Cologne si fort le viendront plaindre
Que le grand groppe au Ryn sera ietté.

To quench the great thirst the great one of Mainz
Will be deprived of his great dignity:
Those of Cologne will come to complain so loudly
That the great rump will be thrown into the Rhine.

VI 41
Le second chef du regne Dannemarc,
Par ceux de Frise & l'isle Britannique,
Fera despendre plus de cent mille marc.
Vain exploiter voyage en Italique.

The second chief of the realm of Annemark,
Through those of Frisia and of the British Isle,
Will spend more than one hundred thousand marks,
Exploiting in vain the voyage to Italy.

VI 42
A logmyon sera laissé le regne,
Du grand Selin qui plus fera de faict,
Par les Itales estendra son enseigne,
Regy sera par prudent contrefait.

To Ogmios will be left the realm
Of the great Selin, who will in fact do more:

Throughout Italy will he extend his banner,
He will be ruled by a prudent deformed one.

VI 43
Long temps sera sans estre habitee,
Ou Seine & Marne autour vient arrouser
De la Tamise & martiaux temptee,
Deceus les gardes en cuidant repousser,

For a long time will she remain uninhabited,
Around where the Seine and the Marne she comes to water:
Tried by the Thames and warriors,
The guards deceived in trusting in the repulse.

VI 44
De nuict par Nantes Lyris apparoistra,
Des arts marins susciteront la pluye :
Arabiq goulfre grand classe parfondra,
Vn monstre en Saxe naistra d'ours & truye.

By night the Rainbow will appear for Nantes,
By marine arts they will stir up rain:
In the Gulf of Arabia a great fleet will plunge to the bottom,
In Saxony a monster will be born of a bear and a sow.

VI 45
Le gouuerneur du regne bien sçauant,
Ne consentir voulant au fait Royal :
Mellile classe par le contraire vent,
Le remettra à son plus desloyal.

The very learned governor of the realm,
Not wishing to consent to the royal deed:
The fleet at Melilla through contrary wind
Will deliver him to his most disloyal one.

VI 46
Vn iuste sera en exil renuoyé,
Par pestilence aux confins de Nonseggle,
Response au rouge le fera desouyer,
Roy retirant à la Rane & l'aigle,

A just one will be sent back again into exile,

Through pestilence to the confines of Nonseggle,
His reply to the red one will cause him to be misled,
The King withdrawing to the Frog and the Eagle.

VI 47
Entre deux monts les deux grands assemblees,
Delaisseront leur simulte secrette :
Bruxelles & Dolle par Langres accablees,
Pour a Malignes executer leur peste.

The two great ones assembled between two mountains
Will abandon their secret quarrel:
Brussels and Dôle overcome by Langres,
To execute their plague at Malines.

VI 48
La saincteté trop saincte & seductiue,
Accompagnée d'vne langue diserte :
La cité vieile & Palme trop hastiue,
Florence & Sienne rendront plus desertes.

The too false and seductive sanctity,
Accompanied by an eloquent tongue:
The old city, and Parma too premature,
Florence and Siena they will render more desert.

VI 49
De la partie de Mammer grand pontife,
Subiuguera les confins du Dannube :
Chasser les croix par fer raffe ne riffe,
Captif, or, bagues, plus de cent mille rubes.

The great Pontiff of the party of Mars
Will subjugate the confines of the Danube:
The cross to pursue, through sword hook or crook,
   Captives, gold, jewels more than one hundred thousand
rubies.

VI 50
Dedans le puits seront trouuez les os,
Sera l'incest commis par la marastre;
L'estat changé on querra bruit & los,
Et aura Mars ascendant pour son astre.

159

Within the pit will be found the bones,
Incest will be committed by the stepmother:
The state changed, they will demand fame and praise,
And they will have Mars attending as their star.

VI 51
Peuple assemblé voir nouueau expectacle
Princes & Roys par plusieurs assistans,
Pilliers faillir, murs, mais comme miracle,
Le Roy sauué & trente des instans.

People assembled to see a new spectacle,
Princes and Kings amongst many bystanders,
Pillars walls to fall: but as by a miracle
The King saved and thirty of the ones present.

VI 52
En lieu du grand qui sera condamné,
De prison hors son amy en sa place :
L'espoir Troyen en six mois ioint mort nay.
Le Sol à l'vrne seront prins fleuues en glace.

In place of the great one who will be condemned,
Outside the prison, his friend in his place:
The Trojan hope in six months joined, born dead,
The Sun in the urn rivers will be frozen.

VI 53
Le grand Prelant Celtique à Roy suspect,
De nuict par cours sortira hors du regne :
Par duc fertille à son grand Roy, Bretagne
Bisance à Cypres & Tunes insuspect.

The great Celtic Prelate suspected by the King,
By night in flight he will leave the realm:
Through a Duke fruitful for his great British King,
Byzantium to Cyprus and Tunis unsuspected.

VI 54
Au poinct du iour au second chant du coq
Ceux de Tunes, de Fez, & de Bugie :
Par les Arabes captif le Roy Maroq,

L'an mil six cens & sept de Liturgie.

At daybreak at the second crowing of the cock,
Those of Tunis, of Fez and of Bougie,
By the Arabs the King of Morocco captured,
The year sixteen hundred and seven, of the Liturgy.

VI 55
Au Chalmé Duc en arrachant l'esponce,
Voille arabesque voir, subit descouuerte :
Tripolis, Chio, & ceux de Trapesonce,
Duc prins, Marnegro, & sa cité deserte.

By the appeased Duke in drawing up the contract,
Arabesque sail seen, sudden discovery:
Tripoli, Chios, and those of Trebizond,
Duke captured, the Black Sea and the city a desert.

VI 56
La crainte armee de l'ennemy Narbon,
Effrayera si fort les Hesperiques :
Parpignan vuide par l'aueugle darbon,
Lors Barcelon par mer donra les piques.

The dreaded army of the Narbonne enemy
Will frighten very greatly the Hesperians:
Perpignan empty through the blind one of Arbon,
Then Barcelona by sea will take up the quarrel.

VI 57
Celuy qu'estoit bien auant dans le regne,
Ayant chef rouge proche à la hierarchie :
Aspre & cruel, & se fera tant craindre,
Succedera a sacree monarchie.

He who was well forward in the realm,
Having a red chief close to the hierarchy,
Harsh and cruel, and he will make himself much feared,
He will succeed to the sacred monarchy.

VI 58
Entre les deux monarques eslongnez,
Lors que Sol par Selin cler perduë :

161

Simulte grande entre deux indignez,
Qu'aux isles & Sienne la liberté renduë.

Between the two distant monarchs,
When the clear Sun is lost through Selin:
Great enmity between two indignant ones,
So that liberty is restored to the Isles and Siena.

VI 59
Dame en fureur par rage d'adultere,
Viendra à son prince coniurer non de dire
Mais bref cogneu sera le vitupere,
Que seront mis dixsept à martire.

The Lady in fury through rage of adultery,
She will come to conspire not to tell her Prince:
But soon will the blame be made known,
So that seventeen will be put to martyrdom.

VI 60
Le prince hors de son terroir Celtique,
Sera trahy deceu par interprete :
Roüan, Rochelle par ceux d'Armorique,
Au port de Blaye deceus par moine & prestre.

The Prince outside his Celtic land
Will be betrayed, deceived by the interpreter:
Rouen, La Rochelle through those of Brittany
At the port of Blaye deceived by monk and priest.

VI 61
Le grand tapis plié ne monſtrera
Fors qu'à demi la plus part de l'hiſtoire.
Chaſſé du regne aſpre LOIN paroiſtra :
Au fait bellique chacun le viendra croire.

Le grand tapis plié ne montrera,
Fors qu'à demy la pluſpart de l'hiſtoire :
Chaſſe du regne loin aſpre apparoiſtra,
Qu'au fait bellique chacun le viendra croire.

Le grand tappis plié ne monstrera,
Fors qu'a demy la pluspart de l'histoire :

162

Chassé du regne loing aspre apparoistra,
Qu'au fait bellique chacun le viendra croire.

The great carpet folded will not show
But by halved the greatest part of history:
Driven far out of the realm he will appear harsh,
So that everyone will come to believe in his warlike deed.

VI 62
Trop tard tous deux, les fleurs seront perduës,
Conre la loy serpent ne voudra faire :
Des ligueurs forces par gallots confonduës,
Sauone, Albinge par monech grand martire.

Too late both the flowers will be lost,
The serpent will not want to act against the law:
The forces of the Leaguers confounded by the French,
Savona, Albenga through Monaco great martyrdom.

VI 63
La dame seulle au regne demeurée,
L'vnic estaint premier au lict d'honneur
Sept ans sera de douleur explorée,
Plus longue vie au regne par grand heur.

The lady left alone in the realm
By the unique one extinguished first on the bed of honor:
Seven years will she be weeping in grief,
Then with great good fortune for the realm long life.

VI 64
On ne tiendra pache aucune arreſté,
Tous receuans iront par tromperie.
De paix & trefue terre & mer proteſté
Par Barcelonne claſſe prins d'induſtrie,

On ne tiendra pache aucun arreſté,
Tous receuans iront par tromperie.
De trefue & paix terre & mer proteſté.
Par Barcelonne claſſe pris d'induſtrie.

On ne tiendra pache aucun arresté,
Tous receuans iront par tromperie :

De paix & trefue terre & mer protesté;
Par Barcelone classe prins d'industrie.

No peace agreed upon will be kept,
All the subscribers will act with deceit:
In peace and truce, land and sea in protest,
By Barcelona fleet seized with ingenuity.

VI 65
Gris & Bureau, demie ouuerte guerre,
De nuict seront assailliz & pillez :
Le bureau prins passera par la serre,
Son temple ouuert deux aux plastres grillez,

Gray and brown in half-opened war,
By night they will be assaulted and pillaged:
The brown captured will pass through the lock,
His temple opened, two slipped in the plaster.

VI 66
Au fondement de la nouuelle secte,
Seront les os du grand Romain trouuez,
Sepulchre en marbre apparoistra ouuerte,
Terre trembler en Auril, mal enfoüez.

At the foundation of the new sect,
The bones of the great Roman will be found,
A sepulcher covered by marble will appear,
Earth to quake in April poorly buried.

VI 67
Au grand Empire paruiendra tout vn autre
Bonté distant plus de felicité :
Regi par vn issu non loing du peautre,
Corruer regnes grande infelicité.

Quite another one will attain to the great Empire,
Kindness distant more so happiness:
Ruled by one sprung not far from the brothel,
Realms to decay great bad luck.

VI 68
Lors que soldats fureur seditieuse,

Contre leur chef feront de nuict fer luire :
Ennemy d'Albe soit par main furieuse,
Lors vexer Rome & principaux seduire.

When the soldiers in a seditious fury
Will cause steel to flash by night against their chief:
The enemy Alba acts with furious hand,
Then to vex Rome and seduce the principal ones.

VI 69
La pitié grande ƒera ƒans loing tarder,
Ceux qui donnoient ƒeront contraints de prendre
Nuds affamez de froid, ƒoif, ƒoy bander,
Les mons paƒƒer commettant grand eƒclandre.

Grande pitié ƒera ƒans long tarder !
Ceux qui donnoyent ƒeront contrains de prendre.
Nuds, affamez, de froid, ƒoif, ƒoy bander :
Paƒƒer les monts en faiƒant grand eƒclandre.

La grand pitié sera sans long tarder,
Ceux qui dônoient seront contraints de prendre
Nuds affamez de froid, soif, soy bander,
Passer les monts en faisant grand esclandre.

The great pity will occur before long,
Those who gave will be obliged to take:
Naked, starving, withstanding cold and thirst,
To pass over the mountains committing a great scandal.

VI 70
Vn chef du monde le grand Chiren sera :
Plus ovtre apres aymé, craint, redouté :
Son bruit & los les cieux sur passera,
Et du seul titre Victeur, fort contenté.

Vn Chef du monde le grand CHIREN ƒera :
PLVS OVTRE apres aimé, craint, redoubté.
Son bruit & lor les cieux ƒurpaƒƒera,
Et du ƒeul titre Vi¢teur, fort contenté.

An chef du monde le grand CHIREN ƒera,
PLUS OUTRE, apres aymé, craint, redouté,

165

Son bruit & los les cieux *ſurpaſſera*,
Et du *ſeul* tiltre vi¢teur fort contenté.

Chief of the world will the great Chyren be,
Plus Ultra behind, loved, feared, dreaded:
His fame and praise will go beyond the heavens,
And with the sole title of Victor will he be quite satisfied.

VI 71
Quand on viendra le grand Roy parenter,
Auant qu'il ait du tout l'ame renduë :
Celuy qui moins le viendra lamenter,
Par Lyons, d' Aigles, croix, couronne venduë.

Quand on viendra le grand Roy parenter,
Auant qu'il ait du tout l'ame rendue :
An le verra bien tost apparenter
D'Aigles, Lions, Croix, Couronne venduë.

Quand on viendra le grand Roy parenter,
Auant qu'il ait du tout l'ame rendue,
An le verra bien to*ſt* apparenter
D'Aigles, Lions, Croix. Couronne vendue.

When they will come to give the last rites to the great King
Before he has entirely given up the ghost:
He who will come to grieve over him the least,
Through Lions, Eagles, cross crown sold.

VI 72
Par fureur faincte d'esmotion diuine,
Sera la femme du grand fort violée :
Iuges voulans damner telle doctrine,
Victime au peuple ignorant immolée.

Through feigned fury of divine emotion
The wife of the great one will be violated:
The judges wishing to condemn such a doctrine,
She is sacrificed a victim to the ignorant people.

VI 73
En cité grande vn moyne & artisan,
Pres de la porte logez & aux murailles :

166

Contre Modene secret, caue disant,
Trahis pour faire sous couleur d'espousailles.

In a great city a monk and artisan,
Lodged near the gate and walls,
Secret speaking emptily against Modena,
Betrayed for acting under the guise of nuptials.

VI 74
Là dechassée au regne tournera,
Ses ennemis trouuez des coniurez :
Plus que iamais son temps triomphera.
Trois & septante à mort trop asseurez.

She chased out will return to the realm,
Her enemies found to be conspirators:
More than ever her time will triumph,
Three and seventy to death very sure.

VI 75
Le grand Pilot sera par Roy mandé,
Laisser la classe, pour plus haut lieu attaindre :
Sept ans apres sera contrebandé,
Barbare armée viendra Venise craindre.

Le grand Pilote *f*era par Roy mandé
Lai*ff*er la cla*ff*e, à plus haut lieu atteindre.
Sept ans apres *f*era contrebandé.
Barbare armée viendra Veni*f*e caindre.

Le grand pillot par Roy *f*era mandé,
Lai*ff*er la cla*ff*e pour plus haut lieu atteindre :
Sept ans apres *f*era contrebandé,
Barbare armée viendra Veni*f*e craindre.

The great Pilot will be commissioned by the King,
To leave the fleet to fill a higher post:
Seven years after he will be in rebellion,
Venice will come to fear the Barbarian army.

VI 76
La cité antique d'antenorée forge,
Plus ne pouuant le tyran supporter :

Le manche fainct au temple couper gorge,
Les siens le peuple à mort viendra bouter.

The ancient city the creation of Antenor,
Being no longer able to bear the tyrant:
The feigned handle in the temple to cut a throat,
The people will come to put his followers to death.

VI 77
Par la victoire du deceu fraudulente,
Deux classes vne, la reuolte Germaine,
Le chef meurtry & son fils dans la tente,
Florence, Imole pourchassez dans Romaine.

Through the fraudulent victory of the deceived,
Two fleets one, German revolt:
The chief murdered and his son in the tent,
Florence and Imola pursued into Romania.

VI 78
Crier victoire du grand Selin croissant,
Par les Romains sera l'Aigle clamé,
Ticcin, Milan & Gennes ny consent,
Puis par eux mesmes Basil grand reclamé.

To proclaim the victory of the great expanding Selin:
By the Romans will the Eagle be demanded,
Pavia, Milan and Genoa will not consent thereto,
Then by themselves the great Lord claimed.

VI 79
Pres du Tesin les habitans de Loyre,
Garonne & Saone, Seine, Tain, & Gironde,
Outre les monts dresseront promontoire,
Conflict donné, Pau granci, submergé onde.

Near the Ticino the inhabitants of the Loire,
Garonne and Saône, the Seine, the Tain and Gironde:
They will erect a promontory beyond the mountains,
Conflict given, Po enlarged, submerged in the wave.

VI 80
De Fez le regne paruiendra à ceux d'Europe,

Feu leur cité, & lame trenchera :
Le grand d'Asie terre & mer à grand troupe,
Quebleux, pers, croix à mort dechassera.

From Fez the realm will reach those of Europe,
Their city ablaze and the blade will cut:
The great one of Asia by land and sea with great troop,
So that blues and Pers[ians] the cross will pursue to death.

VI 81
Pleurs, cris & plaincts, hurlemens, effrayeurs,
Cœur inhumain, cruel, noir, & transy :
Leman, les Isles, de Gennes les maieurs,
Sang espancher, frofaim, à nul mercy.

Tears, cries and laments, howls, terror,
Heart inhuman, cruel, black and chilly:
Lake of Geneva the Isles, of Genoa the notables,
Blood to pour out, wheat famine to none mercy.

VI 82
Par les deserts de lieu, libre, & farouche,
Viendra errer nepueu du grand Pontife :
Assommé à sept auecques lourde souche,
Par ceux qu'apres occuperont le cyphe.

Through the deserts of the free and wild place,
The nephew of the great Pontiff will come to wander:
Felled by seven with a heavy club,
By those who afterwards will occupy the Chalice.

VI 83
Celuy qu'aura tant d'honneur & caresses,
A son entrée en la Gaule Belgique,
Vn temps apres fera tant de rudesses,
Et sera contre à la fleur tant bellique.

Celuy qu'aura tant d'honneurs & care∫∫es
A ∫on entrée en la Gaule Belgique,
Vn temps apres fera tant de rude∫∫es :
Et ∫era contre à la fleur tant bellique.

Celuy qu'aura tant d'honneur & care∫∫e,

169

A ſon entrée en la Gaule Belgique :
Vn temps apres fera tant de rudeſſe,
Et ſera contre à la fleur tant bellique.

He who will have so much honor and flattery
At his entry into Belgian Gaul:
A while after he will act very rudely,
And he will act very warlike against the flower.

VI 84

Celuy qu'en Sparte Claude ne peut regner,
Il fera tant par voye seductiue :
Que du court, long, le fera araigner,
Que contre Roy fera sa perspectiue.

The Lame One, he who lame could not reign in Sparta,
He will do much through seductive means:
So that by the short and long, he will be accused
Of making his perspective against the King.

VI 85

La grand cité de Tharse par Gaulois
Sera destruite, captifs tous à Turban :
Secours par mer, du grand Portugalois,
Premier d'esté le iour du sacre Vrban.

The great city of Tarsus by the Gauls
Will be destroyed, all of the Turban captives:
Help by sea from the great one of Portugal,
First day of summer Urban's consecration.

VI 86

Le grand Prelat vn iour apres son songe
Interpreté au rebours de son sens :
De la Gascongne luy suruiendra vn monge,
Qui fera eslire le grand Prelat de Sens.

The great Prelate one day after his dream,
Interpreted opposite to its meaning:
From Gascony a monk will come unexpectedly,
One who will cause the great prelate of Sens to be elected.

VI 87

L'election faicte dans Francfort,
N'aura nul lieu, Milan s'opposera :
Le sien plus proche semblera si grand fort,
Qu'outre le Rhin és mareschs chassera.

The election made in Frankfort
Will be voided, Milan will be opposed:
The follower closer will seem so very strong
That he will drive him out into the marshes beyond the
Rhine.

VI 88
Vn regne grand demourra desolé,
Aupres del Hebrose feront assemblees :
Mont Pyrenées le rendront consolé,
Lors que dans May seront terres tremblées.

A great realm will be left desolated,
Near the Ebro an assembly will be formed:
The Pyrenees mountains will console him,
When in May lands will be trembling.

VI 89
Entre deux cymbex pieds & mains estachez,
De miel face oingt, & de laict substanté :
Guespes & mouches fitine amour fachez,
Poccilateurs faucer, Cyphe tenté.

Feet and hands bound between two boats,
Face anointed with honey, and sustained with milk:
Wasps and flies, paternal love vexed,
Cup-bearer to falsify, Chalice tried.

VI 90
L'honnissement puant abominable,
Apres le faict sera felicité :
Grand excusé, pour n'estre fauorable.
Qu'à paix Neptune ne sera incité.

The stinking abominable disgrace,
After the deed he will be congratulated:
The great excuse for not being favorable,
That Neptune will not be persuaded to peace.

171

VI 91
Du conducteur de la guerre nauale,
Reuge effrené, seuere, horrible grippe,
Captif eschappé de l'aisné dans la baste :
Quand il naistra du grand vn fils Agrippe.

Of the leader of the naval war,
Red one unbridled, severe, horrible whim,
Captive escaped from the elder one in the bale,
When there will be born a son to the great Agrippa.

VI 92
Prince de beauté tant venuste,
Au chef menée, le second faict trahy :
La cité au glaiue de poudre face aduste,
Par trop grand meurtre le chef du Roy hay.

Prince of beauty so comely,
Around his head a plot, the second deed betrayed:
The city to the sword in dust the face burnt,
Through too great murder the head of the King hated.

VI 93
Prelat auare d'ambition trompé,
Rien ne fera que trop cuider viendra :
Ses me*f*agers, & luy bien attrapé,
Tout au rebours voit qui le bois fendra.

Prelat auare, d'ambition trompé,
Rien ne fera que trop cuider viendra.
Ses messagers, & luy bien attrapé,
Tout au rebours voir qui le bois fendra.

Prelat auare, d'ambition trompé
Rien ne fera que trop cuider viendra.
Ses me*f*agers & luy bien attrapé.
Tout au rebours voir qui le bois fendra.

The greedy prelate deceived by ambition,
He will come to reckon nothing too much for him:
He and his messengers completely trapped,
He who cut the wood sees all in reverse.

VI 94

Vn Roy iré sera aux sedifragues,
Quand interdicts seront harnois de guerre :
La poison taincte au succre par les fragues,
Par eaux meurtris, morts disant serre serre.

A King will be angry with the see-breakers,
When arms of war will be prohibited:
The poison tainted in the sugar for the strawberries,
Murdered by waters, dead, saying land, land.

VI 95

Par detracteur calomnié à puis nay :
Quand istront faicts enormes & martiaux :
La moindre part dubieuse a l'aisné,
Et tost au regne seront faicts partiaux.

Calumny against the cadet by the detractor,
When enormous and warlike deeds will take place:
The least part doubtful for the elder one,
And soon in the realm there will be partisan deeds.

VI 96

Grand cité à soldats abandonnée,
Onc ny eut mortel tumult si proche,
O qu'elle hideuse calamité s'approche,
Fors vne offense n'y sera pardonnée.

Great city abandoned to the soldiers,
Never was mortal tumult so close to it:
Oh, what a hideous calamity draws near,
Except one offense nothing will be spared it.

VI 97

Cinq & quarante degrez ciel bruslera,
Feu approcher de la grand cité neuue,
Instant grand flamme esparse sautera,
Quand on voudra des Normans faire preuue,

At forty-five degrees the sky will burn,
Fire to approach the great new city:
In an instant a great scattered flame will leap up,

When one will want to demand proof of the Normans.

VI 98
Ruyné aux Volsques de peur si fort terribles,
Leur grand cité taincte, faict pestilent :
Piller Sol, Lune, & violer leurs temples :
Et les deux fleuues rougir de sang coulant.

Ruin for the Volcae so very terrible with fear,
Their great city stained, pestilential deed:
To plunder Sun and Moon and to violate their temples:
And to redden the two rivers flowing with blood.

VI 99
L'ennemy docte se tournera confus,
Grand camp malade, & de faict par embusches,
Monts Pyrenées & Pœnus luy seront faicts refus,
Proche du fleuue descouurant antiques oruches.

The learned enemy will find himself confused,
His great army sick, and defeated by ambushes,
The Pyrenees and Pennine Alps will be denied him,
Discovering near the river ancient jugs.

VI 100
Fille de l'Aure, aſyle du mal ſain,
Ou iuſqu'au ciel ſe void l'amphitheatre,
Prodige veu. ton mal eſt fort prochain,
Seras captiue, & des fois plus de quatre.

Fille de l'Aure, aſyle du mal ſain,
Ou jusqu'au ciel ſe void l'amphitteatre
Prodige veu, ton mal eſt fort prochain
Seras captive, & deux fois plus de quatre.

Fille de l'Aure, asyle du mal sain,
Où iusqu'au ciel se void l'amphitheatre,
Prodige veu, ton mal est fort prochain,
Seras captiue, & des fois plus de quatre.

VI 100
*Daughter of the Breeze, asylum of the unhealthy,
Where the amphitheater is seen on the horizon:

174

Prodigy seen, your evil is very near,
You will be captive, and more than four times.

INCANTATION OF THE LAW AGAINST INEPT
CRITICS
LEGIS CAUTIO CONTRA INEPTOS CRITICOS

Qui legent hos versus, mature censunto;
Prophanum vulgus & inscium ne attrectato.
Omnesque Astrologi, Blenni, Barbari procul sunto,
Qui aliter faxit, is rite sacer esto.

INCANTATION OF THE LAW AGAINST INEPT
CRITICS

Let those who read this verse consider it profoundly,
Let the profane and the ignorant herd keep away:
And far away all Astrologers, Idiots and Barbarians,
May he who does otherwise be subject to the sacred rite.

Century VII

VII 0
Qui legent hosce versus, maturé censunte :
Prophanum vulgus & inscium ne attrectato :
Omnesque Astrologi, Blenni, Barbari procul sunto,
Qui aliter faxit, is rité sacer esto.

VII 1
L'Arc du thresor par Achilles deceu.
Aux procrees sceu la quadrangulaire :
Au faict Royal le comment sera sceu,
Corps veu pendu au veu du populaire.

The arc of the treasure deceived by Achilles,
the quadrangle known to the procreators.
The invention will be known by the Royal deed;
a corpse seen hanging in the sight of the populace.

VII 2
Par Mars ouuert Arles ne donra guerre,

175

De nuict seront les soldats estonnez :
Noir, blanc à l'inde dissimulé en terre,
Sous la saincte ombre traistre verrez & sonnez.

Opened by Mars Arles will not give war,
the soldiers will be astonished by night.
Black and white concealing indigo on land
under the false shadow you will see traitors sounded.

VII 3
Apres de France la victoire nauale,
Les Barchinons, Sallinons, les Phocens,
Lierre d'or, l'enclume serré dedans la balle,
Ceux de Prolon au fraud seront contens.

After the naval victory of France,
the people of Barcelona the Saillinons and those of
Marseilles;
the robber of gold, the anvil enclosed in the ball,
the people of Ptolon will be party to the fraud.

VII 4
Le Duc de Langres assiegé dedans Dole,
Accompagné d'Ostun & Lyonnois :
Ceneue, Auspourg ioinct ceux de Mirandole,
Passer les monts conter les Anconnois.

The Duke of Langres besieged at Dôle
accompanied by people from Autun and Lyons.
Geneva, Augsburg allied to those of Mirandola,
to cross the mountains against the people of Ancona.

VII 5
Vin sur la table en sera respandu,
Le tiers n'aura celle qu'il pretendoit :
Deux fois du noir de Parme descendu :
Perouse à Pise fera ce qu'il cuidoit.

Some of the wine on the table will be spilt,
the third will not have that which he claimed.
Twice descended from the black one of Parma,
Perouse will do to Pisa that which he believed.

176

VII 6
Naples, Palerme, & toute la Cecile,
Par main babare sera inhabitée,
Corsicque, Salerne & de Sardeigne l'Isle,
Faim, peste guerre, fin de maux intemptée.

Naples, Palerma and all of Sicily
will be uninhabited through Barbarian hands.
Corsica, Salerno and the island of Sardinia,
hunger, plague, war the end of extended evils.

VII 7
Sur le combat des grands cheuaux legers,
On criera le grand croissant confond.
De nuict tuer mont, habits de bergers,
Abismes rouges dans le fossé profond.

Upon the struggle of the great light horses,
it will be claimed that the great crescent is destroyed.
To kill by night, in the mountains,
dressed in shepherd's' clothing, red gulfs in the deep ditch.

VII 8
Flora, fuis, fuis le plus proche Romain,
Au Fesulan sera conflict donné :
Sang espandu, les plus grands prins à main,
Temple ne sexe ne sera pardonné.

Florense, flee, flee the nearest Roman,
at Fiesole will be conflict given:
blood shed, the greatest one take by the hand,
neither temple nor sex will be pardoned.

VII 9
Dame à l'absence de son grand capitaine,
Sera priée d'amour du Viceroy,
Faincte promesse & mal'heureuse estreine.
Entre les mains du grand Prince Barroys.

The lady in the absence of her great master
will be begged for love by the Viceroy.
Feigned promise and misfortune in love,
in the hands of the great Prince of Bar.

VII 10
Par le grand Prince limitrophe du Mans,
Preux & vaillant chef de grand exercite :
Par mer & terre de Gallois & Normans,
Caspre passer Barcelonne pillé Isle.

By the great Prince bordering Le Mans,
brave and valiant leader of the great army;
by land and sea with Bretons and Normans,
to pass Gibraltar and Barcelona to pillage the island.

VII 11
L'enfant Royal contemnera la mere,
Oeil, pieds blessez, rude, inobeissant,
Nouuelle à dame estrange & bien amere,
Seront tuez des siens plus de cinq cens.

eye, feet wounded rude disobedient;
strange and very bitter news to the lady;
more than five hundred of here people will be killed.

VII 12
Le grand puisnay fera fin de la guerre.
Aux dieux assemble les excusez :
Cahors, Moissac iront long de la serre,
Reffus Lestore, les Agenois rasez.

The great younger son will make an end of the war,
he assembles the pardoned before the gods;
Cahors and Moissac will go far from the prison,
a refusal at Lectoure, the people of Agen shaved.

VII 13
De la cité marine & tributaire,
La teste raze prendra la satrapie :
Chasser sordide qui puis sera contraire,
Par quatorze ans tiendra la tyrannie.

From the marine tributary city,
the shaven head will take up the satrapy;
to chase the sordid man who will the be against him.
For fourteen years he will hold the tyranny.

VII 14
Faux exposer viendra topographie,
Seront les cruches des monuments ouuertes :
Pulluler secte, faincte philosophie,
Pour blanches, noires, & pour antiques vertes.

He will come to expose the false topography,
the urns of the tombs will be opened.
Sect and holy philosophy to thrive,
black for white and the new for the old.

VII 15
Deuant cité de l'Insobre contrée,
Sept ans sera le siege deuant mis :
Le tresgrand Roy y fera son entrée,
Cité puis libre hors de ses ennemis.

Before the city of the Insubrian lands,
for seven years the siege will be laid;
a very great king enters it,
the city is then free, away from its enemies.

VII 16
Entrée profonde par la grand Royne faicte;
Rendra le lieu puissant inaccessible :
L'armée des trois Lyons sera deffaicte,
Faisant dedans cas hideux & terrible.

The deep entry made by the great Queen
will make the place powerful and inaccessible;
the army of the three lions will be defeated
causing within a thing hideous and terrible.

VII 17
Le Prince rare en pitié & clemence,
Apres auoir la paix aux siens baillé,
Viendra changer par mort grand cognoissance,
Par grand repos le regne trauaillé.

Le Prince rare en pitié & clemence,
Apres auoir la paix aux *f*iens baillé,
Viendra changer par mort grand congnoi*ff*ance.

179

Par grand repos le regne trauaillé.

Le prince rare de pitié & clemence
Par grand repos le regne trauaillé,
Viendra changer par mort grand connoi$\int\int$ance,
Lors que le grand to$\int$t $\int$era e$\int$trillé.

The prince who has little pity of mercy
will come through death to change (and become) very
knowledgeable.
The kingdom will be attended with great tranquillity,
when the great one will soon be fleeced.

VII 18
Les assiegez couleront leurs paches,
Sept iours apres feront cruelle issuë,
Dans repoulsez, feu sang. Sept mis à l'hache
Dame captiue qu'auoit la paix tissuë.

The besieged will color their pacts,
but seven days later they will make a cruel exit:
thrown back inside, fire and blood, seven put to the ax
the lady who had woven the peace is a captive.

VII 19
Le fort Nicene ne sera combatu,
Vaincu sera par rutilant metal,
Son faict sera vn long temps debatu
Aux citadins estrange espouuantal.

The fort at Nice will not engage in combat,
it will be overcome by shining metal.
This deed will be debated for a long time,
strange and fearful for the citizens.

VII 20
Ambassadeurs de la Toscane langue,
Auril & May Alpes & mer passer :
Celuy de veau exposera l'harangue,
Vie Gauloise ne venant effacer.

Ambassadors of the Tuscan language
will cross the Alps and the sea in April and May.

180

The man of the calf will deliver an oration,
not coming to wipe out the French way of life.

VII 21
Par pestilente inimitié Volsicque,
Dissimulée chassera le tyran :
Au pont de Sorgues se fera la traffique,
De mettre à mort luy & son adherant.

By the pestilential enmity of Languedoc,
the tyrant dissimulated will be driven out.
The bargain will be made on the bridge at Sorgues
to put to death both him and his follower

VII 22
Les Citoyens de Mesopotamie,
Irez encontre amis de Tarraconne,
Ieux, rits, banquets, toute gent endormie
Vicaire au Rosne, prins cité, ceux d'Ausone.

The citizens of Mesopotamia
angry with their friends from Tarraconne;
games, rites, banquets, every person asleep,
the vicar at Rhône, the city taken and those of Ausonia.

VII 23
Le Royal sceptre sera contrainct de prendre,
Ce que ses predecesseurs auoient engagé :
Puis que l'aneau on fera mal entendre,
Lors qu'on viendra le palais saccager.

The Royal scepter will be forced to take
that which his predecessors had pledged.
Because they do not understand about the ring
when they come to sack the palace.

VII 24
L'enseuely sortira du tombeau,
Fera de chaines lier le fort du pont :
Empoisonné auec œufs de Barbeau,
Grand de Lorraine par le Marquis du Pont.

He who was buried will come out of the tomb,

He will cause the fort of the bridge to be tied in chains:
Poisoned with the spawn of a pimp,
the great one from Lorraine by the Marquis du Pont.

VII 25
Par guerre longue tout l'exercice expuiser,
Que pour soldats ne trouueront pecune :
Lieu d'or d'argent, cuir on viendra cuser,
Gaulois aerain, signe croissant de Lune :

Through long war all the army exhausted,
so that they do not find money for the soldiers;
instead of gold or silver, they will come to coin leather,
Gallic brass, and the crescent sign of the Moon.

VII 26
Fustes & galees autour de sept nauires,
Sera liurée vne mortelle guerre :
Chef de Madric receura coup de vires,
Deux eschapées, & cinq menées à terre.

Foists and galleys around seven ships,
a mortal war will be let loose.
The leader from Madrid will receive a wound from arrows,
two escaped and five brought to land.

VII 27
Au cainct de Vast la grand caualerie,
Proche à Ferrage empesché au bagage,
Pompe a Turin feront tel volerie,
Que dans le fort rauiront leur hostage.

At the wall of Vasto the great cavalry
are impeded by the baggage near Ferrara.
At Turin they will speedily commit such robbery
that in the fort they will ravish their hostage.

VII 28
Le capitaine conduira grande proye,
Sur la montagne des ennemis plus proche :
Enuironné, par feu fera telle voye,
Tous eschappez, or trente mis en broche.

The captain will lead a great herd
on the mountain closest to the enemy.
Surrounded by fire he makes such a way,
all escape except for thirty put on the spit.

VII 29
Le grand Duc d'Albe se viendra rebeller,
A ses grands peres fera le tradiment :
Le grand de Guise le viendra debeller,
Captif mené & dressé monument.

The great one of Alba will come to rebel,
he will betray his great forebears.
The great man of Guise will come to vanquish him,
led captive with a monument erected.

VII 30
Le sac s'approche, feu, grand song espandu,
Po, grand fleuues, aux bouuiers l'entreprinse,
De Gennes, Nice, apres long attendu,
Foussan, Turin, à Sauillan la prinse.

The sack approaches, fire and great bloodshed.
Po the great rivers, the enterprise for the clowns;
after a long wait from Genoa and Nice,
Fossano, Turin the capture at Savigliano.

VII 31
De Languedoc, & Guienne plus de dix,
Mille voudront les Alpes repasser :
Grans Allobroges marcher contre Brundis,
A quin & Bresse les viendront recasser.

From Languedoc and Guienne more than ten
thousand will want to cross the Alps again.
The great Savoyards march against Brindisi,
Aquino and Bresse will come to drive them back.

VII 32
Du mont Royal naistra d'vne casane,
Qui caue, & compte viendra tyranniser,
Dresser copie de la marche Millane,
Fauene, Florence d'or & gens espuiser.

183

From the bank of Montereale will be born one
who bores and calculates becoming a tyrant.
To raise a force in the marches of Milan,
to drain Faenza and Florence of gold and men

VII 33
Par fraude, regne, forces expolier,
La classe obsesse, passages à l'espie :
Deux faincts amis se viendront t'allier,
Esueiller haine de long temps assoupie.

The kingdom stripped of its forces by fraud,
the fleet blockaded, passages for the spy;
two false friends will come to rally
to awaken hatred for a long time dormant.

VII 34
En grand regret sera la gent Gauloise,
Cœur vain, leger croira temerité :
Pain, sel, ne vin, eau, venin ne ceruoise,
Plus grand captif, faim, froid, necessité.

The French nation will be in great grief,
vain and lighthearted, they will believe rash things.
No bread, salt, wine nor water, venom nor ale,
the greater one captured, hunger, cold and want.

VII 35
La grande po*f*che viendra plaindre, plorer,
D'auoir e*f*leu, trompez *f*eront en l'aage :
Guiere auec eux ne voudra demourer,
Deceu *f*era par ceux de *f*on langage.

La grande poche viendra plaindre, pleurer
D'auoir e*f*leu : trompez *f*eront en l'age.
Guiere auec eux ne voudra demeurer :
Deceu *f*era par ceux de *f*on langage.

La grande poche viendra plaindre, pleurer,
D'auoir esleu : trompez seront en l'aage.
Guiere auec eux ne voudra demeurer :
Deceu sera par ceux de son langage.

The great fish will come to complain and weep
for having chosen, deceived concerning his age:
he will hardly want to remain with them,
he will be deceived by those (speaking) his own tongue.

VII 36

Dieu, le ciel tout le diuin verbe à l'onde,
Porté par rouges sept razes à Bizance,
Contre les oingts trois cens de Trabisconde
Deux loix mettront, & borreur, puis credence.

God, the heavens, all the divine words in the waves,
carried by seven red-shaven heads to Byzantium:
against the anointed three hundred from Trebizond,
will make two laws, first horror then trust.

VII 37

Dix enuoyez, chef de nef mettre à mort,
D'vn aduerty, en classe guerre ouuerte :
Confusion chef, l'vn se picque & mord,
Leryn, stecades nefs, cap dedans la nerte.

Ten sent to put the captain of the ship to death,
are altered by one that there is open revolt in the fleet.
Confusion, the leader and another stab and bite each other
at Lerins and the Hyerès, ships, prow into the darkness.

VII 38

L'aisné Royal sur coursier voltigeant,
Picquer viendra si rudement courir :
Gueulle, lepée, pied dans l'estrein pleignant,
Trainé, tire, horriblement mourir.

The elder royal one on a frisky horse
will spur so fiercely that it will bolt.
Mouth, mouthful, foot complaining in the embrace;
dragged, pulled, to die horribly.

VII 39

Le conducteur de l'armée Françoise,
Cuidant perdre le principale phalange :
Par sus paué de l'auaigne & d'ardoise,

185

Soy parfondra par Gennes gent estrange.

The leader of the French army
will expect to lose the main phalanx.
Upon the pavement of oats and slate
the foreign nation will be undermined through Genoa.

VII 40
Dedans tonneaux hors oingts d'huile & gresse,
Seront vingt vn deuant le port fermez,
Au second guet par mort feront proüesse,
Gaigner les portes, & du guet assommez.

Within casks anointed outside with oil and grease
twenty-one will be shut before the harbor,
at second watch; through death they will do great deeds;
to win the gates and be killed by the watch.

VII 41
Les os des pieds & des mains enserrez,
Par bruit maison long temps inhabitée,
Seront par songes concauant deterrez,
Maison salubre & sans bruit habitee.

The bones of the feet and the hands locked up,
because of the noise the house is uninhabited for a long
time.
Digging in dreams they will be unearthed,
the house healthy in inhabited without noise.

VII 42
Deux de poison saisis nouueaux venus,
Dans la cuisine du grand Prince verser :
Par le soüillard tous deux au faict cogneus,
Prins qui cuidoit de mort l'aisné vexer.

Two newly arrived have seized the poison,
to pour it in the kitchen of the great Prince.
By the scullion both are caught in the act,
taken he who thought to trouble the elder with death.

VII 43 *
When one will se two unicorns,

186

The one lifting, the other lowering,
World in the middle, to bend to the limit
The nephew will run away laughing.

VII 44 *
When a Bourbon will really be good,
Bearing in his person the marks of justice,
Bearing then the longest name of his blood
Through flight unjustly he will receive his punishment.

VII 73
REnfort de sieges manubis & maniples
Changez le sacre & passe sur le prosne,
Prins & captifs n'arreste les prez triples
Plus par fonds mis, esleué, mis au trosne.

VII 73 *
Reinforcement of sieges plunder and maniples
The holy one changes and passes over the sermon,
Taken and captives it does not stop the triple meadows,
Put in the uttermost depths, raised, put on the throne.

VII 80
L'Occident libres les Isles Britanniques
Le recogneu passer le bas, puis haut
Ne content triste Rebel. corff. Escotiques
Puis rebeller par plus & par nuict chaut.

VII 80 *
The West free the British Isles
The recognized one to pass low, then high
Discontented sad Rebel Scottish corsairs
Then to rebel much more and by warm night.

VII 81
La stratageme simulte sera rare
La mort en voye rebelle par contrée,
Par le retour du voyage Barbare
Exalteront la protestante entrée.

VII 82 *
The stratagem in the quarrel will be uncommon
The death en route in the coutry rebellion:

187

On the return from the Barbarian voyage
They will exalt the Protestant entry.

VII 83
Vent chaut, conseil pleurs, timidité,
De nuict au lit assailly sans les armes,
D'oppression grande calamité,
L'epithalame conuerty pleurs & larmes.

VII 83 *
Wind warm, counsels, tears, timidity,
By night in bed assailed without arms:
Great calamity from oppression,
The wedding song converted, weeping and tears.

Century VIII

VIII 1
PAv, nay, loron plus feu qu'à sang sera,
Laude nager, fuir grand aux surrez.
Les agassas entrée refusera,
Pampon, Durance les tiendra enserrez.

Pau, Nay, Loron will be more of fire than blood,
  to swim in praise, the great one to flee to the confluence (of
rivers).
  He will refuse entry to the magpies
  Pampon and the Durance will keep them confined.

VIII 1 *
Several will be confused in their waiting,
Pardon will not be given the inhabitants:
Those who thought well of persisting in the waiting,
But not much spare time will be given them.

VIII 2
Condon & Aux & autour de Mirande
Ie voy du ciel feu qui les enuironne.
Sol Mars conioint au Lyon, puis Marmande
Foudre, grand gresle, mur tombe dans Garonne.

188

Condom and Auch and around Mirande,
I see fire from the sky which encompasses them.
Sun and Mars conjoined in Leo, then at Marmande,
lightning, great hail, a wall falls into the Garonne.

VIII 2 *
Several will come, and speak of peace,
Between Monarchs and very powerful lords:
But it will not be accorded so soon,
Unless they become more obedient than the others.

VIII 3
Au fort chasteau de Vigilanue & Resuiers
Sera serré le puisnay de Nancy :
Dedans Turin seront ards les premiers,
Lors que de dueil Luon sera transy.

Within the strong castle of Vigilance and Resviers
the younger born of Nancy will be shut up.
In Turin the first ones will be burned,
when Lyons will be transported with grief.

VIII 3 *
Alas what a fury ! Alas what a pity
Will there be between people:
never did one see such a friendship
As the wolves will have diligent in running.

VIII 4
Dedans Monech le coq sera receu,
Le Cardinal de France apparoistra
Par Logarion Romain sera deceu,
Foiblesse à l'Aigle, & force au Coq naistra.

The cock will be received into Monace,
the Cardinal of France will appear;
He will be deceived by the Roman legation;
weakness to the eagle, strength will be born to the cock.

VIII 4 *
Many people will want to come to terms
With the great lords who will bring war upon them:
They will not want to hear anything of it from them,

189

Alas! if Gos does not send peace to the earth.

VIII 5
Apparoistra temple luisant orné,
La lampe & cierge à Borne & Bretueil,
Pour la Lucerne le canton destorné,
Quand on verra le grand Coq au cercueil.

There will appear a shining ornate temple,
the lamp and the candle at Borne and Breteuil.
For the canton of Lucerne turned aside,
when one will see the great cock in his shroud.

VIII 5 *
Varieties of aid will come from all sides,
From distant people who will want to resist:
Suddenly they will be much urged on,
But they will be unable to assist at that hour.

VIII 6
Clarté fulgure à Lyon apparante
Luysant, print Malte, subit sera estrainte,
Sardon, Mauris traitera deceuante,
Geneue à Londres à Coq trahison fainte.

Lighting and brightness are seen at Lyons shining,
Malta is taken, suddenly it will be extinguished.
Sardon, Maurice will act deceitfully,
Geneva to London, feigning treason towards the cock.

VIII 6 *
Alas, what ambition foreign Princes have,
Take careful heed lest they come into your country:
There should be terrible dangers
And in many countries, even in Vienna.

VIII 7
Verceil, Milan donra intelligence,
Dedans Tycin sera faite la paye.
Courir par Seine eau, sang feu par Florence,
Vnique choir d'hault en bas faisant maye.

Vercelli, Milan will give the news,
the wound will be given at Pavia.
To run in the Seine, water, blood and fire through Florence,
the unique one falling from high to low calling for help.

VIII 8
Prés de Linterne dans de tonnes fermez,
Chiuaz fera pour l'Aigle la menée,
L'esleu cassé luy ses gens enfermez,
Dedans Turin rapt espouse emmenée.

Near Focia enclosed in some tuns
Chivasso will plot for the eagle.
The elected one driven out, he and his people shut up,
rape with Turin, the bride led away.

VIII 9
Pendant que l'Aigle & le Coq à Sauone
Seront vnis, Mer, Leuant & Ongrie.
L'armée à Naples, Palerme, Marque d'Ancone
Rome, Venise par Barbe horrible crie.

While the eagle is united with the cock at Savonna,
the Eastern Sea and Hungary.
The army at Naples, Palermo, the marches of Ancona,
Rome and Venice a great outcry by the Barbarian.

VIII 10
Puanteur grande sortira de Lausanne,
Qu'on ne sçaura l'origine du fait.
Lon mettra hors tout la gent loingtaine
Feu veu au ciel, peuple estranger deffait.

A great stench will come from Lausanne,
but they will not know its origin,
they will put out all people from distant places,
fire seen in the sky, a foreign nation defeated.

VIII 11
Peuple infiny paroistra à Vicence
Sans force feu brusler la basilique
Prés de Lunage deffait grand de Valence,
Lors que Venise par mort prendra pique.

191

A multitude of people will appear at Vicenza
without force, fire to burn the Basilica.
Near Lunage the great one of Valenza defeated:
at a time when Venice takes up the quarrel through custom.

VIII 12
Apparoistra aupres de Buffalore
L'hault & procere entré dedans Milan
L'abbé de Foix auec ceux de sainct Morre
Feront la forbe habillez en vilain.

He will appear near to Buffalora
the highly born and tall one entered into Milan.
The Abbe of Foix with those of Saint-Meur
will cause damage dressed up as serfs.

VIII 13
Le croisé frere par amour effrenée
Fera par Praytus Bellerophon mourir,
Classe à mil ans la femme forcenée
Beu le breuuage, tous deux apres perir.

The crusader brother through impassioned love
will cause Bellerophon to die through Proteus;
the fleet for a thousand years, the maddened woman,
the potion drunk, both of them then die.

VIII 14
Le grand credit d'or & d'argent l'abondance
Fera aueugler par libide l'honneur.
Sera cogneu sera d'adultere l'offense
Qui paruiendra à ƒon grand deshonneur.

Le grand credit, d'or, d'argent l'abondance
Aueuglera par libide l'honneur.
Cogneu ƒera d'adultere l'offenƒe,
Qui paruiendra à ƒon grand deshonneur.

Le grand credit, d'or d'argent l'abondance
Aueuglera par libide l'honneur :
Cogneu sera d'adultere l'offense,
Qui paruiendra à son grand deshonneur.

The great credit of gold and abundance of silver
will cause honor to be blinded by lust;
the offense of the adulterer will become known,
which will occur to his great dishonor.

VIII 15
Vers Aquilon grands efforts par hommasse
Presque l'Europe & l'vniuers vexer,
Les deux eclypses mettra en telle chasse,
Et aux Pannons vie & mort renforcer.

Great exertions towards the North by a man-woman
to vex Europe and almost all the Universe.
The two eclipses will be put into such a rout
that they will reinforce life or death for the Hungarians.

VIII 16
Au lieu que Hieron feit sa nef fabriquer
Si grand deluge sera & si subite,
Qu'on n'aura lieu ne terres s'ataquer,
L'onde monter Fesulant Olympique.

At the place where HIERON has his ship built,
there will be such a great sudden flood,
that one will not have a place nor land to fall upon,
the waters mount to the Olympic Fesulan.

VIII 17
Les bien-aiſez ſubit feront deſmis,
Par les trois freres le monde mis en trouble.
Cité marine ſaiſiront ennemis,
Faim, feu, ſang, peſte, & de tous maux le double.

Les bien aisez subit seront desmis,
Le monde mis par les trois freres en trouble.
Cité marine saisiront ennemis,
Faim, feu, sang, peste, & de tous maux le double

Les bien aiſez ſubit feront demis.
Le monde mis par les trois freré en trouble.
Cité marine ſaiſiront ennemis.
Faim, feu, ſang, peſte, & de tous maux le double.

193

Those at ease will suddenly be cast down,
the world put into trouble by three brothers;
their enemies will seize the marine city,
hunger, fire, blood, plague, all evils doubled.

VIII 18
De Flore issuë de sa mort sera cause,
Vn temps deuant par ieusne & vieille bueyre
Car les trois lys luy feront telle pause,
Par son fruit sauue comme chair cruë mueyre.

De FLORE iſſue de ſa mort ſera cauſe :
Vn temps deuant par ieune & vieille bueyre.
Car les trois Lis luy feront telle pauſe,
Par ſon fruit ſauue, *

De Flore iſſuë de ſa mort ſera cauſe,
Un temps deuant par ieune & vieille bueyre.
Car les trois lys luy feront telle poſe,
Par ſon fruit ſauue comme chair cruë mueyre.

The cause of her death will be issued from Florence,
one time before drunk by young and old;
by the three lilies they will give her a great pause.
Save through her offspring as raw meat is dampened.

VIII 19
A soustenir la grand cappe troublée,
Pour l'esclaircir les rouges marcheront,
De mort famille sera presque accablée,
Les rouges rouges le rouge assommeront.

To support the great troubled Cappe;
the reds will march in order to clarify it;
a family will be almost overcome by death,
the red, red ones will knock down the red one.

VIII 20
Le faux message par election fainte
Courir par vrben rompuë pache arreste,
Voix aceptées, de sang chapelle tainte,
Et à vn autre l'empire contraincte.

194

The false message about the rigged election
to run through the city stopping the broken pact;
voices bought, chapel stained with blood,
the empire contracted to another one.

VIII 21

Au port de Agde trois fustes entreront
Portant l'infect non foy & pestilence
Passant le pont mil milles embleront,
Et le pont rompre à tierce resistance.

Three foists will enter the port of Agde
carrying the infection and pestilence, not the faith.
Passing the bridge they will carry off a million,
the bridge is broken by the resistance of a third.

VIII 22

Gorsan, Narbonne, par le sel aduertir
Tucham, la grace Parpignan trahie,
La vie rouge n'y voudra consentir,
Par haulte voldrap gris vie faillie.

Coursan, Narbonne through the salt to warn
Tuchan, the grace of Perpignan betrayed;
the red town will not wish to consent to it,
in a high flight, a copy flag and a life ended.

VIII 23

Lettres trouuées de la Royne les coffres,
Point de subscrit sans aucun nom d'autheur,
Par la police seront cachez les offres,
Qu'on ne sçaura qui sera l'amateur.

Letters are found in the queen's chests,
no signature and no name of the author.
The ruse will conceal the offers;
so that they do not know who the lover is.

VIII 24

Lieutenant à l'entrée de l'huys
Assommera le grand de Parpignan,
En se cuidant sauuer à Montpertuis.

Sera deceu bastard de Lusignan.

The lieutenant at the door of the house,
will knock down the great man of Perpignan.
Thinking to save himself at Montpertuis,
the bastard of Lusignan will be deceived.

VIII 25
Cœur de l'amant ouuert d'amour fertiue
Dans le ruisseau fera rauir la Dame,
Le demy mal contrefera lassiue,
Le pere à deux priuera corps de l'ame.

The heart of the lover, awakened by furtive love
will ravish the lady in the stream.
She will pretend bashfully to be half injured,
the father of each will deprive the body of its soul.

VIII 26
De Caton es trouuez en Barselonne,
Mys descouuers lieu terrouers & ruyne,
Le grand qui tient ne tient voudra Pamplonne.
Par l'abbage de Montferrat bruyne.

The bones of Cato found in Barcelona,
placed, discovered, the site found again and ruined.
The great one who holds, but does not hold,
wants Pamplona, drizzle at the abbey of Montserrat.

VIII 27
La voye auxelle l'vn sur l'autre fornix.
Du muy de ser hor mis braue & genest,
L'escript d'empereur le fenix
Veu en celuy ce gu'à nul autre n'est.

The auxiliary way, one arch upon the other,
Le Muy deserted except for the brave one and his genet.
The writing of the Phoenix Emperor,
seen by him which is (shown) to no other.

VIII 28
Les simulachres d'or et d'argent enflez,
Qu'apres le rapt lac au feu furent iettez

Au descouuert estaincts tous & troublez.
Au marbre escripts, perscripts interiettez.

The copies of gold and silver inflated,
which after the theft were thrown into the lake,
at the discovery that all is exhausted and dissipated by the
debt.
All scrips and bonds will be wiped out.

VIII 29
Au quart pillier l'on sacre à Saturne.
Par tremblant terre & deluge fendu
Sous l'edifice Saturin trouuée vrne,
D'or Capion rauy & puis rendu.

At the fourth pillar which they dedicate to Saturn
split by earthquake and by flood;
under Saturn's building an urn is found
gold carried off by Caepio and then restored.

VIII 30
Dedans Tholose non loing de Beluzer
Faisant vn puis loing, palais d'espectacle
Thresor trouué vn chacun ira vexer,
Et en deux locs tout & prés des vesacle.

In Toulouse, not far from Beluzer
making a deep pit a palace of spectacle,
the treasure found will come to vex everyone
in two places and near the Basacle.

VIII 31
Premier grand fruict le Prince de Pesquiere :
Mais puis viendra bien & cruel malin,
Dedans Venise perdra sa gloire fiere,
Et mis à mal par plus ioyue Celin.

The first great fruit of the prince of Perchiera,
then will come a cruel and wicked man.
In Venice he will lose his proud glory,
and is led into evil by then younger Selin.

VIII 32

197

Garde toy roy Gaulois de ton nepueu,
Qui fera tant que ton vnique fils
Sera meurtry à Venus faisant vœu,
Accompagné denuict que trois & six.

French king, beware of your nephew
who will do so much that your only son
will be murdered while making his vows to Venus;
accompanied at night by three and six.

VIII 33
Le grand naistra de Veronne & Vincence,
Qui portera vn surnom bien indigne.
Qui à Venise vouldra faire vengeance.
Luy mesme prins homme du guet & signe.

The great one who will be born of Verona and Vincenza
who carries a very unworthy surname;
he who at Venice will wish to take vengeance,
himself taken by a man of the watch and sign.

VIII 34
Apres victoire du Lyon au Lyon,
Sus la montagne de Ivra Secatombe,
Delues & brodes septiesme million,
Lyon, Vlme à Mausol mort & tombe.

After the victory of the Lion over the Lion,
there will be great slaughter on the mountain of Jura;
floods and dark-colored people of the seventh (of a
million),
Lyons, Ulm at the mausoleum death and the tomb.

VIII 35
Dedans l'entrée de Garonne & Bayse,
Et la forest non loing de Damazan
Du marsaues gelées, puis gresle & bize
Dordonnois gelle par erreur de Mezan.

At the entrance to Garonne and Baise
and the forest not far from Damazan,
discoveries of the frozen sea, then hail and north winds.
Frost in the Dardonnais through the mistake of the month.

VIII 36
Sera commis conte oindre aduché
De Saulne & sainct Aulbin & Belœuure
Pauer de marbre de tous loing espluché
Non Bleteran resister & chef d'œuure.

It will be committed against the anointed brought
from Lons le Saulnier, Saint Aubin and Bell'oeuvre.
To pave with marble taken from distant towers,
not to resist Bletteram and his masterpiece.

VIII 37
La forteresse aupres de la Tamise
Cherra par lors, le Roy dedans serré,
Aupres du pont sera veu en chemise
Vn deuant mort, puis dans le fort barré.

The fortress near the Thames
will fall when the king is locked up inside.
He will be seen in his shirt near the bridge,
one facing death then barred inside the fortress.

VIII 38
Le Roy de Bloys dans Auignon regner
Vn autre fois le peuple emonopolle,
Dedans le Rosne par murs fera baigner
Iusques à cinq le dernier prés de Nolle.

The King of Blois will reign in Avignon,
once again the people covered in blood.
In the Rhône he will make swim
near the walls up to five, the last one near Nolle.

VIII 39
Qu'aura esté par prince Bizantin,
Sera tollu par prince de Tholose :
La foy de Foix par le chef Tholentin,
Luy faillira ne refusant l'espouse.

He who will have been for the Byzantine prince
will be taken away by the prince of Toulouse.
The faith of Foix through the leader of Tolentino

will fail him, not refusing the bride.

VIII 40
Le ſang du iuſte par Taurer la Daurade,
Pour ſe venger contre les Saturnins
Au nouueau lac plongeront la maynade,
Puis marcheront contre les Albanins.
Le ſang du iuſte par Taur & la Dorade,

Pour ſe vanger contre les Saturnins,
Au nouueau lac plongeront la mainade :
Puis marcheront contre les Albanins.
Le sang du Iuste par Taur & la Dorade.

Pour se venger contre les Saturins
Au nouueau lac plongeront la mainade,
Puis marcheront contre les Albanins.

The blood of the Just for Taur and La Duarade
in order to avenge itself against the Saturnines.
They will immerse the band in the new lake,
then they will march against Alba.

VIII 41
Esleu sera Renad ne sonnant mot,
Faisant le saint public viuant pain d'orge,
Tyrannizer apres tant à vn cop,
Mettant à pied des plus grands sur la gorge,

A fox will be elected without speaking one word,
appearing saintly in public living on barley bread,
Afterwards he will suddenly become a tyrant
putting his foot on the throats of the greatest men.

VIII 42
Par auarice, par force & violence
Viendra vexer les siens chefs d'Orleans,
Prés sainct Memire assault & resistance,
Mort dans sa tante diront qu'il dort leans.

Through avarice, through force and violence
the chief of Orléans will come to vex his supporters.
Near St. Memire, assault and resistance.

200

Dead in his tent they will say he is asleep inside.

VIII 43
Par le decide de deux choses bastars,
Nepueu du sang occupera le regne,
Dedans lectoyre seront les coups de dards
Nepueu par pleira l'enseigne.

Through the fall of two bastard creatures
the nephew of the blood will occupy the throne.
Within Lectoure there will be blows of lances,
the nephew through fear will fold up his standard.

VIII 44
Le procreé naturel dogmion,
De sept à neuf du chemin destorner
A roy de longue & amy au my hom,
Doit à Nauarre fort de Pav prosterner.

The natural offspring off Ogmios
will turn off the road from seven to nine.
To the king long friend of the half man,
Navarre must destroy the fort at Pau.

VIII 45
La main escharpe & la iambe bandée,
Longs puis nay de Calais portera,
Au mot du guet la mort sera tardée,
Puis dans le temple à Pasques saignera.

With his hand in a sling and his leg bandaged,
the younger brother of Calais will reach far.
At the word of the watch, the death will be delayed,
then he will bleed at Easter in the Temple.

VIII 46
Pol mensolée mourra trois lieuës du rosne,
Fuis les deux prochains tarasc destrois :
Car mars fera le plus horrible trosne,
De coq & d'Aigle de France freres trois.

Paul the celibate will die three leagues from Rome,
the two nearest flee the oppressed monster.

When Mars will take up his horrible throne,
the Cock and the Eagle, France and the three brothers.

VIII 47
Lac Trasmenien portera tesmoignage,
Des coniurez sarez dedans Perouse
Vn despolle contrefera le sage,
Tuant Tedesq de sterne & minuse.

Lake Trasimene will bear witness
of the conspirators locked up inside Perugia.
A fool will imitate the wise one,
killing the Teutons, destroying and cutting to pieces.

VIII 48
Saturne en Cancer, Iupiter auec Mars,
Dedans Feurier Caldondon saluaterre.
Sault Castallon assaily de trois pars,
Pres de Verbiesque conflit mortelle guerre.

Saturn in Cancer, Jupiter with Mars
in February Chaldondon'salva tierra.
Sierra Morena besieged on three sides
near Verbiesque, war and mortal conflict.

VIII 49
Satur au beuf ioue en l'cau, Mars en fleiche,
Six de Feurier mortalité donra,
Ceux de Tardaigne à Bruge si grand breche,
Qu'à Pontereso chef Barbarin mourra.

Saturn in Taurus, Jupiter in Aquarius. Mars in Sagittarius,
the sixth of February brings death.
Those of Tardaigne so great a breach at Bruges,
that the barbarian chief will die at Ponteroso.

VIII 50
La pestilence l'entour de Capadille,
Vne autre faim pres de Sagone s'appreste :
Le cheualier bastard de bon senille,
Au grand de Thunes fera trancher la teste.

The plague around Capellades,

another famine is near to Sagunto;
the knightly bastard of the good old man
will cause the great one of Tunis to lose his head.

VIII 51
Le Bizantin faisant oblation,
Apres auoir Cordube à soy reprinse :
Son chemin long repos pamplation,
Mer passant proy par la Colongna prinse.

The Byzantine makes an oblation
after having taken back Cordoba.
A long rest on his road, the vines cut down,
at sea the passing prey captured by the Pillar.

VIII 52
Le roy de Bloys Auignom regner,
D'Amboise & seme viendra le long de Lyndre
Ongle à Poytiers sainctes aisles ruyner
Deuant Boni.

The king of Blois to reign in Avignon,
from Amboise and Seme the length of the Indre:
claws at Poitiers holy wings ruined
before Boni. . . .

VIII 53
Dedans Bologne voudra lauer ses fautes,
Il ne pourra au temple du soleil,
Il volera faisant chose si hautes,
En hierarchie n'en fut oncq vn pareil.

Within Boulogne he will want to wash away his misdeeds,
he cannot at the temple of the Sun.
He will fly away, doing very great things:
In the hierarchy he had never an equal.

VIII 54
Soubs la couleur du traicté mariage,
Fait magnanime par grand Chyren selin,
Quintin, Arras recouurez au voyage
D'espagnols fait second banc macelin.

Under the color of the marriage treaty,
a magnanimous act by the Chyren Selin:
St. Quintin and Arras recovered on the journey;
By the Spanish a second butcher's bench is made.

VIII 55
Entre deux fleuues se verra enserré,
Tonneaux & caques vnis à passer outre,
Huict ponts rompus chef à tant enferré,
Enfans parfaicts sont igulez en coultre.

He will find himself shut in between two rivers,
casks and barrels joined to cross beyond:
eight bridges broken, their chief run through so many times,
perfect children's throats slit by the knife.

VIII 56
La bande foible le tertre occupera
Ceux du haut lieu feront horribles cris,
Le gros troupeau d'estre coin troublera,
Tombe pres D. nebro descouuers les escris.

The weak band will occupy the land,
those of high places will make dreadful cries.
The large herd of the outer corner troubled,
near Edinburgh it falls discovered by the writings.

VIII 57
De souldat simple paruiendra en empire,
De robe courte paruiendra à la lonque
Vaillant aux armes en eglise ou plus pyre,
Vexer les prestres comme l'eau faict l'esponge.

From simple soldier he will attain to Empire,
from the short robe he will grow into the long.
Brave in arms, much worse towards the Church,
he vexes the priests as water fills a sponge.

VIII 58
Regne en querelle aux freres diuisé,
Prendre les armes & le nom Britannique
Tiltre d'Anglican sera tard aduisé,
Surprins de nuict mener à l'air Gallique.

204

A kingdom divided by two quarreling brothers
to take the arms and the name of Britain.
The Anglican title will be advised to watch out,
surprised by night (the other is), led to the French air.

VIII 59
Par deux fois haut, par deux fois mis à bas
L'orient aussi l'occident foiblira
Son aduersaire apres plusieurs combats,
Par mer chassé au besoing faillira.

Twice put up and twice cast down,
the East will also weaken the West.
Its adversary after several battles
chased by sea will fail at time of need.

VIII 60
Premier en Gaule, premier en Romanie,
Par mer & terre aux Anglois & Paris,
Merueillex faits par celle grand meſnie,
Violant Terax perdra le NORLARIS.

Premier en Gaule, premier en Romanie,
Par mer & terre, aux Anglois & Paris.
Merueillex faits par celle grand meſnie.
Violant, tenax perdra le NORLARIS.

Premier en Gaule, premier en Romanie,
Par mer & terre aux Anglois & Paris
Merueillex faits par celle grand mesnie
Violant, terax perdra le Norlaris.

First in Gaul, first in Romania,
over land and sea against the English and Paris.
Marvelous deeds by that great troop,
violent, the wild beast will lose Lorraine.

VIII 61
Iamais par le decouurement du iour
Ne paruiendra au signe sceptrifere
Que tous ses sieges ne soient en seiour,
Portant au coq don du Tag amifere.

205

Never by the revelation of daylight
will he attain the mark of the scepter bearer.
Until all his sieges are at rest,
bringing to the Cock the gift of the armed legion.

VIII 62
Lors qu'on verra expiler le sainct temple,
Plus grand du Rhosne & sacres prophaner
Par eux naistra pestilence si ample,
Roy faict iniuste ne fera condamner.

Lors qu'on verra expiler le ƒainȼt, Temple,
Plus grand du Roƒne leur ƒacrez profanez,
Par eux naiƒtra peƒtilence ƒi ample,
Roy fuit iniuƒte ne fera condamner.

Lors qu'on voirra expiler le ƒaint temple
Plus grand du Rhoƒne & ƒacres profanez,
Par eux naiƒtra peƒtilence ƒi ample.
Roy fait iniuƒte ne fera condamner.

When one sees the holy temple plundered,
the greatest of the Rhône profaning their sacred things;
because of them a very great pestilence will appear,
the king, unjust, will not condemn them.

VIII 63
Quand l'adultere blessé sans coup aura
Meurdry la femme & le fils par despit,
Femme assoumée l'enfant estranglera :
Huict captifs prins, s'estouffer sans respit.

When the adulterer wounded without a blow
will have murdered his wife and son out of spite;
his wife knocked down, he will strangle the child;
eight captives taken, choked beyond help.

VIII 64
Dedans les Isles les enfans transportez,
Les deux de sept seront en desespoir :
Ceux de terroüer en seront supportez,
Nom pelle prins des ligues fuy l'espoir.

206

The infants transported into the islands,
two out of seven will be in despair.
Those of the soil will be supported by it,
the name 'shovel' taken, the hope of the leagues fails.

VIII 65

Le vieux frustré du principal espoir,
Il paruiendra au chef de son empire :
Vingt mois tiendra le regne à grand pouuoir,
Tiran, cruel en delaissant vn pire.

The old man disappointed in his main hope,
will attain to the leadership of his Empire.
Twenty months he will hold rule with great force,
a tyrant, cruel, giving way to one worse.

VIII 66

Quand l'escriture D. M. trouuée,
Et caue antique à lampe descouuerte,
Loy, Roy & Prince Vlpian esprouuée,
Pauillon Royne & Duc sous la couuerte.

When the inscription D.M. is found
in the ancient cave, revealed by a lamp.
Law, the King and Prince Ulpian tried,
the Queen and Duke in the pavilion under cover.

VIII 67

Par. car. nersaf, à ruine grand discorde,
Ne l'vn ne l'autre n'aura election,
Nersaf du peuple aura amour & concorde,
Ferrare, Collonne grande protection :

Paris, Carcassone, France to ruin in great disharmony,
neither one nor the other will be elected.
France will have the love and good will of the people,
Ferara, Colonna great protection.

VIII 68

Vieux Cardinal par le ieune deceu,
Hors de sa charge se verra desarmé,
Arles ne monstres double soit aperceu,

Et Liqueduct & le Prince embaumé.

The old Cardinal is deceived by the young one,
he will find himself disarmed, out of his position:
Do not show, Arles, that the double is perceived,
both Liqueduct and the Prince embalmed.

VIII 69
Aupres du ieune se vieux Ange baisser,
Et le viendra sur monter à la fin :
Dix ans esgaux aux plus vieux rabaisser,
De trois deux l'vn huictiesme Seraphin.

Beside the young one the old angel falls,
and will come to rise above him at the end;
ten years equal to most the old one falls again,
of three two and one, the eighth seraphim.

VIII 70
Il entrera viain, meschant, infame
Tyrannisant la Mesopotamie
Tous amis faict d'adulterine dame.
Terre horrible noir de phisomie.

He will enter, wicked, unpleasant, infamous,
tyrannizing over Mesopotamia.
All friends made by the adulterous lady,
the land dreadful and black of aspect.

VIII 71
Croistra le nombre si grand des Astronomes
Chassez, bannis & liures censurez,
L'an mil six cens & sept par sacre glomes,
Que nul aux sacres ne seront asseurez.

The number of astrologers will grow so great,
that they will be driven out, banned and their books
censored.
In the year 1607 by sacred assemblies
so that none will be safe from the holy ones.

VIII 72
Champ Perusin ô l'enorme deffaite

208

Et le conflict tout aupres de Rauenne
Passage sacre lors qu'on fera la feste,
Vainqueur vaincu cheual manger l'auenne.

Oh what a huge defeat on the Perugian battlefield
and the conflict very close to Ravenna.
A holy passage when they will celebrate the feast,
the conqueror banished to eat horse meat.

VIII 73
Soldat Barbare le grand Roy frappera,
Iniustement non eslongné de mort,
L'auare mere du faict cause sera
Coniurateur & regne en grand remort.

The king is struck by a barbarian soldier,
unjustly, not far from death.
The greedy will be the cause of the deed,
conspirator and realm in great remorse.

VIII 74
En terre neufue bien auant Roy entré
Pendant subges luy viendront faire acueil,
Sa perfidie aura tel rencontré,
Qu'aux citadins lieu de feste & recueil.

A king entered very far into the new land
while the subjects will come to bid him welcome;
his treachery will have such a result
that to the citizens it is a reception instead of a festival.

VIII 75
Le pere & fils seront meurdris ensemble,
Le prefecteur dedans son pauillon
La mere à Tours du fils ventre aura enfle,
Cache verdure de fueilles papillon.

The father and son will be murdered together,
the leader within his pavilion.
The mother at Tours will have her belly swollen with a son,
a verdure chest with little pieces of paper.

VIII 76

Plus Macelin que Roy en Angleterre,
Lieu obscur nay par force aura l'empire :
Lasche sans foy sans loy seignera terre.
Son temps s'aproche si pres que ie souspire.

More of a butcher than a king in England,
born of obscure rank will gain empire through force.
Coward without faith, without law he will bleed the land;
His time approaches so close that I sigh.

VIII 77
L'antechrist trois bien tost annichilez,
Vingt & sept ans sang durera sa guerre,
Les heretiques morts, captifs exilez,
Son corps humain eau rougie gresler terre.

The antichrist very soon annihilates the three,
twenty-seven years his war will last.
The unbelievers are dead, captive, exiled;
with blood, human bodies, water and red hail covering the
earth.

VIII 78
Vn Bragamas auec la langue torte
Viendra des dieux le sanctuaire,
Aux heretiques il ouurira la porte
En suscitant l'eglise militaire.

A soldier of fortune with twisted tongue
will come to the sanctuary of the gods.
He will open the door to heretics
and raise up the Church militant.

VIII 79
Qui par fer pere perdra nay de Nonnaire
De Gorgon sur la fera sang perfetant,
En terre estrange fera si tout de taire,
Qui bruslera luy mesme & son entant.

He who loses his father by the sword, born in a Nunnery,
upon this Gorgon's blood will conceive anew;
in a strange land he will do everything to be silent,
he who will burn both himself and his child.

VIII 80
Des innocens le sang de vefue & vierge.
Tant de maux faicts par moyen se grand Roge,
Saincts simulachres trempez en ardant cierge,
De frayeur craincte ne verra nul que boge.

The blood of innocents, widow and virgin,
so many evils committed by means of the Great Red One,
holy images placed over burning candles,
terrified by fear, none will be seen to move.

VIII 81
Le neuf empire en desolation,
Sera changé du pole aquilonaire,
De la Sicile viendra l'emotion,
Troubler l'emprise à Philip. tributaire.

The new empire in desolation
will be changed from the Northern Pole.
From Sicily will come such trouble that
it will bother the enterprise tributary to Philip.

VIII 82
Ronge long, sec faisant du bon vallet,
A la parfin n'aura que son congie,
Poignant poyson, & lettres au collet,
Sera saisi eschappé en dangie.

Thin tall and dry, playing the good valet
in the end will have nothing but his dismissal;
sharp poison and letters in his collar,
he will be seized escaping into danger.

VIII 83
Le plus grand voile hors du port de Zara,
Prés de Bisance fera son entreprise.
D'ennemy perte & l'amy ne fera,
Le tiers à deux fera grand pille & prise.

The largest sail set out of the port of Zara,
near Byzantium will carry out its enterprise.
Loss of enemy and friend will not be,

a third will turn on both with great pillage and capture.

VIII 84
Paterne aura de la Sicile crie,
Tous les aprests du goulphre de Trieste,
Qui s'entendra iusques à la Trina rie,
De tant de voiles fuy, fuy l'horrible peste.

Paterno will hear the cry from Sicily,
all the preparations in the Gulf of Trieste;
it will be heard as far as Sicily
flee oh, flee, so may sails, the dreaded pestilence !

VIII 85
Entre Bayonne & à sainct Iean de Lux,
Sera pose de Mars la promottoire :
Aux Hanis d'Aquilon Nanar hostera lux,
Puis suffoqué au lict sans adiutoire.

Between Bayonne and St. Jean de Luz
will be placed the promontory of Mars.
To the Hanix of the North, Nanar will remove the light,
then suffocate in bed without assistance.

VIII 86
Par Arnani Tholoser Ville Franque,
Bande infinie par le mont Adrian,
Passe riuiere, Hutin par pont la planque,
Bayonne entrer tous Bichoro criant.

Through Emani, Tolosa and Villefranche,
an infinite band through the mountains of Adrian.
Passes the river, Cambat over the plank for a bridge,
Bayonne will be entered all crying Bigoree.

VIII 87
Mort conspirée viendra en plein effect,
Charge donnée & voyage de mort.
Esleu, creé, receu, par siens deffaict,
Sang d'innocence deuant soy par remort.

Mort con*ƒ*pirée viendra en plein effe¢t.
Charge donnée & voyage de mort.

Esleu, creé, receu. par ſiens defait.
Sang d'innocence deuant ſoy par remord.

Mort conſpirée viendra en plain effet,
Charge donnée & voyage de mort :
Eſleu, creé, receu, per ſiens deffaict,
Sang d'innocent deuant ſoy par remort.

A death conspired will come to its full effect,
the charge given and the voyage of death.
Elected, created, received (then) defeated by its followers,
in remorse the blood of innocence in front of him.

VIII 88
Dans la Sardaigne vn noble Roy viendra,
Qui ne tiendra que trois ans le Royaume,
Plusieurs couleurs auec soy conioindra,
Luy mesme apres soin sommeil marrit scome.

A noble king will come to Sardinia,
who will only rule for three years in the kingdom.
He will join with himself several colors;
he himself, after taunts, care spoils slumber.

VIII 89
Pour ne tomber entre mains de son oncle,
Qui les enfans par regner trucidez,
Orant au peuple mettant pied sur Peloncle
Mort & traisné entre cheuaux bardez.

In order not to fall into the hands of his uncle
who slaughtered his children in order to reign.
Pleasing with the people, putting his foot on Peloncle,
dead and dragged between armored horses.

VIII 90
Quand des croisez vn trouué de sens trouble
En lieu du sacre verra vn bœuf cornu
Par vierge porc son lieu lors sera comble,
Par Roy plus ordre ne sera soustenu.

When those of the cross are found their senses troubled,
in place of sacred things he will see a horned bull,

213

through the virgin the pig's place will then be filled,
order will no longer be maintained by the king.

VIII 91
Frimy les champs de Rodanes entrées
Où les croisez seront presque vnis,
Les deux brassierez en pisces rencontrées,
Et vn grand nombre par deluge punis.

Entered among the field of the Rhône
where those of the cross are almost united,
the two lands meeting in Pisces
and a great number punished by the flood.

VIII 92
LOIN hors du regne, mis en hazard voyage :
Grand o∫t duira, pour ∫oy l'occupera.
Le Roy tiendra les ∫iens captifs ho∫tage.
A ∫on retour tout pays pillera.

Loin hors du regne mis en hazard voyage,
Grand o∫t duira pour ∫oy l'occupera,
Le Roy tiendra les ∫iens captif o∫tage
A ∫on retour tout pays pillera.

Loin hors du regne mis en hazard voyage
Grand ost duyra, pour soy l'occupera,
Le Roy tiendra les siens captif, ostage,
A son retour tout pays pillera.

Far distant from his kingdom, sent on a dangerous journey,
he will lead a great army and keep it for himself.
The king will hold his people captive and hostage,
he will plunder the whole country on his return.

VIII 93
Sept mois sans plus obtiendra prelature
Par son decez grand scisme fera naistre :
Sept mois tiendra vn autre la preture,
Pres de Venise paix vnion renaistre.

For seven months, no longer, will he hold the office of
prelate,

through his death a great schism will arise;
for seven months another acts as prelate near Venice,
peace and union are reborn.

VIII 94
Deuant le lac où plus cher fut getté
De sept mois, & son ost desconfit
Seront Hispans par Albannois gastez,
Par delay perte en donnant le conflit.

In front of the lake where the dearest one was destroyed
for seven months and his army routed;
Spaniards will be devastating by means of Alba,
through delay in giving battle, loss.

VIII 95
Le seducteur sera mis en la fosse,
Et estaché iusques à quelque temps,
Le clerc vny le chef auec sa crosse
Pycante droite attraira les contens.

The seducer will be placed in a ditch
and will be tied up for some time.
The scholar joins the chief with his cross.
The sharp right will draw the contented ones.

VIII 96
La Synagogue sterile sans nul fruit
Sera receuë entre les infideles
De Babylon la fille du porsuit
Misere & triste luy trenchera les aisles.

The sterile synagogue without any fruit,
will be received by the infidels,
the daughter of the persecuted (man) of Babylon,
miserable and sad, they will clip her wings.

VIII 97
Aux fins du Var changer le Pompotans,
Prés du riuage les trois beaux enfans naistre,
Ruyne au peuple par aage competans
Regne au pays charger plus croistre.

215

At the end of the Var the great powers change;
near the bank three beautiful children are born.
Ruin to the people when they are of age;
in the country the kingdom is seen to grow and change more.

VIII 98
Des gens d'Eglise sang sera espanché,
Comme de l'eau en si grande abondance
Et d'vn long temps ne sera restranché
Ve vë au clerc ruy & doleance.

Des gens d'E∫gli∫e ∫ang ∫era e∫panché
Comme de l'eau, en ∫i grande abondance,
Que d'vn long temps ne ∫era re∫tanché.
Vé, vé au Clerc ruine & doleance.

Des gens d'Egli∫e ∫ang ∫era e∫panché,
Comme de l'eau en ∫i grande abondance :
Et d'vn long-temps ne ∫era retranché,
Ve, ve au clerc ruine & doleance.

Of the church men the blood will be poured forth
as abundant as water in (amount);
for a long time it will not be restrained,
woe, woe, for the clergy ruin and grief.

VIII 99
Par la puissance des trois Roys temporels,
En autre lieu sera mis le saint siege :
Où la substance de l'esprit corporel,
Sera remis & receu pour vray siege.

Through the power of three temporal kings,
the sacred seat will be put in another place,
where the substance of the body and the spirit
will be restored and received as the true seat.

VIII 100
Pour l'abondance de l'arme respanduë
Du haut en bas par le bas au plus haut
Trop grande foy par ieu vie perduë,
De soif mourir par habondant deffaut.

216

By the great number of tears shed,
from top to bottom and from the bottom to the very top,
a life is lost through a game with too much faith,
to die of thirst through a great deficiency.

VIIIa 1

Eront confus plusieurs de leurs attente,
Aux habitans ne sera pardonné,
Qui bien pensoient perseuerer l'attente
Mais grand loisir ne leur sera donné.

VIIIa 2

Plusieurs viendront, & parleront de paix
Entre Monarques & seigneurs bien puissans,
Mais ne sera accordé de si prés,
Que ne se rendent plus qu'autres obeissans,

VIIIa 3

Las quelle fureur! helas quelle pitié,
Il u aura entre beaucoup de gens!
On ne vit onc vne telle amitié,
Qu'auront les loups à courir diligens.

VIIIa 4

Beaucoup de gens voudront parlementer
Aux grands seigneurs qui leur feront la guerre,
On ne voudra en rien les escouter,
Helas! si Dieu n'enuoye paix en terre.

VIIIa 5

Plusieurs secours viendront de tous costez,
De gens loingtains qui voudront resister :
Ils seront tout à coup bien hastez,
Mais ne pourront pour ceste heure assister.

VIIIa 6

Las quel desir ont Princes estrangers!
Garde toy bien qu'en ton pays ne vienne
Il y auroit de terribles dangers
En maints contrées, mesme en la Vienne.

Century IX

IX 1

DAns la maison du traducteur de Bourc
Seront les lettres trouuées sur la table,
Borgne, roux blanc, chenu tiendra de cours,
Qui changera au nouueau Connestable.

In the house of the translator of Bourg,
The letters will be found on the table,
One-eyed, red-haired, white, hoary-headed will hold the
course,
Which will change for the new Constable.

IX 2

Du hault du mont Auentin voix ouye,
Vuidez, vuidez de tous les deux costez,
Du sang des rouges sera l'ire assomie,
D'Arimin Prato, Columna debotez.

From the top of the Aventine hill a voice heard,
Be gone, be gone all of you on both sides:
The anger will be appeased by the blood of the red ones,
From Rimini and Prato, the Colonna expelled.

IX 3

La magna vaqua à Rauenne grand trouble,
Conduicts par quinze enserrez à Fornase :
A Rome naistra deux monstres à teste double,
Sang, feu, deluge, les plus grands à l'espase.

The "great cow" at Racenna in great trouble,
Led by fifteen shut up at Fornase:
At Rome there will be born two double-headed monsters,
Blood, fire, flood, the greatest ones in space.

IX 4

L'an ensuyuant descouuerts par deluge,
Deux chefs esleuz, le premier ne tiendra
De fuyr ombre à l'vn d'eux le refuge,
Saccagée case qui premier maintiendra.

The following year discoveries through flood,

Two chiefs elected, the first one will not hold:
The refuge for the one of them fleeing a shadow,
The house of which will maintain the first one plundered.

IX 5
Tiers doibt du pied au premier semblera
A vn nouueau Monarque de bas haut
Qui Pyse & Luques Tyran occupera
Du precedent corriger le deffault.

The third toe will seem first
To a new monarch from low high,
He who will possess himself as a Tyrant of Pisa and Lucca,
To correct the fault of his predecessor.

IX 6
Par la Guyenne infinité d'Anglois
Occuperont par nom d'Anglaquitaine
Du Languedoc I palme Bourdelois.
Qu'ils nommeront apres Barboxitaine.

An infinity of Englishmen in Guienne
Will settle under the name of Anglaquitaine:
In Languedoc, Ispalme, Bordelais,
Which they will name after Barboxitaine.

IX 7
Qui ouurira le monument trouué,
Et ne viendra le serrer proprement,
Mal luy viendra, & ne pourra prouué
Si mieux doit estre Roy Breton ou Normand.

He who will open the tomb found,
And will come to close it promptly,
Evil will come to him, and one will be unable to prove,
If it would be better to be a Breton or Norman King.

IX 8
Puisnay Roy fait son pere mettre à mort,
Apres conflict de mort tres-inhonneste :
Escrit trouué soubson donra remort,
Quand loup chassé pose sur la couchette.

The younger son made King will put his father to death,
After the conflict very dishonest death:
Inscription found, suspicion will bring remorse,
When the wolf driven out lies down ion the bedstead.

IX 9
Quand lampe ardante de feu inextinguible
Sera trouuée au temple des Ve*f*tales,
Enfant trouué. feu. eau pa*ff*ant par crible,
Ni*f*me eau perir. Tholo*f*e choir les hales.

Quand lampe ardente de feu inextinguible
Sera trouue au temple des Ve*f*tales :
Enfant trouué feu, eau pa*ff*ant par crible :
Perir eau, Nysmes, Tholo*f*e cheoir les alles.

Quand lampe ardente de feu inextinguible
Sera trouuée au temple des Vestales,
Enfant trouué, feu, eau passant par crible :
Nismes eau perir. Tholose cheoir les hales.

When the lamp burning with inextinguishable fire
Will be found in the temple of the Vestals:
Child found in fire, water passing through the sieve:
To perish in water Nîmes, Toulouse the markets to fall.

IX 10
Moyne moynesse d'enfant mort exposé,
Mourir par ourse & rauy par verrier.
Par Fois & Pamyes le camp sera posé
Contre Tholose Carcas dresser forrier.

The child of a monk and nun exposed to death,
To die through a she-bear, and carried off by a boar,
The army will be camped by Foix and Pamiers,
Against Toulouse Carcassonne the harbinger to form.

IX 11
Le iuste à tort à mort l'on viendra mettre
Publiquement, & du milieu estaint :
Si grande peste en ce lieu viendra naistre,
Que les iugeans fouyr seront contraints.

Wrongly will they come to put the just one to death,
In public and in the middle extinguished:
So great a pestilence will come to arise in this place,
That the judges will be forced to flee.

IX 12
Le tant d'argent de Diane & Mercure
Les simulachres au lac seront trouuez :
Le figulier cherchant argille neufue
Luy & les siens d'or seront abbreuuez.

So much silver of Diana and Mercury,
The images will be found in the lake:
The sculptor looking for new clay,
He and his followers will be steeped in gold.

IX 13
Les Exilez autour de la Solongne
Conduicts de nuict pour marcher en l'Auxois,
Deux de Modene truculent de Bologne.
Mis. descouuerts par feu de Burançois.

Les exilez autour de la Solongne
Conduits de nui¢t pour marcher à Lauxois,
Deux de Modenne truculent de Bolongne,
Mis de*f*couuerts par feu de Burançois.

Les Exilez autour de la Solongne
Conduits de nui¢t pour marcher en Lauxois.
Deux de Modene, truculant de Bologne
Mis. decouuers par feu de Burançois.

The exiles around Sologne,
Led by night to march into Auxois,
Two of Modena for Bologna cruel,
Placed discovered by the fire of Buzanais.

IX 14
Mis en planure chauderon d'infecteurs,
Vin, miel & huyle, & bastis sur fourneaux
Seront plongez, sans mal dit mal facteurs
Sept. fum. extaint au canon des borneaux.

221

Dyers' caldrons put on the flat surface,
Wine, honey and oil, and built over furnaces:
They will be immersed, innocent, pronounced malefactors,
Seven of Bordeaux smoke still in the cannon.

IX 15
Prés de Parpan les rouges detenus,
Ceux du milieu parfondrez menez loing :
Trois mis en pieces, & cinq mal soustenus,
Pour le Seigneur & Prelat de Bourboing.

Near Perpignan the red ones detained,
Those of the middle completely ruined led far off:
Three cut in pieces, and five badly supported,
For the Lord and Prelate of Burgundy.

IX 16
De castel Franco sortira l'assemblée,
L'ambassadeur non plaisant fera scisme :
Ceux de Ribiere seront en la meslée,
Et au grand goulphre desnier ont l'entrée.

Out of Castelfranco will come the assembly,
The ambassador not agreeable will cause a schism:
Those of Riviera will be in the squabble,
And they will refuse entry to the great gulf.

IX 17
Le tiers premier pis que ne fit Neron,
Vuidez vaillant que sang humain respandre
R'édifier fera le forneron,
Siècle d'or, mort, nouueau Roy grand esclandre.

The third one first does worse than Nero,
How much human blood to flow, valiant, be gone:
He will cause the furnace to be rebuilt,
Golden Age dead, new King great scandal.

IX 18
Le lys Dauffois portera dans Nansi,
Iusques en Flandres Electeur de l'Empire,
Neufue obturée au grand Montmorency,
Hors lieux prouez deliure à clere peyne.

The lily of the Dauphin will reach into Nancy,
As far as Flanders the Elector of the Empire:
New confinement for the great Montmorency,
Outside proven places delivered to celebrated punishment.

IX 19
Dans le milieu de la forest Mayenne,
Sol au Lyon la foudre tombera,
Le grand bastard yssu du grand du Maine,
Ce iour Fougeres pointe en sang entrera.

In the middle of the forest of Mayenne,
Lightning will fall, the Sun in Leo:
The great bastard issued from the great one Maine,
On this day a point will enter the blood of Fougères.

IX 20
De nuict viendra par la forest de Reines,
Deux pars voltorte Herne la pierre blanche,
Le moine noir en gris dedans Varennes
Esleu cap. cause tempeste, feu, sang tranche.

By night will come through the forest of Reines,
Two couples roundabout route Queen the white stone,
The monk king in gray in Varennes:
Elected Capet causes tempest, fire, blood, slice.

IX 21
Au temple haut de Bloys sacre Salonne,
Nuict pont de Loyre, Prelat, Roy pernicant :
Cuiseur victoire aux marests de la Lone,
D'où prelature de blancs abormeant.

At the tall temple of Saint-Solenne at Blois,
Night Loire bridge, Prelate, King killing outright:
Crushing victory in the marshes of the pond,
Whence prelacy of whites miscarrying.

IX 22
Roy & sa court au lieu de langue halbe,
Dedans le temple vis à vis du palais
Dans le iardin Duc de Mantor & d'Albe,

Albe & Mantor poignard langue & palais.

The King and his court in the place of cunning tongue,
Within the temple facing the palace:
In the garden the Duke of Mantua and Alba,
Alba and Mantua dagger tongue and palace.

IX 23
Puisnay ioüant au fresch dessous la tonne,
Le haut du toict du milieu sur la teste :
Le pere Roy au temple sainct Solonne,
Sacrifiant sacrera fum de feste.

The younger son playing outdoors under the arbor,
The top of the roof in the middle on his head,
The father King in the temple of Saint-Solonne,
Sacrificing he will consecrate festival smoke.

IX 24
Sur le palais au rocher des fenestres
Seront rauis les deux petits royaux,
Passer aurelle Luthece Denis cloistres,
Nonnain, mallods aualler verts noyaux.

Upon the palace at the balcony of the windows,
The two little royal ones will be carried off:
To pass Orléans, Paris, abbey of Saint-Denis,
Nun, wicked ones to swallow green pits.

IX 25
Passant les Ponts venir prés des rosiers,
Tard arriué plustost qu'il cuydera,
Viendront les noues Espagnols à Besiers,
Qui icelle chasse emprinse cassera.

Crossing the bridges to come near the Roisiers,
Sooner than he thought, he arrived late.
The new Spaniards will come to Béziers,
So that this chase will break the enterprise.

IX 26
Nice sortie sur nom des lettres aspres,
La grande cappe fera present non sien :

Proche de vultry aux murs de vertes capres
Apres plombim le vent à bon essien.

Departed by the bitter letters the surname of Nice,
The great Cappe will present something, not his own;
Near Voltai at the wall of the green columns,
After Piombino the wind in good earnest.

IX 27
De bois la garde, vent clos rond pont sera,
Haut le receu frappera le Dauphin,
Le vieux teccon bois vnis passera,
Passant plus outre du Duc le droict confin.

The forester, the wind will be close around the bridge,
Received highly, he will strike the Dauphin.
The old craftsman will pass through the woods in a
company,
Going far beyond the right borders of the Duke.

IX 28
Voille Symacle pour Massiliolique,
Dans Venise port marcher aux Pannons :
Partir du goulfre & Synus Illyrique,
Vast à Socille, Ligurs coups de canons.

The Allied fleet from the port of Marseilles,
In Venice harbor to march against Hungary.
To leave from the gulf and the bay of Illyria,
Devastation in Sicily, for the Ligurians, cannon shot.

IX 29
Lors que celuy qu'à nul ne donne lieu,
Abandonner voudra lieu prins non prins :
Feu nef par saignes, bitument à Charlieu,
Seront Quintin Balez reprins.

When the man will give way to none,
Will wish to abandon a place taken, yet not taken;
Ship afire through the swamps, bitumen at Charlieu,
St. Quintin and Calais will be recaptured.

IX 30

Au port de Pvola & de sainct Nicolas,
Peril Normande au goulfre Phanatique
Cap. de Bisance rues crier helas,
Secors de Gaddes & du grand Philippique.

At the port of Pola and of San Nicolo,
A Normand will punish in the Gulf of Quarnero:
Capet to cry alas in the streets of Byzantium,
Help from Cadiz and the great Philip.

IX 31
Le tremblement de terre à Mortara,
Cassich sainct Georges à demy perfondrez,
Paix assoupie, la guerre esueillera,
Dans temple à Pasques abysmes enfondrez.

The tin island of St. George half sunk;
Drowsy with peace, war will arise,
At Easter in the temple abysses opened.

IX 32
De fin porphire profond collon trouuée
Dessous la laze escripts capitolin :
Os poil retors Romain force prouuée,
Classe agiter au port de Methelin.

A deep column of fine porphyry is found,
Inscriptions of the Capitol under the base;
Bones, twisted hair, the Roman strength tried,
The fleet is stirred at the harbor of Mitylene.

IX 33
Hercules Roy de Rome & d'Annemarc,
De Gaule trois Guion surnommé,
Trembler l'Itale & l'vnde de sainct Marc,
Premier sur tous Monarque renommé.

Hercules King of Rome and of "Annemark,"
With the surname of the chief of triple Gaul,
Italy and the one of St. Mark to tremble,
First monarch renowned above all.

IX 34

La part sous mary sera mitré,
Retour conflict passera sur la thuille :
Par cinq cens vn trahyr sera tiltré,
Narbon & Saulce par contaux auons d'huille.

The single part afflicted will be mitered,
Return conflict to pass over the tile:
For five hundred one to betray will be titled
Narbonne and Salces we have oil for knives.

IX 35
Et Ferdinand blonde sera descorte,
Quitter la fleur, suyure le Macedon,
Au grand besoing defaillira sa routte,
Et marchera contre le Myrmiden.

And fair Ferdinand will be detached,
To abandon the flower, to follow the Macedonian:
In the great pinch his course will fail,
And he will march against the Myrmidons.

IX 36
Vn grand Roy prins entre les mains d'vn ieune
Non loin de Pasques, confusion, coup cultre,
Perpet. cattif temps! que foudre en la hune
Trois freres lors se blesseront, & murtre.

A great King taken by the hands of a young man,
Not far from Easter confusion knife thrust:
Everlasting captive times what lightning on the top,
When three brothers will wound each other and murder.

IX 37
Pont & molins en Decembre versez
En si hault lieu montera la Garonne :
Murs, edifice, Tholose renuersez,
Qu'on ne sçaura son lieu autant matronne.

Bridge and mills overturned in December,
The Garonne will rise to a very high place:
Walls, edifices, Toulouse overturned,
So that none will know his place like a matron.

227

IX 38

L'entrée de Blaye par Rochelle & l'Anglois,
Passera outre le grand Aemathien,
Non loing d'Agen attendra le Gaulois,
Secours Narbonne deceu par entretien.

The entry at Blaye for La Rochelle and the English,
The great Macedonian will pass beyond:
Not far from Agen will wait the Gaul,
Narbonne help beguiled through conversation.

IX 39

En Arbissel à Veront & Carcari,
De nuict conduicts par Sauone attraper,
Le vif Gascon Turby, & la Scerry,
Derrier mur vieux & neuf palais gripper.

In Albisola to Veront and Carcara,
Led by night to seize Savona:
The quick Gascon La Turbie and L'Escarène:
Behind the wall old and new palace to seize.

IX 40

Prés de Quintin dans la forest bourlis,
Dans l'Abbaye seront Flamans ranchés :
Les deux puisnais de coups my estourdis,
Suitte oppressée & garde tous achés.

Near Saint-Quintin in the forest deceived,
In the Abbey the Flemish will be cut up:
The two younger sons half-stunned by blows,
The rest crushed and the guard all cut to pieces.

IX 41

Le grand Chyren soy saisir d'Auignom,
De Rome lettres en miel plein d'amertume
Lettre ambassade partir de Chanignon,
Carpentras prins par duc noir rouge plume.

The great "Chyren" will seize Avignon,
From Rome letters in honey full of bitterness:
Letter and embassy to leave from Chanignon,
Carpentras taken by a black duke with a red feather.

IX 42

De Barcelonne, de Gennes & Venise,
De la Secille peste Monet vnis,
Contre Barbare classe prendront la vise,
Barbar poulsé bien loing iusqu'à Thunis.

From Barcelona, from Genoa and Venice,
From Sicily pestilence Monaco joined:
They will take their aim against the Barbarian fleet,
Barbarian driven 'way back as far as Tunis.

IX 43

Proche à descendre l'armée Crucigere,
Sera guettée par les Ismaëlites,
De tous costez batus par nef Rauier,
Prompt assaillis de dix galeres eslites.

On the point of landing the Crusader army
Will be ambushed by the Ishmaelites,
Struck from all sides by the ship Impetuosity,
Rapidly attacked by ten elite galleys.

IX 44

Migrés, migrés de Genefue trestous,
Saturne d'or en fer se changera,
Le contre Raypoz exterminera tous,
Auant l'aruent le Ciel signes fera.

Leave, leave Geneva every last one of you,
Saturn will be converted from gold to iron,
Raypoz will exterminate all who oppose him,
Before the coming the sky will show signs.

IX 45

Ne *f*era *f*oul iamais de demander.
Grand MENDOSVS obtiendra *f*on empire.
Loin de la Cour fera contremander
Piedmont, Picar. Paris, Tyrren le pire.

Ne *f*era *f*aoul iamais de demander,
Grand Mendo*f*us obtiendra *f*on empire :
Loin de la Gour fera contrc-mander,

Pymont, Picart, Paris, Tyrten le pire.

Ne sera soul iamais de demander,
Grand Mendosvs obtiendra son empire
Loing de la court fera contremander,
Piedmont, Picart, Paris Tyrhen le pire.

None will remain to ask,
Great Mendosus will obtain his dominion:
Far from the court he will cause to be countermanded
Piedmont, Picardy, Paris, Tuscany the worst.

IX 46
Vuydez, fuyez de Tholose les rouges
Du sacrifice faire expiation,
Le chef du mal dessous l'ombre des courges
Mort estrangler carne omination.

Be gone, flee from Toulouse ye red ones,
For the sacrifice to make expiation:
The chief cause of the evil under the shade of pumpkins:
Dead to strangle carnal prognostication.

IX 47
Les soulz signez d'indigne deliurance,
Et de la multe auront contre aduis,
Change monarque mis en perille pence,
Serrez en cage se verront vis à vis.

The undersigned to an infamous deliverance,
And having contrary advice from the multitude:
Monarch changes put in danger over thought,
Shut up in a cage they will see each other face to face.

IX 48
La grand' cite d'Occean maritime,
Enuironnée de marets en cristal :
Dans le solstice hyemal & la prime,
Sera tentée de vent espouuental.

The great city of the maritime Ocean,
Surrounded by a crystalline swamp:
In the winter solstice and the spring,

It will be tried by frightful wind.

IX 49
Grand & Bruceles marcheront contre Anuers
Senat de Londres mettront à mort leur Roy
Le sel & vin luy seront à l'enuers,
Pour eux auoir le regne en desarroy.

Ghent and Brussels will march against Antwerp,
The Senate of London will put to death their King:
Salt and wine will overthrow him,
To have them the realm turned upside down.

IX 50
Mendosvs tost viendra à son haut regne,
Mettant arriere vn peu le Norlaris.
Le Rouge blesme, le masle à l'interregne.
Le ieune crainte & frayeur Barbaris.

Mendosus will soon come to his high realm,
Putting behind a little the Lorrainers:
The pale red one, the male in the interregnum,
The fearful youth and Barbaric terror.

IX 51
Contre les rouges sectes se banderont,
Feu, eau, fer, corde par paix se minera,
Au point mourir ceux qui machineront,
Fors vn que monde sur tout ruynera.

Against the red ones sects will conspire,
Fire, water, steel, rope through peace will weaken:
On the point of dying those who will plot,
Except one who above all the world will ruin.

IX 52
La paix s'approche d'vn coſté & la querre :
Oncques ne fut la pourſuite ſi grande.
Plaindre homme femme, ſang innocent par terre,
Et ce ſera de France à toute bande.

La paix s'approche d'vn coſté, & la querre,
Oncques ne fut la pourſuite ſi grande :

231

Plaindre homme, femme, ſang innocent par terre,
Et ce ſera de France à toute bande.

La paix s'approche d'vn costé & la querre
Oncques ne fut la poursuite si grande,
Plaindre homme, femme, sang innocent par terre
Et ce sera de France à toute bande.

Peace is nigh on one side, and war,
Never was the pursuit of it so great:
To bemoan men, women innocent blood on the land,
And this will be throughout all France.

IX 53
Le Neron ieune dans les trois cheminées
Fera de paiges vifs pour ardoir ietter,
Heureux qui loing sera de tels menées,
Trois de son sang le feront mort guetter.

The young Nero in the three chimneys
Will cause live pages to be thrown to burn:
Happy those who will be far away from such practices,
Three of his blood will have him ambushed to death.

IX 54
Arriuera au port de Corsibonne,
Prés de Rauenne qui pillera la dame,
En mer profonde legat de la Vlisbonne
Sous roc cachez rauiront septante ames.

There will arrive at Porto Corsini,
Near Ravenna, he who will plunder the lady:
In the deep sea legate from Lisbon,
Hidden under a rock they will carry off seventy souls.

IX 55
L'horrible guerre qu'en l'Occident s'appreſte,
L'an enſuiuant viendra la peſtilence
Si fort horrible qne ieune, vieux ne beſte,
Sang, feu, Mercure, Mars, Iupiter en France.

L'horrible guerre qu'en Occident s'appreſte!
L'an enſuiuant viendra la peſtilence

232

Si fort terrible, que ieune, vieil, ne be*f*te.
Sang, feu, Mercu. Mars, Iupiter en France.

The horrible war which is being prepared in the West,
The following year will come the pestilence
So very horrible that young, old, nor beast,
Blood, fire Mercury, Mars, Jupiter in France.

IX 56 55
L'horrible guerre qu'en Occident s'appreste!
L'an ensuiuant viendra la pestilence
Si fort terrible, que ieune, vieil, ne beste,
Sang, feu, Mercu. Mars, Iupiter en France.

IX 56
The army near Houdan will pass Goussainville,
And at Maiotes it will leave its mark:
In an instant more than a thousand will be converted,
Looking for the two to put them back in chain and firewood.

IX 57
Au lieu de Drvx vn Roy reposera,
Et cherchera loy changeant d'Anatheme,
Pendant le ciel si tresfort tonnera,
Portée neufue Roy tuera soy-mesme.

In the place of Drux a King will rest,
And will look for a law changing Anathema:
While the sky will thunder so very loudly,
New entry the King will kill himself.

IX 57 56
Camp pres de Noudam passera Goussan ville,
Et à Maiotes laissera son enseigne,
Conuertira en instant plus de mille,
Cherchant les deux remettre en chaine & legne.

IX 58
Au costé gauche à l'endroit de Vitri,
Seront guettez les trois rouges de France
Tous assoumez rouge, noir non meurdry,
Par les Bretons remis en asseurance.

On the left side at the spot of Vitry,
The three red ones of France will be awaited:
All felled red, black one not murdered,
By the Bretons restored to safety.

IX 59
A la Ferté prendra la Vidame,
Nicol tenu rouge qu'auoit produit la vie,
La grand Loyse naistra que fera clame.
Donnant Bourgongne à Bretons par enuie.

At La Ferté-Vidame he will seize,
Nicholas held red who had produced his life:
The great Louise who will act secretly one will be born,
Giving Burgundy to the Bretons through envy.

IX 60
Conflict Barbar en la Cornere noire,
Sang espandu trembler la Dalmatie,
Grand Ismaël mettra son promontoire,
Ranes trembler, secours Lusitanie.

Conflict Barbarian in the black Headdress,
Blood shed, Dalmatia to tremble:
Great Ishmael will set up his promontory,
Frogs to tremble Lusitania aid.

IX 61
La pille faite à la coste marine,
Incita noua & parens amenez,
Plusieurs de Malte par le fait de Messine,
Estroit serrez seront mal guerdonnez.

The plunder made upon the marine coast,
In Cittanova and relatives brought forward:
Several of Malta through the deed of Messina
Will be closely confined poorly rewarded.

IX 62
Au grand de Cheramonagora
Seront croisez par ranc tous attachez,
Le pertinax Oppi, & Mandragora,
Raugon d'Octobre le tiers seront laschez.

To the great one of Ceramon-agora,
The crusaders will all be attached by rank,
The long-lasting Opium and Mandrake,
The Raugon will be released on the third of October.

IX 63
Plainctes & pleurs, cris & grands hurlements
Prés de Narbon à Bayonne & en Foix
O quels horribles calamitez changemens,
Auant que Mars reuolu quelques fois.

Complaints and tears, cries and great howls,
Near Narbonne at Bayonne and in Foix:
Oh, what horrible calamities and changes,
Before Mars has made several revolutions.

IX 64
L'Aemathion passer monts Pyrenées,
En Mars Narbon ne fera resistance,
Par mer & terre fera si grand menée,
Cap. n'ayant terre seure pour demeurance.

The Macedonian to pass the Pyrenees mountains,
In March Narbonne will not offer resistance:
By land and sea he will carry on very great intrigue,
Capetian having no land safe for residence.

IX 65
Dedans le coing de Luna viendra rendre,
Où sera prins & mis en terre estrange,
Les fruicts immeurs seront à grand esclandre,
Grand vitupere, à l'vn grande loüange.

He will come to go into the corner of Luna,
Where he will be captured and put in a strange land:
The unripe fruits will be the subject of great scandal,
Great blame, to one great praise.

IX 66
Paix, vnion sera & changement,
Estats, Offices, bas hault, & hault bien bas.
Dresser voyage, le fruict premier, torment,

Guerre cesser, ciuils proces, debats.

Paix, vnion ƒera & changement
Eƒtats, offices. bas haut, & haut bien bas.
Dreƒƒer voyage. le fruit premier, torment.
Guerre ceƒƒer. ciuils procez, debats.

Paix, vnion ƒera & changement,
Eƒtats, offices bas, haut, & haut bien bas
Dreƒƒer voyage, le frui¢t premier torment,
Guerre ceƒƒer, ciuil procez, debats.

There will be peace, union and change,
Estates, offices, low high and high very low:
To prepare a trip, the first offspring torment,
War to cease, civil process, debates.

IX 67
Du hault des monts à l'entour de Dizére
Port à la roche Valent, cent assemblez
De chasteau neuf Pierre late en douzere,
Contre le Crest Romans foy assemblez.

From the height of the mountains around the Isère,
One hundred assembled at the haven in the rock Valence:
From Châteauneuf, Pierrelatte, in Donzère,
Against Crest, Romans, faith assembled.

IX 68
Du mont Aymar sera noble obscurcie,
Le mal viendra au ioinct de Saone & Rosne,
Dans bois cachez soldats iour de Lucie,
Qui ne fut onc vn si horrible throsne.

The noble of Mount Aymar will be made obscure,
The evil will come at the junction of the Saône and Rhône:
Soldiers hidden in the woods on Lucy's day,
Never was there so horrible a throne.

IX 69
Sur le mont de Bailly & la Bresle
Seront cachez de Grenoble les fiers,
Outre Lyon, Vien, eulx si grand gresle,

Langoult en terre n'en restera vn tiers.

One the mountain of Saint-Bel and L'Arbresle
The proud one of Grenoble will be hidden:
Beyond Lyons and Vienne on them a very great hail,
Lobster on the land not a third thereof will remain.

IX 70
Harnois trenchans dans les flambeaux cachez
Dedans Lyon le iour du Sacrement,
Ceux de Vienne seront trestous hachez
Par les Cantons Latins. Masconneront.

Harnois trenchans dans les flambeaux cachez
Dedans Lyon, le iour du Sacrement,
Cieux de Vienne feront treſtouz hachez,
Par les cantons Latins Maſconnement.

Harnois tranchans dans les flambeaux cachez
Dedans Lyon le iour du Sacrement.
Ceux de Vienne feront treſtous hachez
Par les Cantons Latins. Maſcon ne ment.

Sharp weapons hidden in the torches.
In Lyons, the day of the Sacrament,
Those of Vienne will all be cut to pieces,
By the Latin Cantons Mâcon does not lie.

IX 71
Aux liex sacrez animaux veu à trixe,
Auec celuy qui n'osera le iour,
A Carcassonne pour disgrace propice,
Sera posé pour plus ample seiour.

At the holy places animals seen with hair,
With him who will not dare the day:
At Carcassonne propitious for disgrace,
He will be set for a more ample stay.

IX 72
Encor seront les saincts temples pollus,
Et expillez par Senat Tholosain,
Saturne deux trois siecles reuollus,

Dans Auril, May, gens de nouueau leuain.

Again will the holy temples be polluted,
And plundered by the Senate of Toulouse:
Saturn two three cycles completed,
In April, May, people of new leaven.

IX 73
Dans Fois entrez Roy ceiulee Turban,
Et regnera moins euolu Saturne,
Roy Turban blanc Bizance cœur ban,
Sol, Mars, Mercure prés la hurne.

The Blue Turban King entered into Foix,
And he will reign less than an evolution of Saturn:
The White Turban King Byzantium heart banished,
Sun, Mars and Mercury near Aquarius.

IX 74
Dans la cité de Fert sod homicide,
Fait & fait multe beuf arant ne macter,
Retour encores aux honneurs d'Artemide,
Et à Vulcan corps morts sepulturer.

In the city of Fertsod homicide,
Deed, and deed many oxen plowing no sacrifice:
Return again to the honors of Artemis,
And to Vulcan bodies dead ones to bury.

IX 75
De l'Ambraxie & du pays de Thrace,
Peuple par mer mal & secours Gaulois,
Perpetuelle en Prouence la trace,
Auec vestiges de leur coustume & loix.

From Ambracia and the country of Thrace
People by sea, evil and help from the Gauls:
In Provence the perpetual trace,
With vestiges of their custom and laws.

IX 76
Auec le noir Rapax & sanguinaire,
Yssu du peaultre de l'inhumain Neron,

Emmy deux fleuues main gauche militaire,
Sera murtry par Ioyne chaulueron.

With the rapacious and blood-thirsty king,
Issued from the pallet of the inhuman Nero:
Between two rivers military hand left,
He will be murdered by Young Baldy.

IX 77

Le regne prins le Roy conutera,
La dame prinse à mort iurez à sort,
La vie à Royne fils on desniera,
Et la pellix au fort de la consort.

The realm taken the King will conspire,
The lady taken to death ones sworn by lot:
They will refuse life to the Queen and son,
And the mistress at the fort of the wife.

IX 78

La dame Grecque de beauté laydique,
Heureuse faicte de proces innumerable,
Hors translatée au regne Hispanique,
Captiue prinse mourir mort miserable.

The Greek lady of ugly beauty,
Made happy by countless suitors:
Transferred out to the Spanish realm,
Taken captive to die a miserable death.

IX 79

Le chef de classe, par fraude stratageme,
Fera timides sortir de leurs galleres,
Sortis meurtris chef renieux de cresme,
Puis par l'embusche luy rendront le saleres.

The chief of the fleet through deceit and trickery
Will make the timid ones come out of their galleys:
Come out, murdered, the chief renouncer of chrism,
Then through ambush they will pay him his wages.

IX 80

Le Duc voudra les siens exterminer,

239

Enuoyera les plus forts lieux estranges,
Par tyrannie Bize & Luc ruyner,
Puis les Barbares sans vin feront vendanges.

The Duke will want to exterminate his followers,
He will send the strongest ones to strange places:
Through tyranny to ruin Pisa and Lucca,
Then the Barbarians will gather the grapes without vine.

IX 81
Le Roy rusé entendra ses embusches
De trois quartiers ennemis assaillir,
Vn nombre estrange larmes de coqueluches
Viendra Lemprin du traducteur faillir.

The crafty King will understand his snares,
Enemies to assail from three sides:
A strange number tears from hoods,
The grandeur of the translator will come to fail.

IX 82
Par le deluge & pestilence forte
LA cité grande de long temps assiegée,
La sentinelle & garde de main morte,
Subite prinse, mains de nul oultragée.

By the flood and fierce pestilence,
The great city for long besieged:
The sentry and guard dead by hand,
Sudden capture but none wronged.

IX 83
Sol vingt de Taurus si fort terre trembler,
Le grand theatre remply ruinera,
L'air, ciel & terre obscurcir & troubler,
Lors l'infidele Dieu & saincts voguera.

Sun twentieth of Taurus the earth will tremble very mightily,
It will ruin the great theater filled:
To darken and trouble air, sky and land,
Then the infidel will call upon God and saints.

IX 84

Roy exposé parfaira l'hecatombe,
Apres auoir trouué son origine,
Torrent ouurir de marbre & plomb la tombe
D'vn grand Romain d'enseigne Medusine.

The King exposed will complete the slaughter,
After having discovered his origin:
Torrent to open the tomb of marble and lead,
Of a great Roman with Medusine device.

IX 85
Passer Guienne, Languedoc & le Rosne,
D'Agen tenans de Marmande & la Roole,
D'ouurir par foy parroy, Phocen tiendra son trosne,
Conflict aupres sainct Pol de Manseole.

To pass Guienne, Languedoc and the Rhône,
From Agen holding Marmande and La Réole:
To open through faith the wall, Marseilles will hold its
throne,
Conflict near Saint-Paul-de-Mausole.

IX 86
Du bourg Lareyne paruiêdrot droit à Chartes
Et feront prés du pont Anthoni pause.
Sept pour la paix cauteleux comme Martres
Feront entrée d'armée à Paris clause.

From Bourg-la-Reine they will come straight to Chartres,
And near Pont d'Antony they will pause:
Seven crafty as Martens for peace,
Paris closed by an army they will enter.

IX 87
Par la forest de Touphon essartée,
Par hermitage sera posé le temple,
De Duc d'Estempes par sa ruse inuentée,
Du mont Lehori prelat donra exemple.

In the forest cleared of the Tuft,
By the hermitage will be placed the temple:
The Duke of Étampes through the ruse he invented
Will teach a lesson to the prelate of Montlhéry.

241

IX 88
Calais, Arras secours à Theroanne,
Paix & semblant simulera l'escoute,
Soul de d'Alobrox descendre par Roane
Destornay peuple qui defera la routte.

Calais, Arras, help to Thérouanne,
Peace and semblance the spy will simulate:
The soldiery of Savoy to descend by Roanne,
People who would end the rout deterred.

IX 89
Sept ans sera Philip, fortune prespere,
Rabaissera des Barbares l'effort.
Puis son mydi perplex, rebours affaire,
Ieune ogmion abysmera son fort.

Sept ans aura PHILIP fortune preſpere.
Rabaiſſera des Barbares l'effort.
Puis ſon midy perplex, rebours affaire.
Ieune Ogmion abyſmera ſon fort.

Sept ans ſera Philipp. fortune preſpere,
Rabaiſſera des Arabes l'effort,
Puis ſon midy perplex, rebours affaire,
Ieuſne oignion abiſmera ſon fort.

For seven years fortune will favor Philip,
He will beat down again the exertions of the Arabs:
Then at his noon perplexing contrary affair,
Young Ogmios will destroy his stronghold.

IX 90
Vn grand Capitaine de la grand Germanie
Se viendra rendre par simulé secours
A Roy des Roys ayde de Pannonie,
Que sa reuolte fera de sang grand cours.

A captain of Great Germany
Will come to deliver through false help
To the King of Kings the support of Pannonia,
So that his revolt will cause a great flow of blood.

242

IX 91

L'horrible peste Perynte & Nicopolle,
Le Chersonnez tiendra & Marceloyne,
La Thessalie vastera l'amphipolle,
Mal incogneu, & le refus d'Anthoine.

The horrible plague Perinthus and Nicopolis,
The Peninsula and Macedonia will it fall upon:
It will devastate Thessaly and Amphipolis,
An unknown evil, and from Anthony refusal.

IX 92

Le Roy voudra dans cité neufue entrer
Par ennemis expugner l'on viendra
Captif libere faulx dire & perpetrer,
Roy dehors estre, loin d'ennemis tiendra.

The King will want to enter the new city,
Through its enemies they will come to subdue it:
Captive free falsely to speak and act,
King to be outside, he will keep far from the enemy.

IX 93

Les ennemis du fort bien esloignez,
Par chariots conduict le bastion,
Par sur les murs de Bourges esgrongnez
Quand Hercules battra l'Haemathion.

The enemies very far from the fort,
The bastion brought by wagons:
Above the walls of Bourges crumbled,
When Hercules the Macedonian will strike.

IX 94

Foibles galeres seront vnis ensemble,
Ennemis faux le plus fort en rempart :
Faible assaillies Vratislaue tremble,
Lubecq & Mysne tiendront barbare part.

Weak galleys will be joined together,
False enemies the strongest on the rampart:
Weak ones assailed Bratislava trembles,

Lübeck and Meissen will take the barbarian side.

IX 95

Le nouueau faict conduira l'exercite,
Proche apamé iusqu'aupres du riuage,
Tendant secours de Millanoile eslite,
Duc yeux priue à Milanfer de cage.

The newly made one will lead the army,
Almost cut off up to near the bank:
Help from the Milanais elite straining,
The Duke deprived of his eyes in Milan in an iron cage.

IX 96

Dans cité entrer exercit desniée,
Duc entrera par persuasion,
Aux foibles portes clam armée amenée,
Mettront feu, mort, de sang effusion.

The army denied entry to the city,
The Duke will enter through persuasion:
The army led secretly to the weak gates,
They will put it to fire and sword, effusion of blood.

IX 97

De mer copies en trois parts diuisées,
A la seconde les viures failleront,
Desesperez cherchant champs Helisées,
Premiers en breches entrez victoire auront.

The forces of the sea divided into three parts,
The second one will run out of supplies,
In despair looking for the Elysian Fields,
The first ones to enter the breach will obtain the victory.

IX 98

Les affligez par faute d'vn seul taint,
Contremenant à partie opposite,
Aux Lygonnois mandera aue contraint
Seront de rendre le grand chef de Molite.

Those afflicted through the fault of a single one stained,
The transgressor in the opposite party:

He will send word to those of Lyons that compelled
They be to deliver the great chief of Molite.

IX 99
Vent Aquilon fera partir le siege,
Par murs ietter cendres, chaulx, & poussiere :
Par pluye apres qui leur fera bien piege,
Dernier secours encontre leur frontiere.

The "Aquilon" Wind will cause the siege to be raised,
Over the walls to throw ashes, lime and dust:
Through rain afterwards, which will do them much worse,
Last help against their frontier.

IX 100
Naualle pugne nuict sera superée,
Le feu, aux naues à l'Occident ruine :
Rubriche neufue, la grand nef colorée,
Ire à vaincu, & victoire en bruine.

Naval battle night will be overcome,
Fire in the ships to the West ruin:
New trick, the great ship colored,
Anger to the vanquished, and victory in a drizzle.

Century X

X 1
A l'ennemy, l'ennemy foy promiſe
Ne ſe tiendra, les captifs retenus :
Prins preme mort, & le reſte en chemiſe :
Damné le reſte pour eſtre fouſtenus.

A l'ennemi l'ennemi foy promiſe
Ne ſe tiendra. les captifs retenus.
Prins preme mort, & le reſte en chemiſe,
Donnant le reſte pour eſtre ſecourus.

A L'ennemy, l'ennemy foy promise
Ne se tiendra, les captifs retenus :
Prins preme mort, & le reste en chemise,

245

Donnant le reste pour estre secourus.

To the enemy, the enemy faith promised
Will not be kept, the captives retained:
One near death captured, and the remainder in their shirts,
The remainder damned for being supported.

X 2
Voile gallere voil de nef cachera,
La grande classe viendra sortir la moindre,
Dix naues proches le tourneront poulser,
Grande vaincue vnies à soy ioindre.

The ship's veil will hide the sail galley,
The great fleet will come the lesser one to go out:
Ten ships near will turn to drive it back,
The great one conquered the united ones to join to itself.

X 3
En apres cinq troupeau ne mettra hors
Vn fuytif pour Penelon laschera,
Faux murmurer secours venir par lors,
Le chef, le siege lors abandonnera.

After that five will not put out the flock,
A fugitive for Penelon he will turn loose:
To murmur falsely then help to come,
The chief will then abandon the siege.

X 4
Sus la minuict conducteur de l'armée
Se sauuera subit esuanouy,
Sept ans apres la fame non blasmée,
A son retour ne dira oncq ouy.

At midnight the leader of the army
Will save himself, suddenly vanished:
Seven years later his reputation unblemished,
To his return they will never say yes.

X 5
Albi & Castres feront nouuelle ligue,
Neuf Arriens Lisbon & Portugués,

Carcas, Tholose consumeront leur brigue,
Quand chef neuf monstre de Lauragués.

Albi and Castres will form a new league,
Nine Arians Lisbon and the Portuguese:
Carcassonne and Toulouse will end their intrigue,
When the chief new monster from the Lauraguais.

X 6
Sardon Nemans si hault desborderont,
Qu'on cuidera Deucalion renaistre,
Dans le colosse la plus part fuyront,
Vesta sepulchre feu estaint apparoistre.

The Gardon will flood Nîmes so high
That they will believe Deucalion reborn:
Into the colossus the greater part will flee,
Vesta tomb fire to appear extinguished.

X 7
Le grand conflit qu'on appreste à Nancy,
L'Aemathien dira tout ie soubmets,
L'Isle Britanne par vin, sel en solcy,
Hem. mi. deux Phi. long temps ne tiendra Mets.

The great conflict that they are preparing for Nancy,
The Macedonian will say I subjugate all:
The British Isle in anxiety over wine and salt,
"Hem. mi." Philip two Metz will not hold for long.

X 8
Index & poulse parfondera le front
De Senegalia le Comte à son fils propre
La Myrnamée par plusieurs de prin front
Trois dans sept iours blessez more.

With forefinger and thumb he will moisten the forehead,
The Count of Senigallia to his own son:
The Venus through several of thin forehead,
Three in seven days wounded dead.

X 9
De Castillon figuieres nour de brune,

247

De femme infame naistra souuerain prince
Surnom de chausses perhume luy posthume,
Onc Roy ne fut si pire en sa prouince.

In the Castle of Figueras on a misty day
A sovereign prince will be born of an infamous woman:
Surname of breeches on the ground will make him
posthumous,
Never was there a King so very bad in his province.

X 10
Tasche de murdre, enormes adulteres,
Grand ennemy de tout le genre humain
Que sera pire qu'ayeuls, oncles, ne peres
En fer, feu eau, sanguin & inhumain.

Stained with murder and enormous adulteries,
Great enemy of the entire human race:
One who will be worse than his grandfathers, uncles or
fathers,
In steel, fire, waters, bloody and inhuman.

X 10 11
Dessous Ionchere du dangereux passage
Fera passer le posthume sa bande,
Les monts Pyrens passer hors son bagage
De Parpignan couurira Duc à Tende.

X 11
At the dangerous passage below Junquera,
The posthumous one will have his band cross:
To pass the Pyrenees mountains without his baggage,
From Perpignan the duke will hasten to Tende.

X 12
Esleu en Pape, d'esleu sera mocqué,
Subit soudain esmeu prompt & timide,
Par trop bon doux à mourir prouoqué,
Crainte estainte la nuit de sa mort guide.

Elected Pope, as elected he will be mocked,
Suddenly unexpectedly moved prompt and timid:
Through too much goodness and kindness provoked to die,

248

Fear extinguished guides the night of his death.

X 13
Soulz la pasture d'animaux ruminants
Par eux conduicts au ventre herbipolique
Soldats cachez, les armes bruit menants,
Non loing temptez de cité Antipolique.

Beneath the food of ruminating animals,
led by them to the belly of the fodder city:
Soldiers hidden, their arms making a noise,
Tried not far from the city of Antibes.

X 14
Vrnel Vaucile sans conseil de soy mesmes
Hardit timide, par crainte prins vaincu,
Accompagné de plusieurs putains blesmes
A Barcellonne aux chartreux conuaincu.

Urnel Vaucile without a purpose on his own,
Bold, timid, through fear overcome and captured:
Accompanied by several pale whores,
Convinced in the Carthusian convent at Barcelona.

X 15
Pere Duc vieux d'ans & de soif chargé,
Au iour extreme fils desniant les guiere
Dedans le puis vif mort viendra plongé,
Senat au fil la mort longue & legere.

Father duke old in years and choked by thirst,
On his last day his don denying him the jug:
Into the well plunged alive he will come up dead,
Senate to the thread death long and light.

X 16
Heureux au regne de France heureux de vie
Ignorant sang mort fureur & rapine,
Par non flateurs seras mis en enuie,
Roy desrobé trop de foy en cuisine.

Happy in the realm of France, happy in life,
Ignorant of blood, death, fury and plunder:

For a flattering name he will be envied,
A concealed King, too much faith in the kitchen.

X 17
La Royne Ergaste voyant sa fille blesme,
Par vn regret dans l'estomach enclos,
Crys lamentables seront lors d'Angolesme,
Et au germain mariage forclos.

The convict Queen seeing her daughter pale,
Because of a sorrow locked up in her breast:
Lamentable cries will come then from Angoulême,
And the marriage of the first cousin impeded.

X 18
Le ranc Lorrain fera place a Vandosme,
Le hault mis bas, & le bas mis en hault,
Le fils d'Hamon sera esleu dans Rome,
Et les deux grands seront mis en defaut.

The house of Lorraine will make way for Vendôme,
The high put low, and the low put high:
The son of Mammon will be elected in Rome,
And the two great ones will be put at a loss.

X 19
Iour que sera par Royne saluéë,
Le iour apres le salut, la priere :
Le comte fait raison & valbuéë,
Par auant humble oncques ne fut si fiere.

X 20
Tous les amys qu'auront tenu party,
Pour rude en lettres mis mort & saccagé,
Biens publiez par fixe grand neanty,
Onc Romain peuple ne fut tant outragé.

All the friend who will have belonged to the party,
For the rude in letters put to death and plundered:
Property up for sale at fixed price the great one annihilated.
Never were the Roman people so wronged.

X 21

Par le despit du Roy soustenant moindre
Sera meurdry luy resentant les bagues,
Le pere au fils voulant noblesse poindre
Fait comme à Perse iadis feirent les Magues.

Through the spite of the King supporting the lesser one,
He will be murdered presenting the jewels to him:
The father wishing to impress nobility on the son
Does as the Magi did of yore in Persia.

X 22
Pour ne vouloir consentir au diuorce,
Qui puis apres sera cogneu indigne,
Le Roy des Isles sera chassé par force,
Mis à son lieu qui de Roy n'aura signe.

For not wishing to consent to the divorce,
Which then afterwards will be recognized as unworthy:
The King of the Isles will be driven out by force,
In his place put one who will have no mark of a king.

X 23
Au peuple ingrat faictes les remonstrances,
Par lors l'armée se saisira d'Antibe,
Dans l'arc Monech feront les doleances,
Et à Freius l'vn l'autre prendra ribe.

The remonstrances made to the ungrateful people,
Thereupon the army will seize Antibes:
The complaints will place Monace in the arch,
And at Fréjus the one will take the shore from the other

X 24
Le Captif prince aux Itales vaincu
Passera Gennes par mer iusqu'à Marseille,
Par grand effort des forens suruaincu
Sauf coup de feu, barril liqueur d'abeille.

The captive prince conquered in Italy
Will pass Genoa by sea as far as Marseilles:
Through great exertion by the foreigners overcome,
Safe from gunshot, barrel of bee's liquor.

251

X 25
Par Nebro ouurir de Brisanne passage,
Bien esloignez el tago fara muestra,
Dans Pelligouxe sera commis l'outrage
De la grand dame assise sur l'orchestra.

Through the Ebro to open the passage of Bisanne,
Very far away will the Tagus make a demonstration:
In Pelligouxe will the outrage be committed,
By the great lady seated in the orchestra.

X 26
Le successeur vengera son beau frere,
Occuper regne souz ombre de vengeance,
Occis ostacle son sang mort vitupere,
Long temps Bretagne tiendra auec la France.

The successor will avenge his brother-in-law,
To occupy the realm under the shadow of vengeance:
Obstacle slain his blood for the death blame,
For a long time will Brittany hold with France.

X 27
Par le cinquiesme & vn grand Herculés
Viendront le temple ouurir de main bellique,
Vn Clement, Iule & Ascans reculés,
Lespe, clef, aigle, n'eurent onc si grand picque.

Through the fifth one and a great Hercules
They will come to open the temple by hand of war:
One Clement, Julius and Ascanius set back,
The sword, key, eagle, never was there such a great
animosity.

X 28
Second & tiers qui font prime muſique
Sera par Roy en honneur ſublimée,
Par grace & maigre preſque demy eticque
Rapport de Venus faux rendra deprimée.

Second & tiers qui font prime muſique,
Sera par Roy en honneur ſublimée.
Par graſſe & maigre preſque à demi etique

Rapport de Venus faux rendra deprimée.

Second & tiers qui font prime musique
Sera par Roy en honneur sublimée,
Par grasse & maigre presque à demy eticque
Rapport de Venus faux rendra deprimée.

Second and third which make prime music
By the King to be sublimated in honor:
Through the fat and the thin almost emaciated,
By the false report of Venus to be debased.

X 29
De Pol Mansol dans cauerne caprine
Caché & prins extraict hors par la barbe,
Captif mené comme beste mastine
Par Begourdans amenée prés de Tarbe.

In a cave of Saint-Paul-de-Mausole a goat
Hidden and seized pulled out by the beard:
Led captive like a mastiff beast
By the Bigorre people brought to near Tarbes.

The day that she will be hailed as Queen,
The day after the benediction the prayer:
The reckoning is right and valid,
Once humble never was one so proud.

X 30
Nepueu & sang du sainct nouueau venu,
Par le surnom soustient arcs & couuert
Seront chassez mis à mort chassez nu,
En rouge & noir conuertiront leur vert.

Nephew and blood of the new saint come,
Through the surname he will sustain arches and roof:
They will be driven out put to death chased nude,
Into red and black will they convert their green.

X 31
Le sainct empire viendra en Germanie,
Ismaëlites trouueront lieux ouuerts.
Anes voudront aussi la Carmanie,

Les soustenans de terre tous couuerts.

The Holy Empire will come into Germany,
The Ishmaelites will find open places:
The asses will want also Carmania,
The supporters all covered by earth.

X 32
Le grand empire chacun an deuoit estre,
Vn sur les autres le viendra obtenir,
Mais peu de temps sera son regne & estre,
Deux ans aux naues se pourra soustenir.

The great empire, everyone would be of it,
One will come to obtain it over the others:
But his realm and state will be of short duration,
Two years will he be able to maintain himself on the sea.

X 33
La faction cruelle à robbe longue
Viendra cacher souz les pointus poignards
Saisir Florence le duc & lieu diphlongue,
Sa descouuerte par immeurs & flangnards.

The cruel faction in the long robe
Will come to hide under the sharp daggers:
The Duke to seize Florence and the diphthong place,
Its discovery by immature ones and sycophants.

X 34
Gaulois qu'empire par guerre occupera,
Par son beau frere mineur sera trahy,
Par cheual rude voltigeant trainera,
Du fait le frere long temps sera hay.

The Gaul who will hold the empire through war,
He will be betrayed by his minor brother-in-law:
He will be drawn by a fierce, prancing horse,
The brother will be hated for the deed for a long time

X 35
Puisnay royal flagrand d'ardant libide,
Pour se iouyr de cousine germaine

254

Habit de femme au temple d'Arthemide :
Allant murdry par incogneu du Marne.

The younger son of the king flagrant in burning lust
To enjoy his first cousin:
Female attire in the Temple of Artemis,
Going to be murdered by the unknown one of Maine.

X 36
Apres le Roy du soucq guerres parlant,
L'isle Harmotique le tiendra à mespris :
Quelques ans bons rongeant vn & pillant
Par tyrannie à l'isle changeant pris.

Upon the King of the stump speaking of wars,
The United Isle will hold him in contempt:
For several good years one gnawing and pillaging,
Through tyranny in the isle esteem changing.

X 37
L' a∫∫emblée grande pres du lac de Borget,
Se ralieront pres de Montmelian :
Marchans plus outre pen∫if feront proger,
Chambry, Moraine combat ∫ainçt Iulian.

Grande a∫∫emblée pres du lac du Borget,
Se rallieront pres de Montmelian :
Pa∫∫ants plus outre pen∫ifs feront proiet :
Chambry, Moriane. combat Saint-Iulian.

Grande assemblée prés du lac du Borget,
Se rallieront prés de Montmelian :
Passants plus outre pensifs feront projet,
Chambry Moriant combat Sainct-Iulian.

The great assembly near the Lake of Bourget,
They will meet near Montmélian:
Going beyond the thoughtful ones will draw up a plan,
Chambéry, Saint-Jean-de-Maurienne, Saint-Julien combat.

X 38
Amour alegre non loin pose le siege,
Au sainct barbar seront les garnisons,

255

Vrsins Hadrie pour Gaulois feront plaige,
Pour peut rendus de l'armée aux Grisons.

Sprightly love lays the siege not far,
The garrisons will be at the barbarian saint:
The Orsini and Adria will provide a guarantee for the Gauls,
For fear delivered by the army to the Grisons.

X 39
Premier fils vefue malheureux mariage,
Sans nuls enfans. deux i*f*les en di*f*cord.
Auant dixhuit incompetant eage.
De l'autre prés plus bas *f*era l'accord.

Premier fils vefue malheureux mariage,
Sans nuls enfans deux I*f*les en di*f*cord :
Auant dix-hui¢t incompetant aage,
De l'autre pres plus bas *f*era l'accord.

Premier fils vefue mal'heureux mariage,
Sans nuls enfans deux Isles en discord,
Auant dixhuict incompetant eage,
De l'autre prés plus bas sera l'accord.

First son, widow, unfortunate marriage,
Without any children two Isles in discord:
Before eighteen, incompetent age,
For the other one the betrothal will take place while
younger.

X 40
Le ieune nay au regne Britannique,
Qu'aura le pere mourant recommandé,
Iceluy mort Lonole donra topique,
Et à son fils le regne demandé.

The young heir to the British realm,
Whom his dying father will have recommended:
The latter dead Lonole will dispute with him,
And from the son the realm demanded.

X 41
En la frontiere de Caussade & Charlus,

256

Non gueres loing du fond de la valée,
De ville Franche musique à son de luths,
Enuironnez combouls & grand myttée.

On the boundary of Caussade and Caylus,
Not at all far from the bottom of the valley:
Music from Villefranche to the sound of lutes,
Encompassed by cymbals and great stringing.

X 42
Le regne humain d'Angelique geniture,
Fera son regne paix vnion tenir,
Captiue guerre demy de sa closture,
Long temps la paix leur fera maintenir.

The humane realm of Anglican offspring,
It will cause its realm to hold to peace and union:
War half-captive in its enclosure,
For long will it cause them to maintain peace.

X 43
Le trop bon temps, trop de bonté royale,
Faicts & deffaicts prompt, subit, negligence.
Leger croira faux d'espouse loyale.
Luy mis à mort par sa beneuolence.

Too much good times, too much of royal goodness,
Ones made and unmade, quick, sudden, neglectful:
Lightly will he believe falsely of his loyal wife,
He put to death through his benevolence.

X 44
Par lors qu'vn Roy sera contre les siens,
Natif de Bloys subiuguera Ligures :
Mammel, Cordube & les Dalmatiens,
Des sept puis l'ombre à Roy estrennes & lemures.

When a King will be against his people,
A native of Blois will subjugate the Ligurians,
Memel, Cordoba and the Dalmatians,
Of the seven then the shadow to the King, New Year's
money and ghosts.

257

X 45

L'ombre du regne de Nauarre non vray,
Fera la vie de sort illegitime :
La veu promis incertain de Cambray,
Roy Orleans donra mur legitime.

The shadow of the realm of Navarre untrue,
It will make his life one of fate unlawful:
The vow made in Cambrai wavering,
King Orléans will give a lawful wall.

X 46

Vie sort mort de L'or vilaine indigne,
Sera de Saxe non nouueau electeur :
De Brunsuic mandra d'amour signe,
Faux le rendant au peuple seducteur.

In life, fate and death a sordid, unworthy man of gold,
He will not be a new Elector of Saxony:
From Brunswick he will send for a sign of love,
The false seducer delivering it to the people.

X 47

De Bourze ville à la dame Guyrlande,
L'on mettra sus par la trahison faicte,
Le grand prelat de Leon par Formande,
Faux pellerins & rauisseurs deffaicte.

At the Garland lady of the town of Burgos,
They will impose for the treason committed:
The great prelate of Leon through Formande,
Undone by false pilgrims and ravishers.

X 48

Du plus profond de l'Espagne enseigne,
Sortant du bout & des fins de l'Europe,
Toubles passant aupres du pont de Laigne,
Sera deffaicte par bande sa grand troppe.

Banners of the deepest part of Spain,
Coming out from the tip and ends of Europe:
Troubles passing near the bridge of Laigne,
Its great army will be routed by a band.

X 49

Iardin du monde aupres de cité neufue,
Dans le chemin des montagnes cauées,
Sera saisi & plongé dans la cuue,
Beuuant par force eaux soulphre enuenimées.

Garden of the world near the new city,
In the path of the hollow mountains:
It will be seized and plunged into the Tub,
Forced to drink waters poisoned by sulfur.

X 50

La Meuse au iour terre de Luxembourg,
Descouurira Saturne & trois en lurne.
Montagne & plaine, ville, cité & bourg,
Lorrain deluge, trahison par grand hurne.

The Meuse by day in the land of Luxembourg,
It will find Saturn and three in the urn:
Mountain and plain, town, city and borough,
Flood in Lorraine, betrayed by the great urn.

X 51

Des lieux plus bas du pays de Lorraine,
Seront des basses Allemagnes vnis,
Par ceux du siege Picards, Normans, du Maisne
Ey aux cantons se seront reünis.

Some of the lowest places of the land of Lorraine
Will be united with the Low Germans:
Through those of the see Picards, Normans, those of Main,
And they will be joined to the cantons.

X 52

Au lieu où Laye & Scelde se marient,
Seront les nopces de long temps maniées,
Au lieu d'Anuers où la crappe charient,
Ieune vieillesse conforte intaminee.

At the place where the Lys and the Scheldt unite,
The nuptials will be arranged for a long time:
At the place in Antwerp where they carry the chaff,

Young old age wife undefiled.

X 53
Les trois pellices de loing s'entrebatron,
La plus grand moindre demeurera à l'escoute;
Le grand Selin n'en sera plus patron,
Le nommera feu pelte blanche routte.

The three concubines will fight each other for a long time,
The greatest one the least will remain to watch:
The great Selin will no longer be her patron,
She will call him fire shield white route.

X 54
Née en ce monde par concubine fertiue,
A deux hault mise par les tristes nouuelles,
Entre ennemis sera prinse captiue,
Et amenée à Malings & Bruxelles.

She born in this world of a furtive concubine,
At two raised high by the sad news:
She will be taken captive by her enemies,
And brought to Malines and Brussels.

X 55
Les mal'heureuses nopces celebreront
En grande ioye mais la fin mal'heureuse :
Mary & mere nore desdaigneront,
Le Phybe mort, & nore plus piteuse.

The unfortunate nuptials will be celebrated
In great joy but the end unhappy:
Husband and mother will slight the daughter-in-law,
The Apollo dead and the daughter-in-law more pitiful.

X 56
Prelat royal son baissant trop tiré,
Grand flux de sang sortira par sa bouche,
Le regne Anglicque par regne respiré,
Long temps mort vif en Tunis comme souche.

The royal prelate his bowing too low,
A great flow of blood will come out of his mouth:

260

The Anglican realm a realm pulled out of danger,
For long dead as a stump alive in Tunis.

X 57
Le subleué ne cognoistra son sceptre,
Les enfans ieunes des plus grands honnira :
Oncques ne fut vn plus ord cruel estre,
Pour leurs espouses à mort noir bannira.

The uplifted one will not know his scepter,
He will disgrace the young children of the greatest ones:
Never was there a more filthy and cruel being,
For their wives the king will banish them to death.

X 58
A temps du dueil que le felin monarque,
Guerroyera le ieune Aemathien :
Gaule bransler, perecliter la barque,
Tenter Phossens au Ponant entretien.

In the time of mourning the feline monarch
Will make war upon the young Macedonian:
Gaul to shake, the bark to be in jeopardy,
Marseilles to be tried in the West a talk.

X 59
Dedans Lyon vingt-cinq d'vne haltine,
Cinq Citoyens Germains, Brefians, Latins :
Par deffous nobles conduiront longue treine,
Et defcouuerts par abois de maftins.

Dedans Lyon vingt & cinq d'vne halaine,
Cinq citoyens Germains, Bressans, Latins,
Par dessous noble conduiront longue traine,
Et descouuers par abbois de mastins.

Dedans Lyon vint & cinq d'vne haleine,
Cinq citoyens Germains, Breffans, Latins,
Par deffous neble conduiront longue traine,
Et decouuerts par abois de maftins.

Within Lyons twenty-five of one mind,
Five citizens, Germans, Bressans, Latins:

Under a noble one they will lead a long train,
And discovered by barks of mastiffs.

X 60
Ie pleure Nisse, Mannego, Pize, Gennes,
Sauone, Sienne, Capue, Modene, Malte :
Le dessus sang & glaiue par estrennes,
Feu, trembler terre, eau, mal'heureuse nolte.

I weep for Nice, Monaco, Pisa, Genoa,
Savona, Siena, Capua, Modena, Malta:
For the above blood and sword for a New Year's gift,
Fire, the earth will tremble, water an unhappy reluctance.

X 61
Betta, Vienne, Emorre, Sacarbance,
Voudront liurer aux Barbares Pannone :
Par picque & feu, enorme violance,
Les coniurez descouuerts par matrone.

Betta, Vienna, Emorte, Sopron,
They will want to deliver Pannonia to the Barbarians:
Enormous violence through pike and fire,
The conspirators discovered by a matron.

X 62
Prés de Sorbin pour assaillir Ongrie.
L'herault de Brudes les viendra aduertir,
Chef Bizantin, Sallon de Sclauonie,
A loy d'Arabes les viendra conuertir.

Near "Sorbia" to assail Hungary,
The herald of "Brudes" (dark ones?) will come to warn
them:
Byzantine chief, Salona of Slavonia,
He will come to convert them to the law of the Arabs.

X 63
Cydron, Raguse, la cité au sainct Hieron,
Reuerdira le medicant secours,
Mort fils de Roy par mort de deux heron,
L'Arabe, Ongrie feront vn mesme cours.

262

Cydonia, Ragusa, the city of St. Jerome,
With healing help to grow green again:
The King's son dead because of the death of two heroes,
Araby and Hungary will take the same course.

X 64
Pleure Milan, pleure Lucques, Florence,
Que ton grand Duc sur le char montera,
Changer le siege prés de Venise s'aduance,
Lors que Colonne à Rome changera.

Weep Milan, weep Lucca and Florence,
As your great Duke climbs into the chariot:
The see to change it advances to near Venice,
When at Rome the Colonna will change.

X 65
O vaste Rome ta ruyne s'approche,
Non de tes murs, de ton sang & substance :
L'aspre par lettres fera si horrible coche,
Fer poinctu mis à tous iusques au manche.

O vast Rome, thy ruin approaches,
Not of thy walls, of thy blood and substance:
The one harsh in letters will make a very horrible notch,
Pointed steel driven into all up to the hilt.

X 66
Le chef de Londres par regne l'Americh,
L'isle d'Escosse t'empiera par gelée :
Roy Rebauront vn si faux Antechrist,
Que les mettra trestous dans la meslée.

The chief of London through the realm of America,
The Isle of Scotland will be tried by frost:
King and Reb will face an Antichrist so false,
That he will place them in the conflict all together.

X 67
Le tremblement si fort au mois de May,
Saturne, Caper, Iupiter, Mercure au bœuf :
Venus aussi, Cancer, Mars en Nonnay,
Tombera gresle lors plus grosse qu'vn œuf.

263

A very mighty trembling in the month of May,
Saturn in Capricorn, Jupiter and Mercury in Taurus:
Venus also, Cancer, Mars in Virgo,
Hail will fall larger than an egg.

X 68
L'armée de mer deuant cité tiendra,
Puis partira sans faire longue allée :
Citoyens grande proye enterre prendra,
Retourner classe reprendre grande emblée.

The army of the sea will stand before the city,
Then it will leave without making a long passage:
A great flock of citizens will be seized on land,
Fleet to return to seize it great robbery.

X 69
Le fait luysant de neuf vieux esleué,
Seront si grands par midy Aquilon,
De sa seur propre grandes alles leué :
Fuyant murdry au buisson d'ambellon.

The shining deed of the old one exalted anew,
Through the South and Aquilon they will be very great:
Raised by his own sister great crowds,
Fleeing, murdered in the thicket of Ambellon.

X 70
Lœil par obiect fera telle excroissance,
Tant & ardente que tombera la neige,
Champ arrousé viendra en decroissance,
Que le primat succombera à Rege.

Through an object the eye will swell very much,
Burning so much that the snow will fall:
The fields watered will come to shrink,
As the primate succumbs at Reggio.

X 71
La terre & l'air geleront si grand eau,
Lors qu'on viendra pour ieudy venerer :
Ce qui sera iamais ne feut si beau,

Des quatre parts le viendront honorer,

The earth and air will freeze a very great sea,
When they will come to venerate Thursday:
That which will be never was it so fair,
From the four parts they will come to honor it.

X 72
L'an mil neuf cens nonante neuf sept mois
Du ciel viendra vn grand Roy d'effrayeur
Resusciter le grand Roy d'Angolmois,
Auant apres Mars regner par bon heur.

The year 1999, seventh month,
From the sky will come a great King of Terror:
To bring back to life the great King of the Mongols,
Before and after Mars to reign by good luck.

X 73
Le temps present auecques le passé
Sera iugé par grand Iouialiste,
Le monde tard luy sera lassé,
Et desloyal par le clergé iuriste.

The present time together with the past
Will be judged by the great Joker:
The world too late will be tired of him,
And through the clergy oath-taker disloyal.

X 74
Au reuolu du grand nombre septiesme,
Apparoistra au temps ieux d'Hecatombe,
Non esloigné du grand eage milliesme,
Que les entrez sortiront de leur tombe.

The year of the great seventh number accomplished,
It will appear at the time of the games of slaughter:
Not far from the great millennial age,
When the buried will go out from their tombs.

X 75
Tant attendu ne reuiendra iamais
Dedans l'Europe, en Asie apparoistra

Vn de la ligue yssu du grand Hermés,
Et sur tous Roys des Orients croistra.

Long awaited he will never return
In Europe, he will appear in Asia:
One of the league issued from the great Hermes,
And he will grow over all the Kings of the East.

X 76
Le grand Senat decernera la pompe,
A vn qu'apres sera vaincu, chassé :
Des adherans seront à son de trompe,
Biens publiez. ennemy dechassé.

The great Senate will ordain the triumph
For one who afterwards will be vanquished, driven out:
At the sound of the trumpet of his adherents there will be
Put up for sale their possessions, enemies expelled.

X 77
Trente adherans de l'ordre des quirettes
Bannis, leurs biens donnez ses aduersaires,
Tous leurs bienfaits seront pour demerites
Classe espargie deliurez aux corsaires.

Thirty adherents of the order of Quirites
Banished, their possessions given their adversaries:
All their benefits will be taken as misdeeds,
Fleet dispersed, delivered to the Corsairs.

X 78
Subite ioye en subite tristesse
Sera à Rome aux graces embrassées.
Dueil, cris, pleurs, larm. sang excellent liesse :
Contraires bandes surprinses & troulsées.

Sudden joy to sudden sadness,
It will occur at Rome for the graces embraced:
Grief, cries, tears, weeping, blood, excellent mirth,
Contrary bands surprised and trussed up.

X 79
Les vieux chemins seront tous embellis,

L'on passera à Memphis somentrées,
Le grand Mercure d'Hercules fleur de lys
Faisant trembler terre mer, & contrées.

The old roads will all be improved,
One will proceed on them to the modern Memphis:
The great Mercury of Hercules fleur-de-lis,
Causing to tremble lands, sea and country.

X 80
Au regne grand du grand regne regnant,
Par force d'armes les grands portes d'airain
Fera ouurir, le Roy & Duc ioignant,
Port demoly, nef à fons, iour serain.

In the realm the great one of the great realm reigning,
Through force of arms the great gates of brass
He will cause to open, the King and Duke joining,
Fort demolished, ship to the bottom, day serene.

X 81
Mis thresor temple citadins Hesperiques
Dans iceluy retiré en secret lieu
Le temple ouurir les liens fameliques
Reprens, rauis, proye horrible au milieu.

A treasure placed in a temple by Hesperian citizens,
Therein withdrawn to a secret place:
The hungry bonds to open the temple,
Retaken, ravished, a horrible prey in the midst.

X 82
Cris, pleurs, larmes viendront auec coteaux
Semblanyt four donront dernier assault
L'entour parques planter profons plateaux,
Vifs repoussez & murdris de prinsault.

Cries, weeping, tears will come with knives,
Seeming to flee, they will deliver a final attack,
Parks around to set up high platforms,
The living pushed back and murdered instantly.

X 83

De batailler ne sera donné signe,
Du parc seront contraints de sortir hors,
De Gand lentour sera cogneu l'enseigne,
Qui fera mettre de tous les siens a mors.

The signal to give battle will not be given,
They will be obliged to go out of the park:
The banner around Ghent will be recognized,
Of him who will cause all his followers to be put to death.

X 84
Le naturelle à si hault hault non bas
Le tard retour fera marris contens,
Le Recloing ne sera sans debats,
En empliant & perdant tout son temps.

The illegitimate girl so high, high, not low,
The late return will make the grieved ones contended:
The Reconciled One will not be without debates,
In employing and losing all his time.

X 85
Le vieil tribung au point de la trehemide
Sera pressée captif ne deliurer,
Le vueil non vueil le mal parlant timide
Par legitime à ses amis liurer.

The old tribune on the point of trembling,
He will be pressed not to deliver the captive:
The will, non-will, speaking the timid evil,
To deliver to his friends lawfully.

X 86
Côme vn gryphon viendra le Roy d'Europe
Accompagné de ceux d'Aquilon,
De rouges & blancs conduira grane troppe
Et iront contre le Roy de Babylon.

Like a griffin will come the King of Europe,
Accompanied by those of Aquilon:
He will lead a great troop of red ones and white ones,
And they will go against the King of Babylon.

X 87

Grâd roy viendra prendre port prés de Nisse
Le grand empire de la mort si en fera
Aux Antipolles posera son genisse,
Par mer la Pille tout esuanouyra.

A Great King will come to take port near Nice,
Thus the death of the great empire will be completed:
In Antibes will he place his heifer,
The plunder by sea all will vanish.

X 88

Pieds & Cheual à la seconde veille
Feront entrée vastient tout par la mer,
Dedans le poil entrera de Marseille,
Pleurs, crys, & sang, onc nul temps si amer.

Foot and Horse at the second watch,
They will make an entry devastating all by sea:
Within the port of Marseilles he will enter,
Tears, cries, and blood, never times so bitter.

X 89

De brique en marbre serôt les murs reduicts,
Sept & cinquante années pacifique,
Ioye aux humains, renoüé l'aqueduict,
Santé, grands fruits, joye & temps melifique.

The walls will be converted from brick to marble,
Seven and fifty pacific years:
Joy to mortals, the aqueduct renewed,
Health, abundance of fruits, joy and mellifluous times.

X 90

Cent fois mourra le tyran inhumain,
Mis à son lieu sçauant & debonnaire,
Tout le senat sera dessoubs sa main,
Fasché sera par malin teméraire.

A hundred times will the inhuman tyrant die,
In his place put one learned and mild,
The entire Senate will be under his hand,
He will be vexed by a rash scoundrel.

X 91
Clergé Romain l'an mil six cens & neuf,
Au chef de l'an fera élection
D'vn gris & noir de la Compagne yssu,
Qui onc ne fut si maling.

In the year 1609, Roman clergy,
At the beginning of the year you will hold an election:
Of one gray and black issued from Campania,
Never was there one so wicked as he.

X 92
Deuant le pere l'enfant sera tué,
Le pere apres entre cordes de jonc,
Geneuois peuple sera esuertué,
Gisant le chef au milieu comme vn tronc.

Before his father the child will be killed,
The father afterwards between ropes of rushes:
The people of Geneva will have exerted themselves,
The chief lying in the middle like a log.

X 93
La barque neufue receura les voyages,
Là & aupres transfereront l'empire :
Beaucaire, Arles retiendront les hostages,
Prés deux colomnes trouuées de porphire.

The new bark will take trips,
There and near by they will transfer the Empire:
Beaucaire, Arles will retain the hostages,
Near by, two columns of Porphyry found.

X 94
De Nismes, d'Arles, & Vienne contemner,
N'obey tout à l'edict Hesperique :
Aux labouriez pour le grand condamner,
Six eschappez en habit seraphicque.

Scorn from Nîmes, from Arles and Vienne,
Not to obey the Hesperian edict:
To the tormented to condemn the great one,

270

Six escaped in seraphic garb.

X 95
Dans les Espagnes viêdra Roy tres-puissant,
Par mer & terre subjugant or midy :
Ce mal sera, rabaissant le croissant,
Baisser les aesles à ceux du vendredy.

To the Spains will come a very powerful King,
By land and sea subjugating the South:
This evil will cause, lowering again the crescent,
Clipping the wings of those of Friday.

X 96
Religion du nom des mers vaincra,
Contre la secte fils Adaluncatif,
Secte obstinée deplorée craindra,
Des deux blessez par Aleph & Aleph.

The Religion of the name of the seas will win out
Against the sect of the son of Adaluncatif:
The stubborn, lamented sect will be afraid
Of the two wounded by A and A.

X 97
Triremes pleines tout aage captifs,
Temps bon à mal, le doux pour amertume :
Proye à Barbares trop tost seront hastifs,
Cupide de voir plaindre au vent la plume.

Triremes full of captives of every age,
Good time for bad, the sweet for the bitter:
Prey to the Barbarians hasty they will be too soon,
Anxious to see the feather wail in the wind.

X 98
La splendeur claire à pucelle joyeuse
Ne luyra plus long temps sera sans sel :
Auec marchans, russiens, loups odieuse,
Tous pesle mesle mostre vniuersel.

For the merry maid the bright splendor
Will shine no longer, for long will she be without salt:

271

With merchants, bullies, wolves odious,
All confusion universal monster.

X 99
La fin le loup, le lyon, bœuf & l'asne,
Timide dama seront auec mastins,
Plus ne cherra à eux la douce manne,
Plus vigilance & custode aux mastins.

The end of wolf, lion, ox and ass,
Timid deer they will be with mastiffs:
No longer will the sweet manna fall upon them,
More vigilance and watch for the mastiffs.

X 100
Le grand empire sera par Angleterre,
Le Pempotam des ans plus de trois cens :
Grandes copies passer par mer & terre,
Les Lusitains n'en seront pas contens.

The great empire will be for England,
The all-powerful one for more than three hundred years:
Great forces to pass by sea and land,
The Lusitanians will not be satisfied thereby.

X 100 *
When the fork will be supported by two stakes,
With six half-bodies and six open scissors:
The very powerful Lord, heir of the toads,
Then he will subject the entire world to himself.

272

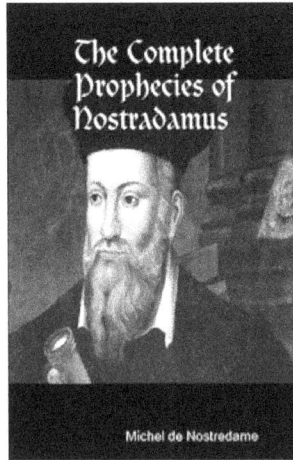

The Complete Prophecies of Nostradamus

The amazing predictions of the "Seer of Provence" are collected in this startling book. Learn the strange, cryptic secrets of the mysterious, legendary Michel de Nostredame, who foretold world wars, Napoleon, Hitler, rockets, nuclear power, automobiles, television, the assassination of John F. Kennedy and Martin Luther King, and the coming of the "Antichrist," and all of this HUNDREDS of years before any of these things actually occurred! Did Nostradamus predict the Apocalypse and the end of the world? Read the amazing prophecies and decide for yourself! An all-time classic masterpiece of the unknown!

492 Pages / Paperback / 12.00 USD / ISBN 9781329742918 / www.lulu.com/zem66

Milton Keynes UK
Ingram Content Group UK Ltd.
UKHW011922170424
441318UK00047B/696

9 781387 864164